The Order and Integration of Knowledge

The Order and Integration of Knowledge

WM. OLIVER MARTIN

ANN ARBOR

THE UNIVERSITY OF MICHIGAN PRESS

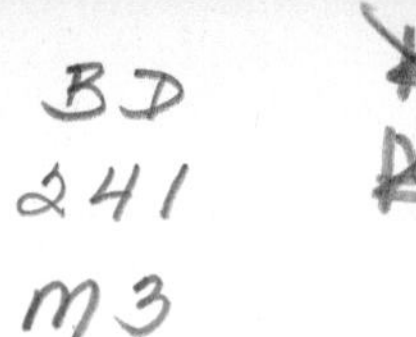

Library of Congress Catalog Card No. 56-11320

PRINTED IN THE UNITED STATES OF AMERICA BY
VAIL-BALLOU PRESS, INC., BINGHAMTON, N.Y.

TO

MY FATHER AND MOTHER

WILLIAM OLIVER MARTIN

THE ORDER AND INTEGRATION OF KNOWLEDGE

Nihil Obstat: JOHN F. FINNEGAN
Censor Librorum

Imprimatur: ✠ ALEXANDER M. ZALESKI
Vicar General,
Archdiocese of Detroit

JANUARY 17, 1957

Preface

Being, knowing, learning, and teaching are related, although they are not identical. Learning and teaching rest upon knowledge, and knowledge in turn presupposes being. How one kind of knowledge is related to another kind is a theoretical problem, but the need to understand that relation is both urgent and practical. Scholars and teachers either see their special subject in the light of the whole of knowledge—or else they see the whole from the narrow perspective of their special discipline, and thus create disorder in knowledge. That disorder is certain to affect the professions, and finally the public at large.

Disorder of knowledge takes its beginnings in higher education, and there it must be corrected. If it is not, the curricula of our colleges and universities, while still using the names of categories of knowledge, will increasingly be abstracted from their real foundation and will more and more reflect mere personal and institutional interests.

The most rational order of knowledge is perhaps still to be found in our technological and medical curricula. There is less in law. In the "arts and sciences" disorder prevails. Subjectivism, and intellectual, moral, and spiritual nihilism are no longer the bookish theories of men of pride—they have become a part of our culture, become respectable, and are being perpetuated by men who are cut off from that continuity of wisdom which alone could provide the cure. The tragedy of our age is the awful incommunicability of souls. In higher education, it is intensified by the "method of consensus" which, in abstraction from knowledge about kinds of knowledge, is simply a power technique masking under the guise of democracy.

It is my hope that this work may prove of value to those scholars, teachers, and administrators who are troubled by the anti-intellectualism and curricular disorder that exist in higher education. I attempt to deal with the general nature of evidence, and my concern is with some of the bases of responsible belief and responsible utterance. Although my treatment is systematic rather than historical, the reader will recognize my debt to the masters, from Aristotle on. He will know that the order of knowledge was not left for me to discover. I have tried only to organize what others have discovered, to rediscover what some of us either have never known or have forgotten—and also, perhaps, to throw some new light on the old problems. I hope that future analyses, by other writers, may help to clarify what is still obscure in certain passages of mine. The brevity with which I have treated history and strict theology as kinds of knowledge may to some be disappointing; it was necessary in order to complete the outline of knowledge. Both theology and history are concerned with the "unique" and the "singular" and are thus closely related. But to treat them adequately would have required another volume. Still, I believe that what has been said about them would not be modified by what more can be said.

I wish to express my gratitude for the many insights obtained in conversations with John Wild and Henry B. Veatch. John Wild has carefully read my manuscript and has offered many helpful suggestions. Not all of them have been followed, and I am fully responsible for any inadequacies that remain. I am deeply grateful for the unfailing help and encouragement of Mary Johnson in the preparation of the manuscript, and also for the aid and concern given by Dr. James A. McGrath.

Finally, I am indebted to the Ford Foundation. This publication has resulted from studies undertaken, in part, during the tenure of a fellowship granted by The Fund for the Advancement of Education for 1952–53, although I am solely responsible for the formulation of the work and its findings.

WM. OLIVER MARTIN

Narragansett, Rhode Island
March, 1956

Contents

The Order and Integration of Knowledge

1

Introduction to the Problem of the Order of Knowledge

There is evidence that specialists in the various fields of knowledge are becoming increasingly concerned with the nature of the kind of knowledge with which they identify themselves professionally. The interest is not new, but the urgency of the concern is. There is a reason for this. The division of labor in the pursuit of truth—in itself both necessary and good—has increased manyfold in modern times. The consequence has been the multiplication of knowledge-categories, the number and variety of which are reflected in the contemporary university catalogue. For example, "physics" no longer has the same meaning that it once had for the ancient Greeks; nor is it identical in meaning with what was called "natural philosophy" in the seventeenth century. While physics today tends to be thought of as a part of experimental science, the latter is often thought of as having little to do with the "natures" of things. At the same time natural philosophy or the philosophy of nature has almost been forgotten, the substitute for it more often than not being something called the "philosophy of science." And of course the term "science" itself has a history.

If the problem were merely verbal, a question of correct naming of kinds of knowledge, the matter would be relatively trivial. In fact it is a very serious one having to do with the nature and order of various kinds of knowledge. For if a person who is professionally identified with a subject does not know clearly its nature, which includes not only what it is but also what it is not, then how can he know when he is a practitioner of his subject and when he is not? How can he know whether a question is relevant to his subject or not? How can he know what evidence is and is not relevant to a problem? What kind of evidence is relevant in the demonstration of the truth of what kind of propositions and what kind of knowledge? If all this is not clear, a person may wander far afield from the subject he knows under the delusion that in some manner or other his special subject "proves" something in a subject about which he may know very little. The consequence is chaos in the order of knowledge, and a breakdown in the possibility of intelligent communication. And so the historian pauses in his research and reflects on the nature of "history" as a subject, a kind of knowledge. The scientist writes on the "meaning" or "logic" of science. The aim is presumably to inform others as to the nature of a certain kind of knowledge.

The problem is an important one, from both a theoretical and a practical standpoint. Is experimental science relevant in the determination of the truth of moral standards, and not just in their application? If this is so, it would be well to know it. On the other hand, if this is theoretically impossible, then it would not only be a waste of time and effort to write constantly as if it were so, but it would also intensify existing confusion.

Again, consider the proposition: *The physical world is finite.* To what kind of knowledge does this belong? If the answer to this question is not clear, then how can one know what is or what is not relevant evidence for its assertion or denial? (1) Is it a proposition of that kind of special metaphysics called "cosmology"? (2) Is it a proposition of experimental science which can be confirmed or disconfirmed as are general laws, by the same kind of data as evidence? (3) Is it a philosophical (cosmological) postulate which seems to be required by modern physical theory—required as a "presupposition," but not as something that is confirmed by physical data? (4) Is it a cosmological postulate, but one that is "postsupposed," and is it partially or wholly confirmed by the data of physics as an experimental science? (5) Or, finally, is it a cosmological proposition that can be known to be true or false on metaphysical grounds alone; and if true, its truth being only illustrated, not confirmed, by the data of physics?

It is to be noted that the answers to these questions are demanded prior to the determination of the truth or falsity of a proposition. Such questions are those concerned with the order of knowledge. *Only by first knowing which of the five alternatives is the case can one know what kind of evidence it is that will be relevant to the demonstration of the truth or falsity of the proposition.* If this fact is not recognized, discussion can be endless and, of course, fruitless. The consequence is the skepticism that comes with frustration and despair. The whole problem may be "solved" by dismissing the proposition in question as a type of linguistic expression which is a "pseudo-proposition," something that cannot be either true or false.

The Confusion of "Knowing" with Other Categories

As a creature who acts man is unique in being conscious of good and evil; having a substantial unity man is a being of a certain kind; as a knower he *discovers* truth about being, beings, and modes of being; as an artist he *makes* (or *creates*) "things" (artifacts). For there to be knowledge, and hence an order of knowledge, the distinctions between *being, knowing, doing* (*acting*), and *making* must be recognized. The road to nihilism (the reduction of something to "nothingness") begins when one or more of these notions is reduced to another. Much of modern philosophy since Kant has been the history of the ways in which men have tried to reduce one of these categories to another. For example, (1) one or more kinds of destructive "activisms" are implied (logically, of course, not psychologically) in the reduction of knowing to doing. (2) When being is reduced to knowing (Hegel) the dialectic ceases to be an instrument in knowing and becomes instead one of creating or making. Marx found that the converse reduction is quite as easily made, so that "changing the world" has been substituted for "knowing the world." Certain forms of pragmatism have consistently followed this reduction in principle, differing only in the conception of the mode of the change, i.e., evolution versus revolution. (3) When knowing and making are confused the philosophy of nature, i.e., natural science, the science of "nature," is reduced to experimental science. The techniques of experimental science then cease to be one means among others by which phenomena are known, and instead become instruments by which nature is manipulated and controlled for use purposes.

The following chapters will explain the general notions in more detail. Thus far we have spoken of the reduction of knowing to other categories. There are, of course, the innumerable forms of reductionism that derive from this primary form, i.e., the reduction of one kind of knowledge to another. For example, if being is reduced to knowing, then metaphysics may be reduced to logic (as with Hegel). But since anything that has a "nature" is what it is partly because it is not something else, the reduction of one to the other is equivalent to the denial of the nature of each. Thus the reduction destroys both logic and metaphysics. Similarly, if knowing is reduced to acting, one may end with neither logic nor ethics except in name. One practical consequence of such theoretical errors is that in colleges and universities, though the names of the philosophical disciplines may remain in the catalogue, what they should stand for is often absent. Of course, the game of "names" can be played by anyone. If logic is really mathematics, for example, it is only a concession to tradition to have philosophers teach it. If metaphysics has no truth, but is merely "ideology," then surely nonphilosophers are equally capable of spinning out their own.

The Problem of the Use of Knowledge-Categories

Thus far we have spoken of the dangers of confusing knowing with other notions, such as being, acting, and making. When the order and kinds of knowledge are not understood there is also the possibility of confusion in the use of the various knowledge-categories themselves. A category may refer to the nature which makes a kind of knowledge what it is; or reference may be to personal or institutional interest in knowledge.

Knowledge-categories as referring to subject matters and as objects of interests. What makes a fundamental kind of knowledge what it is, is the kind of subject matter studied. The term "subject matter" is equivocal. If the thing studied by two kinds of knowledge is the same, then not it but something else must be responsible for the kinds of knowledge being different. The "something else" is the "aspect" of the thing studied. The existential (or "material") object is the same but the aspect (or "formal object") is different, and it is the latter that differentiates the two kinds of knowledge. For example, both experimental science and metaphysics may be concerned with the same existential or material object, but not in the same way. They have different formal objects. When a person says that the human being is a substantial unity, a compound composite of act and potency, he is stating a proposition composed of metaphysical categories. The human being may also be studied by the physicist, chemist, and biologist. Experimental science is defined in terms of another set of categories. Both sets of categories apply to the human being, and at the same time they limit the nature of the two kinds of knowledge.

If there is an identification of the existential or material object and the aspect or formal object, then the two kinds of knowledge must be conceived of as studying the same "thing," the latter term becoming equivocal. Once this confusion is made, other errors logically follow. The two kinds of knowledge are conceived of as being in competition, each presumably doing the same thing, but one claiming to do it better. Over a period of time, in the case in question, experimental science is said to "do it better," and so it "wins out," the victory being acclaimed as "progress." What happens is that the part becomes the whole; an aspect is identified with a whole object or thing. Hence, a limited kind of knowledge becomes "total." But since such a claim could never be made by experimental science in itself, for in itself it is quite innocent, it can only be made by an *interested* party—one whose interest is not so much in the nature of experimental science as a kind of knowledge, but in some end or goal *the attainment of which may be hastened by the use of a knowledge-category as a means, a weapon.*

Interest in the use of a kind of knowledge is not at all incompatible with interest in the nature of the knowledge. The error is to reduce "nature" to "use." Interest in knowledge may be of two kinds, personal or institutional. For example, the term "science" may refer to a particular kind of knowledge having a definite subject matter, namely, experimental science. It may also refer to a professional interest of a person or a group of persons. There is no harm in such equivocal use of the term as long as the equivocation is recognized. It must also be understood that the term "scientist" is to be defined by the fact that a man's interest is in "science" and not that the nature of science is to be defined in terms of a man's interest. It is sometimes said that in this age of atomic power scientists must cease to be neutral and must take responsibility for the weapons they have produced. Taken literally the statement rests upon the confusion between "interest" and "nature" with respect to knowledge. Experimental science is morally neutral. What makes a scientist *what* he is, is the practice of experimental science. Hence, *as* a practitioner of experimental science he is necessarily morally neutral. It is as a *man,* who is a father, citizen, and one perhaps with religious commitments, that a person who happens also to be a scientist should be responsible. But often the incorrect assumption is made that the scientist *as such,* i.e., *because* he is a scientist, has some authority to speak on matters concerned with the moral use of the weapon. If a man who is a scientist has such authority, and if his judgments are of worth, then it is not because he is a scientist but because he has another kind of knowledge, moral wisdom.

Interest in the use of a knowledge-category can be institutional as well as personal. "Natural science" may refer to a kind of subject matter which a department or a group of departments in an institution of higher education professes to teach. The teachers, as "doctors of philosophy," would integrate experimental science and philosophy (metaphysics) in order to understand the *nature* of things, and not merely their phenomenological aspects. In this case the interest of the department respects the nature and order of kinds of knowledge, and thus conforms to one of the aims of proper education. But means and ends may be reversed, the term "natural science" referring to an institutional interest to which subject matter may sometimes be subordinated. The interest may now be that of acquiring prestige. One way is simply to elevate, by institutional power, the "subject" to an importance which it should not have. Instead of "doctors of philosophy" integrating experimental science and philosophy, we now have "experimental scientists" *creating* a philosophy.

Finally, there are knowledge-categories which refer neither to subject matter, formal or material, nor to the perverse subordination of subject matter to institutional interest. Such a category may quite legitimately refer to the practical interest of a department or school. This is the case with such terms as "home economics" or "domestic science." Such a term properly refers to various kinds of knowledge brought to bear upon some practical problem. "Home economics" does not refer to one fundamental kind of knowledge among others. Hence, it is purely an "institutional construct," and cannot be on the same co-ordinate level of classification with subject matter disciplines.

Metaphysics and the Order of Knowledge

The problem of the order of knowledge is to account for each and every kind of knowledge without, in the very process of doing so, eliminating any kind. Since a method is instrumental only, and since a fundamental kind of knowledge must be defined in terms of subject matter, the order of knowledge can be understood only by means of metaphysics. The problem of the order of knowledge is part of the general problem of the metaphysics of knowledge.

To attempt to understand knowledge without allowing the possibility of metaphysics is immediately self-defeating. This is the fatal difficulty of positivism. As a corrective, various kinds of naturalisms have been constructed through "postulation." A plausible thesis could be made out that all historical forms of naturalism and materialism have been postulational, from the atoms of Democritus to the "points" and "instants" of Samuel Alexander. But only in recent times has postulation in ontology become deliberate and intentional. There is a reason for this. Until the nineteenth century naturalism was essentially metaphysical in the sense that subject matter was held to be prior to method. That is, the "scientific method" (or its equivalent) was the only method because only the physical is real. During the last century, with the rise of positivism, naturalism became methodological. It was now said that the "phenomenological" (in the Kantian sense) is all there is because that is all that can be found by the "scientific method," and this method is the only one by which knowledge may be obtained. This position is often called "empiricism" instead of positivism.

In the twentieth century there were only two alternatives for positivism. The first was to intensify its anti-metaphysical tendencies, with a consequent retreat further into a kind of subjectivistic idealism. The phenomenological was absolutized. If methodology was to remain basic and prior, and at the same time the dead-end of skepticism to be avoided, the only alternative was to use the basic methodology obtained from the physical sciences to construct an ontology or metaphysics. By the twentieth century the methodology of experimental science had become (and quite legitimately) somewhat sophisticated, i.e., postulational, in contrast to the more naïve views from Bacon to Mill. It was thought necessary, then, to make metaphysics postulational. This procedure practically defines modern naturalism and materialism.

In contrast, moderate realism, as we shall see later, insists that there are metaphysical protocols, and that metaphysical truth is obtained by abstraction, not postulation. Some questions may occur at this point. What difference does it make? Some arrive at metaphysical propositions in one way, some in another. Furthermore, what difference does it make so far as the order and number of kinds of knowledge are concerned? Is realism in some sort of privileged position with respect to this problem? Cannot anything of importance that is presumably discovered by abstraction and analysis also be accounted for in a postulational system?

These questions are legitimate and will require answering. The answer to the last depends upon the meaning of "accounted for" and the criterion of "importance." However, the general problem is that of the criterion for postulating a certain "content," and the purpose for which it is done. There are ontological "either-or's." As we shall see, from the standpoint of postulation there is no way of knowing which is true. Do or do not universal concepts have a foundation in things? Is "reality" essentially process, becoming or being—i.e., "forms of process" or a "process of forms"? And so on. We may grant that a person may *will* either definition of "reality" in absence of evidence, reason, and of all *knowing*. But this is subjectivism.

Nor does it help to appeal to "consequences." In the first place, although the appeal to consequences has some meaning in the context of methodology of experimental science, it is question-begging when carried over to the ontological. For example, certain metaphysical postulates will allow the possibility of Christianity and/or Judaism and/or Mohammedanism. Other postulates would imply that they are all dangerous bits of historical foolishness. Now that the consequences are thoroughly understood, if either set of postulates is chosen, how does this fact help us choose?

In the second place, if there are no metaphysical protocols, if the ontological is not just as immediately experienced as the phenomenological, then to what kind of consequences does one appeal? Phenomenological fact and/or value? If the former, there is a confusion of evidence, and universal metaphysical propositions are reduced to generalizations. If the latter, then the implication is that value determines the ontological, rather than conversely. But value determination in complete abstraction from all objective grounds is simply the construction of a metaphysics in terms of wishes, wants, desires. If so, then postulation has nothing to do with knowing. Rather, it is an ideological instrument that serves some noncognitive purpose.

For the order of knowledge this means that the *possibility* of theological knowledge is eliminated *a priori*, not by *knowing*, but by postulation. And this means that even metaphysics is not a knowledge discipline. Other than being instrumental for noncognitive purposes, in a university metaphysics becomes a name for a historical study of past postulation by men who thought they were doing something else, not a record of the thought of courageous men who, in the search for total truth, ran the risk of being totally wrong.

For the order of knowledge the moral of all of this is that it would seem that one postulates because it is impossible to know. In contrast, realistic metaphysics has always made a knowledge-claim, not because it postulates itself as true, but because it has carefully distinguished and explained the difference between knowing and postulating (or "making," or "doing"). It is to such metaphysics that we must turn in order to understand the order and kinds of knowledge. By now it should be understood why metaphysics is unique in having a double relation to the problem of the order of knowledge. That is, metaphysics is not only one of the kinds of knowledge to be ordered, but it is also the kind of knowledge in terms of which the order is to be understood. This fact is important, and is true of *any* order of knowledge. Even the positivistic schema is based on subject matter, that of the experimental sciences, and because of this the postulational method is absolutized.

It will be well, now, to consider in some detail, yet briefly, some realistic notions, for they will be assumed in the analyses in the following chapters. Hylomorphism is of especial importance in understanding the nature of knowing.

The Principles of Hylomorphism

In knowing the world of nature, of individual things which exist independently of the cognitive act, sense knowledge is either instrumental or it is not. By "sense knowledge" we refer at present to what are sometimes called sensations, percepts, ideas (Lockean), impressions, i.e., it includes objects of sense *from the standpoint of sense* and not insofar as they are intelligible. The two standpoints are always only distinguishable, never separable. If sense knowledge is instrumental, then it is a *means* by which we know things. If it is not instrumental, then the sense object is *that which* is known. If we consider the latter, then there are three alternatives.

First, either there is a similarity between thing and thing known, or there is not. If there is, then we have the "copy theory" of knowing. This theory need not be slain again, although it is of historical importance. Second, if there is no similarity, then skepticism is the answer. The third alternative is the attempt to avoid skepticism by denying that a structured external world exists independently of cognition and about which we must be skeptical. The so-called external world is to be constructed from sense-experience. Such construction may be direct through an act of the "will" or "intellect," or indirect by postulation through "feeling-selection." In any case, having constructed the world, we can know it. *If we create what we know, then we can know what we create.* This third alternative is quite contemporary; and although terms such as "knowing," "truth," "logic," "intellect," and "mind," are still used, their meanings have been so changed that any identity or historical continuity remains chiefly oral or linguistic.

On the other hand, if what we know are things existing independently of cognition, and sense impressions and concepts are the *means by which* we know, then knowing can be explained by hylomorphic categories. There is in knowing a formal identity and material diversity.

In order to understand the meaning of hylomorphism and its importance in "knowing" let us consider some examples by way of illustration.

In the distance I observe some men and horses. I may also observe *this* man and *that* horse. Each man is an entity in himself, and is exclusive of every other entity of the same kind. The same is true of the horses. I do not confuse the horses and the men. I recognize that they are a different kind of being. We may say that the men and the horses differ because they have different "forms." The term "form," as used here, does not mean "shape"; it is rather a metaphysical concept. There is something about a man that makes him different from a horse;

and conversely. Furthermore, there is something that *this* man has that distinguishes him from *that* man.

Whatever the principle is that distinguishes this man from that man, it is something other than that which distinguishes a man from a horse. A man is different from a horse precisely because he is a man. But we cannot say that one man differs from another because he is a man. A second principle is involved, and that is called "matter." Two men may be formally the same but they differ materially. The form accounts for the men being of the same kind of creature; the material principle accounts for the fact that they are different individuals. "Matter" is called the principle of individuation. This does not mean that matter causes individuality or personality; rather, it is a necessary condition for individuality. We have, then, two principles, form and matter, and it is in terms of these two principles that the things of nature may be understood; for example, the nature of continuous and discontinuous quantity, and the nature of various kinds of change.

There are various kinds of motion or change—generation, corruption, local movement, alteration, augmentation, and diminution. Change is pervasive in nature. The planets move in their orbits, the seasons come and go, a house burns down and the wood is reduced to ashes, the boy becomes a man, and the colt grows into a horse. These changes can and have been explained in terms of the principles of matter and form. Without these principles, one kind of change is reduced to some other kind, and this, in effect, is to reduce or eliminate some kind of being. For example, in the case of mechanistic materialism there was a repudiation of the concepts of matter and form, with the consequence that certain types of change could not be accounted for. Alteration and generation were reduced to the local movements of atoms and molecules. Substantial change in a living organism either becomes a mystery or is implicitly denied.

The wood in the house that burned down is gradually reduced to ashes. Here we have a case of substantial change, not merely an alteration in some unessential quality or accident. In this kind of change something must remain permanent and be the subject of change. If this is not the case, then at some point the nature of the wood is totally annihilated, and the nature of the ashes comes into being or existence out of nothing. This something which is the subject of change, and which accounts for the continuity, is called "matter," or more exactly, "primary matter." This primary matter is determinable, the determining elements being the substantial forms. It is the function of the form to determine a specific nature, and it is the function of primary matter to receive the determination.[1]

The nature of primary matter. The principles of hylomorphism can never be understood if meanings are read into the concepts of matter and form which they do not have in this theory. It will be well to take time to understand these concepts. In so doing we refer generally to the Aristotelian-Aquinas tradition. For the purpose at hand the understanding of these concepts will be sufficient; the consideration of particular metaphysical problems either historically or systematically will not be necessary.

When we say that a horse is a material thing we are speaking of matter in the secondary sense. When we say that the horse is composed of matter and form we are referring to primary matter. It is primary matter that Aristotle is thinking of when, in his *Metaphysics,* he says that "by matter I mean that which, not being a 'this' actually, is potentially a 'this'." [2] Matter is not a particular kind of being, nor can it be identified with being itself. It is potentiality, and considered merely in itself it is pure potentiality. In another place Aristotle says: "Since the substance which exists as underlying and as matter is generally recognized, and this is that which exists potentially, it remains for us to say what is the substance, in the sense of *actuality,* of sensible things." [3] What Aristotle is saying here is that a substance without form cannot actually exist. Without form there would be nothing but mere primary matter, and hence substance in the sense of primary matter alone has only potential existence. Furthermore, primary matter is not a "thing." [4]

In one passage St. Thomas sums up many of the characteristics of primary matter: "Primary matter does not exist by itself in nature, since it is not actual being, but only potential.

Hence it is something con-created rather than created. Nevertheless, primary matter even as a potentiality is not absolutely infinite, but relatively, because its potentiality extends only to natural forms." [5] The implications of these characteristics of primary matter have been given by St. Thomas and other realists, and so a brief statement in exposition is now in order.

As pure potentiality, primary matter is of course completely formless; it is pure indetermination. But potentiality is always potentiality *for* something. What is pure potentiality potential for? Or, what is it relative to? It is pure potentiality relative to form. Cannot all of this be said of secondary matter as well as primary matter? Is not a bit of marble potential relative to the form of the statue which it may eventually become? The answer lies in the distinction between pure potentiality and potentiality. A piece of marble is already actual as marble; it is only potential relative to being a statue. Hence the marble is material in the secondary sense of the term "matter." The marble is said to possess first act and be potential only in relation to second act. In the case of primary matter it is not merely potential relative to form; it is nothing but potentiality, in itself lacking any actuality whatsoever. Whatever being or actuality primary matter has is conferred upon it by form. Hence, it may be said that primary matter is nothing but the possibility of receiving form.[6] Pure potentiality can be said to be the very "essence" of primary matter. On the other hand, for any composite material thing the essence must always include a formal element.

It might seem that pure potentiality or primary matter is equivalent to nothing. It would be a serious mistake to so conceive it. A correct way of stating it is that primary matter has no reality *apart* from form. But that is simply to say that it does not exist alone. If it could exist alone, then it would have to be determinate in some manner or other. But only form can provide determination. Hence, it would be an error to hold that primary matter has any existence apart from form. Primary matter is, then, equivalent to nothing only if it is considered as being apart from form. Since that is impossible, it is also impossible for primary matter to be equivalent to nothing. It does not follow, however, that because primary matter has no character of its own *apart* from form that therefore it has none *distinct* from form. Matter is different from a composite substance in being one of its constituent elements. It is different from nothingness because, though it is not a being in itself, it is a principle of being.

Another characteristic of primary matter is, then, its capacity to receive forms. This would be impossible if primary matter were nothing at all. In its capacity to receive forms it is purely passive; because of such absolute passiveness, indetermination, and formlessness primary matter can be said to be infinite. What makes anything in nature finite is its form, for form limits and determines. Primary matter, in itself, being absolutely indeterminate is not thus limited and finite, and hence is infinite. However, infinity attributed to matter is not the same as infinity attributed to God. God is infinite as to pure form and as pure act, and is not relative in any manner that is determined by the potentiality caused by matter. Matter is infinite in the sense of absolute formlessness and absolute indetermination. The infinity of primary matter is the infinity of imperfection rather than perfection. Perfection is proportional to actuality. Imperfection is proportional to the lack of actuality, the lack of form and determinateness. There is relative imperfection in whatever has potentiality. Pure potentiality would be pure imperfection; and conversely.

For many realists, following St. Thomas, matter is the principle of individuation. This does not mean that it causes an individual to be an individual. Only form can do that. Rather, in the realm of nature, primary matter is the necessary condition for the existence of individual things. This is a metaphysical problem on which there has long been considerable controversy, and one about which, fortunately, we are not forced to make a decision at present. It will be sufficient to emphasize that problem on which there is more general agreement. Without primary matter there could be no change or motion in natural things. And when form is thought of in complete abstraction from matter, such form is irrelevant to space and time. Primary matter, although not identical with, is certainly the foundation for, the spacialization and temporalization of forms. For our problem the concept of primary matter is important in that in the order of being it is the foundation for what from the standpoint of the order of knowledge is called the phenomenological context.

The nature of form. Nature is composed of individual things, of substances. It is the substance which is made or produced and not the constitutive principle which is the form. The form is that which determines the thing to be what it is. Aristotle puts it in this way: "It is obvious, then, from what has been said, that that which is spoken of as form or substance is not produced, but the concrete thing which gets its name from this is produced, and that in everything which is generated matter is present, and one part of the thing is matter and the other form." [7] St. Thomas, in commenting upon this passage, says that "what is made, properly speaking, is the composite; for this, properly speaking, is what subsists. But the form is called a being, not as *that which* is, but as *that by which* something is." [8]

As principles of being, and not beings themselves, matter and form are the metaphysical, and not the physical (or phenomenological), constituents of a natural subject. The confusion of the physical and metaphysical is equivalent to the elimination of the metaphysical. Nominalism is the consequence; and matter and form, instead of being principles of being, become beings themselves. Realism agrees with nominalism that only individuals exist in nature. But the individual that exists is a composite of form and matter and is not reducible to either one. The individual, composite substance is that which *is,* the form is that *by which* the substance is. The form is the principle of determination, of definiteness. It is by means of the form that matter acquires being and existence.

The relation of essence to matter and form. What is the relation of essence to matter and form, and essence to the substantial thing? The concept of essence is often used equivocally. Sometimes it is identified with the form; sometimes it is identified with the thing itself. Add to this the fact that substance itself is often used equivocally, and it is very understandable that confusion may occur. If the essence of the thing is identified with the form merely, then the thing is reduced to form. Matter no longer has any function, and the ideal and the real are identified. On the other hand, if essence is identified with the thing, and the thing is composed of matter and form, then the term essence becomes merely a synonym for the term substance. In this case, since the essence is the substance, and conversely, then if the substance is to have an essence at all it would have to be the form, the thing's form that is contrasted with primary matter. A difficulty now arises in explaining individuation. If the form of horse is the same in every horse, what is it that makes the horses different? If the essence is identified with the form, then all that there is left is primary matter or pure potentiality. Now primary matter is the principle of individuation in the sense that it is a necessary condition in order to have individual things in nature, in this case horses. But pure potentiality or primary matter alone is not sufficient, for although all horses will be composed of matter, what makes *this* horse different from *that* horse is particular or *signate* matter. A particular, individual horse has this flesh and these bones, and not flesh and bones in general.

Now, only in a purely spiritual substance would the essence and the form be identical. In a natural substance, a composite, the essence is composed of the matter and the form. The confusion is eliminated if we remember that the matter referred to here is common matter. It is the matter of bones and flesh *in general* which all horses (in general) have. The matter which makes this particular horse different from that one is a particular quantity of matter, signate matter, which is unique to each horse. Each horse is different from every other horse, and is a substance; it has a *nature*. It is not an existent without an essence, nor is it an essence that does not exist.

Since any composite thing is the union of form and matter, the form and matter are reciprocally related in a causal manner. Neither the form nor the matter is an efficient cause in relationship to the thing, for an efficient cause is always extrinsic to what it produces. The form is the formal cause of a thing, and being a constituent principle of the thing is an intrinsic cause. Primary matter is likewise the material cause of the thing, and is also intrinsic: "The matter and the form are mutually causative; the matter may be called the cause of the form insofar as the form cannot exist except in the matter, and the form may be called the cause of the matter, since the latter has actual existence only by the form." [9]

Only individual substances can suffer the change which is generation and corruption. Forms themselves do not change, but in generation and corruption there may be said to be a change of forms. In generation the forms pre-exist in the matter, but only in the sense that it is of the very essence of pure potentiality or primary matter to have the capacity of taking on the forms. In this connection we may call attention to the fact that in the controversy over preformationism and epigenesis in evolutionary development a misleading interpretation of preformationism has been attributed to the realistic tradition. A given thing is said to be pre-formed, as if it existed actually and *formally* in matter much as the plot and players exist on a moving picture film prior to its unfolding and projection on the screen. Such a view is not implied in hylomorphism. Also, the hylomorphic implication as to evolutionary change would tend to be in the direction of an interpretation in terms of a *process of forms,* and not as *forms of process*—an example of the latter being that which is found in Whitehead's *Process and Reality.*

This exposition of the principles of hylomorphism should be sufficient for our purposes. In summary we may indicate what the form is *not.* Form is not a composite substance; it is not a Platonic idea in a separate realm; it is not the subjective *quale* of modern conceptualism; it is not a datum or essence in the usual meaning of the term as found in what is called "critical realism"; it is not a Kantian "form of the mind"; it is not a Leibnitzian monad or a Whiteheadian "eternal object"; it is not that which makes "formal logic" mathematical. And finally, it is not something that forever covers existence like a veil and hides it from us, as it was for Santayana.

The Knowledge of Things

The paradox of knowledge has often been put in the form of a question: How is knowledge possible if only individual things exist in nature and knowledge of them must come through concepts which are universal? Historically this so-called paradox has sometimes been "solved" by turning it into a contradiction and then choosing one alternative or the other.

On the one hand is the proposition that individuals exist. Concepts then become names, "breaths," sounds, physical marks, propositional functions, linguistic rules, or what not. This is nominalism. The difference between extreme nominalism and conceptualism is of importance only for the nominalist. In neither case do the concepts of things have any foundation in the things themselves. For the former, concepts *qua* concepts do not exist at all. For conceptualism they exist, but their foundation is in the mind, feeling, or will rather than in things. This way leads either to skepticism or to some form of voluntaristic, anti-intellectualistic pragmatism or subjectivism. If we can't know things, we can at least *use* them. The next step is simply to identify "using" and "knowing." The most frequent expression of this identification is the absolutizing of a technique, such as is used in experimental science. Being useful for certain purposes the technique is identified with the very essence of knowing itself.

On the other hand is the proposition that individual substances do not exist, for they become collections of universals. "Existence" is a predicate like "blue" or "round." In effect, existence is reduced to essence. We do not know the thing by means of the concept. What we know are our concepts, and things are identified with concepts. The only real particular is the most universal, the Absolute. All else is appearance. Differences in kind are reduced to differences of degree.

These are the two very general alternatives to realism. In the twentieth century there are no new alternatives; there are only novel expressions of the alternatives. Whichever one is true, we can be sure of this, that the correct answer will allow us to understand the order of all kinds of knowledge, and any other answer will tend to the reduction of one kind of knowledge to another.

In order to understand the paradox, to understand how I can know individual things, substances, there must be an identity of some sort between me and the thing known. The thing must get out of itself and come to me. Also, I must get out of myself and go to it. If I am "here," and the thing is "there," and that is all that can be said, then knowledge remains a mystery. Stated in this fashion we have not gotten beyond the poetic. Yet such knowledge has the truth that poetry has. All philosophers, from Democritus to Whitehead, who have come to grips seriously with the problem have had to admit an identity of some sort in cognition. For realism the identity is found in "form" as well as in existence. If this is rejected, then in order to avoid skepticism the identity must be found elsewhere. In effect, "elsewhere" means in some subintellectual faculty or aspect of man—instinct, feeling, or the arbitrary will. Against these tendencies the intuition of Democritus was fundamentally correct. Particles leave atoms and come straight to our sense organs. Rationalist that he was, Democritus believed that some particles come unmodified straight to our "minds," and then we "see" truly. In other words, there is a formal or intelligible element in knowing—and this in spite of, not because of, his materialism.

Hylomorphism and cognitive identity. How, then, in knowing, can I be identified with the thing known without being the thing? For example, in knowing a horse there must be some cognitive identity between me and the horse. If there is not, then in attempting to know the horse either I modify and change the object or that which I know is some object that is supposed to be similar to the existing horse. If the latter be the case, then we are faced with the fatal difficulties of the "copy theory." On the other hand, in knowing a horse must it be the case that I know by "doing" something to the horse? My purpose is to know, not to do. Doing may be necessary in order to establish the conditions that make a given case of knowing possible. To see the horse, I must open my eyes. Opening the eyes is doing something, but it is not the same as knowing or understanding.

When I know a horse truly I know *what* it is. The "essence" is a formal entity and represents what the horse is, independent of the human mind. I want to know what the horse is *in* and *for itself,* not merely *for me.* Of course, the creature that we call a horse may be classified in many ways, relative to human purposes. For example, it may be classified as a beast of burden used for transportation. But all such classifications presuppose that what we are talking about has a "nature," a "form," that is what it is independent of our purposes. If our interests and purposes did not presuppose that the creature has a nature, an essence, then we would hold the fantastic position that our human purposes determine the nature of anything. It is true that one purpose may be to know the nature of a creature, but this is a theoretical and not a practical purpose, although a practical use may be made of the knowledge. But the "practical" does not constitute the nature of that which is known.

The basis of such knowledge is the individual essence or form. An essence can have two modes of existence. When it exists materially in a thing it constitutes a substance, a singular entity. When it exists formally in my mind, then it constitutes the content of my concept of "horse." There is the same form in each case; only the mode of existence is different. The identity relation in knowing is this formal identity of the content of my concept with the essence of the creature known. It is in this sense that I am, in knowing it, identical with the object known. In knowing a horse I am not identical with it "materially." There is a material diversity and a formal identity.

We see here that the hylomorphic notion of matter and form makes possible an explanation of perceptual knowledge. An epistemological analysis of perceptual knowledge is not our concern. What is important for the problem of the order of knowledge is the contrast in implications between the realistic explanation and its alternatives. For this purpose there are some further essential points in the usual realistic explanation that need emphasis.

The ability to receive the form or essence of a thing immaterially is unique to the human creature, and hence defines the uniqueness of cognition. Any theory that tends to deny that uniqueness also tends to reduce the human being to the subhuman; e.g., a theory that would reduce knowing to stimulus and response. Such a "beaver theory" is not adequate. (Beavers know how to build dams; so do humans. The only difference is that the humans know how to build them bigger and better.) One difference between a horse and a man is that a man can know *what* a horse is. The essence of the horse can be in the mind of man, but not conversely. It is this fact that St. Thomas is stating when he says that "knowing beings are distinguished from non-knowing beings in that the latter possess only their own forms; whereas the knowing being is naturally adapted to have also the form of some other thing, for the species of the thing known is in the knower." [10]

The universality of a concept is the result of a mental act, and hence is an *ens rationis*. The foundation of a concept of the thing is the "species" or "absolute nature" which is in the thing. The subject matter of logic is defined by these concepts *qua* concepts and the propositions composed of them in arguments. Logic is, then, concerned primarily with second intentions. If concepts and propositions are studied in abstraction from what they specifically intend, then we have "formal" logic. It should be noted that even formal logic is intentional logic. Concepts are still treated as intentional entities, otherwise they would not be concepts. The abstraction is only from what they intend specifically. Since a mutual relation is a relation the extremes of which are of the same order of reality, formal logic may be defined as the science of mutual logical relations. "Material" logic is concerned with concepts and propositions in relation to the objects intended. This is also "epistemology" in the sense that it means something other than a substitute for metaphysics.

What is the formula for reducing logic to mathematics, or something else, instead of allowing it to find its place in the order of knowledge? The formula is a simple one: Identify essence and thing, sign and thing signified. The distinction vanishes between that which (*id quod*) is known and that by which (*id quo*) a thing is known. Second intentions are then reduced to first intentions, and logical relations are identified with real relations considered in abstraction from the objects related.[11]

When the formal sign and the thing signified are confused we meet again the alternatives to realism with which we have become familiar. What is obtained depends upon whether the thing or the concept is emphasized. If the thing is stressed some form of nominalistic skepticism is the consequence. If the concept is stressed, some form of idealism or subjectivism follows.

The essence of nominalism, at least from the negative standpoint, lies in its denial that the content of concepts has any objective foundation. Individual material things exist, but the universal either does not exist at all or is a fiction or a construct. The first is an extreme form of nominalism and leads to complete skepticism. The latter is a kind of conceptualism. Concepts exist and are mental entities, but the content of the concept has no foundation in things, and hence, if not empty, is created or constructed by the mind. For Kant such construction was nonvoluntaristic, for the forms of the mind were in a sense "given" and beyond the control of the will. This type of skepticism requires a dualism between thing and thing known, between the thing as it is in itself and the thing as it is for us.

Once the radical change has taken place, and the notion of "construction" is substituted for the realistic notion of "abstraction," then the revolution must be completed. What must be liquidated is the notion of an independent, individual thing or substance. In this case the concept rather than the thing is stressed. *That which* we know becomes identical with *that by which* we know. We do not know the thing by means of, or through, the concept. We know only our concepts. Instead of second intentions being reduced to first intentions, we now have the converse situation in which the real is reduced to the logical, and metaphysics is reduced to logic. But whereas in the former case—the reduction of logic to mathematics—logic remained formal but nonintentional, now with the real reduced to the logical, logic must become "dynamic" and "dialectical" just as is the real world with which it has become identified.

To sum up, in knowing there must be an identity of some

sort between the knower and the thing known. Realism finds such identity in the formal, immaterial element—in the intelligible species which is at once the foundation of the universality of the concept and the formal element constituting the essence of the thing. The concept is the result of abstracting the immaterial, intelligible form from the thing. This formal element in its real mode of existence constitutes the essence of the thing, and hence the thing and the thing known are the same in this respect.

The Alternatives to Hylomorphism

The difference between hylomorphic realism and other metaphysical conceptions does not lie in the acceptance or rejection of the categories of form and matter. The latter are never really eliminated in any metaphysical analysis. The key to the understanding of the difference is to understand that in the analysis of nature matter and form are principles of being, whereas on alternative conceptions they are beings themselves. In the latter case the categories cease to have their realistic meaning. Primary matter is identified with secondary matter or the "physical," while form tends to become "mind," "thought," "will," or "feeling." Since the time of Descartes the difficulties of such constructed dualism have been met in general by the alternatives of idealism and materialism. For reasons which need not now be stated, in historical development idealism tends to become epistemological, while at the same time naturalism or materialism becomes methodological. Hence, it is not an accident at all that each in its own way tends to generate finally its own special kind of positivism or skepticism.

For the order of knowledge the importance of this is that both idealism and naturalism tend to be reductive of some kind of knowledge. Idealism has always had difficulty in taking account of experimental science. (Example: If nature must behave syllogistically, as Hegel thought, then there is little room for experiment in the modern sense.) Materialism has left no room for ethical knowledge or strict theology.

In summation, the problem of the order of knowledge is that

of ordering, and not destroying, kinds of legitimate knowledge-claims. This cannot be done without metaphysical assumptions. We have no right to make assumptions which would eliminate *a priori* any kind of knowledge-claim. On the other hand, it is our duty to recognize as *prima facie* adequate and true those metaphysical principles which are not only compatible with, but make possible the understanding of, all kinds of knowledge. As we have tried to show, such principles are those of moderate or classical realism.

On the Method of Procedure and Certain Difficulties

If by an "empirical approach" is meant "experiential" as opposed to the "arbitrary *a priori*," then the following study is empirical. But it is empirical (experiential) in a double sense. By means of realism all forms of subjectivism are avoided; for realism itself claims to be empirical, based as it is upon abstraction from experience. On the other hand, what in fact various kinds of knowledge historically have been conceived to be is taken into account in two ways. Such facts are *instrumental* in the sense that the study of the problem of the order of knowledge would not be possible if knowledge did not already exist in roughly classified forms. Second, such facts serve as a partial check upon the theoretical development and exposition. For example, there would be something seriously wrong with an order of knowledge in which such categories as (say) history, experimental science, and theology had little to do with anything in the past that has gone under such names.

At this point we call attention to the difficulty which anyone may encounter in dealing with the problem at hand. In the very process of clarifying a knowledge-category one must use it. And yet, because it is still ambiguous in meaning, confusion may occur. The most one can do is forewarn the reader.

The plan of the following chapters. Knowledge-categories may stand for kinds of knowledge that are (*a*) fundamental and relatively autonomous, e.g., mathematics; (*b*) synthetic (or integrative), theoretical or practical, e.g., the moral or social sciences; (*c*) species of (*a*) or (*b*), e.g., chemistry as an experimental science; (*d*) eclectic combinations, e.g., domestic science.

The following questions will be answered:

(1) What kinds of knowledge are there that are autonomous, i.e., not constituted by integration of other kinds?

(2) What kinds of knowledge are there that are synthetic, i.e., constituted by integration of autonomous kinds?

(3) What makes a kind of knowledge what it is?

(4) What is the nature of the evidence to which each kind of knowledge appeals?

(5) What are the loci of compatibility and incompatibility between kinds of knowledge? That is, in what kinds of knowledge is it possible to have the truth-claim of a proposition in one kind of knowledge incompatible with the truth-claim of a proposition in another kind?

In more familiar language, in this volume there is the attempt to define the nature of experimental and natural science, history, mathematics, metaphysics, theology, logic, moral or social science, and the arts. The problem is a limited one. Always the question is: What makes a kind of knowledge what it is? What is its essential nature? We shall see that this raises the question of kinds of evidence.

With the exception of the treatment of theology, it is believed that the analyses given are sufficient to answer the questions that have been raised. The general nature and delimitation of history and theology have been given, but a more detailed treatment must be the subject of a future work. Both their nature and their importance require this special attention.

The problem of the order and integration of knowledge is essentially the same as the problem of the nature and kinds of evidence, which phrase could be used as an alternative title for this volume.

2

Logic, Presupposition, Evidence, and Contexts of Knowledge

The remainder of the volume will be concerned with the fundamental kinds of knowledge and their relations to each other in terms of evidence. But this will presuppose something about "knowing" itself; not merely perceptual knowing, but knowing by means of an intelligible instrument—by logic. A false conception of the instrument may cause a false conception of that for which the instrument exists.

The Nature of Logic

It may be well for a moment to anticipate what will be forthcoming in order to get an over-all view of the problem. Not only is there an order to knowledge, but it is essential to knowledge *qua* knowledge that it be ordered. If a serious error is made concerning any part of the order, then the error may infect the whole order in such a manner that the order is destroyed. Knowledge becomes disordered and fragmented, and becomes something else. If the analogy is not pressed too far, the ordered structure of man's nature may be used to illustrate. If man is a delicate balance of body and spirit, it is very easy to disturb the order, not only in practice but theoretically, by conceiving of man as angel or beast. And by the dialectic of error when man presumes to be the former he only succeeds in becoming the latter. But even this is not quite exact, for he becomes something less than a beast.

And so with knowledge. If the philosophy of nature or natural science should be, as knowledge, an ordered structure of the phenomenological and the ontological, the study of "mobile being," then what happens if a reduction occurs? The phenomenological context is absolutized, and natural science is reduced to experimental science. But now, even experimental science ceases to be a kind of knowledge, and becomes an instrument for controlling nature, not *knowing* it. To anticipate again, if the same process occurs with the study of quantitative being, then mathematics may end conceived of as having nothing to do with quantity. What it is becomes a mystery and the subject of conjectures varying from "manipulation of meaningless marks" to "study of relations." If the latter, then logical relations—those *by which* one reasons—become the subject of mathematics. The distinction between logic and mathematics breaks down. Ontologically this means that intentional being is reduced to quantitative being; or conversely.

But as we have seen, even this, though true, is not quite exact. If *A* and *B* are elementary and distinct kinds of knowledge, then each is what it is, partly but not wholly, only in relation to the other. However, if *A* is *reduced* to *B*, then *B* no longer retains its nature; we now have something else, *C*. If *B* is reduced to *A*, then we have, say, *D*, instead of *A*. The fundamental principle is this, that *if one kind of knowledge is reduced to another, then both are distorted or destroyed.* There is here a sharp "either-or"—if *A* and *B* are kinds of knowledge, then *C* and *D* are but distorted forms; and conversely. And so, when intentional being is reduced to quantitative being, one may wonder what we have. Certainly we have neither intentional nor quantitative being.

The seriousness of reduction in the case of logic cannot be overemphasized. Since logic is an instrument by which we know, if the instrument itself is wrongly conceived, then it may affect everything that can be known, i.e., the whole order of knowledge itself. If realism is correct, logical forms are intentional; they are not "real" relations "out there"; they are mental beings only. A Hegelian type of idealism is generated by reducing real forms to intentional forms. In the words of

Hegel: "The syllogistic form is an universal form of all things." [1] But in the reduction intentionality itself is lost.

If logical forms are reduced to real forms, then the intentional is reduced to the nonintentional, logic to mathematics. Whereas in idealism knowing was conceived as both unique and total, epistemology becoming metaphysics, in this case knowing ceases to be even unique, and thus, *as knowing* becomes nothing at all, for it becomes identified either with "doing" or "making" when there is an attempt to escape the skepticism implicit in such a reduction. In this case intentionality is lost by being directly denied. This is the formalistic or positivistic position.

The relevance of all this to the problem at hand is that whenever reduction occurs the order of knowledge tends toward disorder. In short, the kinds of knowledge which we shall presently define and attempt to understand exist only through *an order.* If it is a matter of fact that realism does not require any reduction of one kind of knowledge to another, it may be well for us to understand why this is so. And this will require the understanding of logic itself, knowing *about* knowing; for, to repeat again, if there is a misconception about this, then other kinds of knowledge may likewise be misconceived.

In a few pages we shall merely indicate the nature of logic sufficiently to delimit it in relation to mathematics, and to show its relation to realistic metaphysics. For further understanding we can only recommend a most excellent and detailed study, *Intentional Logic,* by Henry Veatch.[2]

Logic is concerned with mutual relations between beings of reason, concepts, propositions, and forms of reasoning such as the syllogism. They are objects of "second intention," and are mental creations or constructions that are not found as such in *rerum natura.* There is an active and creative aspect to cognition. The mind is not passive. Knowing is not merely "enjoying" an object as, for example, S. Alexander supposes in his materialist exposition of naïve realism. Reductionism occurs not from recognizing an active factor in cognition, but from misplacing its locus. By recognizing the distinct orders of existence, the logical and the real, we avoid the error of thinking that syllogisms, propositions and concepts are "out there" with trees, men, and planets; and also the contrary error of supposing that because we have concepts of these natural things, therefore they are *merely* mental constructions. These natural things are what are first intended by our concepts. The concepts themselves are second intentions. When we think reflexively about concepts and other logical beings which are instrumental in knowing, then we are considering second intentions as first intentions only for the purpose of analysis.

If the logical and the real are distinct, they must nevertheless be related. That relation must be understood in order to understand the nature of kinds of knowledge. To misunderstand the relation is inevitably to eliminate or distort one or more kinds of knowledge. Although the concept *qua* concept is only logical, it is through the concept that the logical and the real are related. Arguments are built from propositions; the elements related to form propositions are concepts. We derive our concepts from perceiving things in the real, independent world of nature.[3]

It is a fundamental position of realism that beings *are,* and that they can be known, to some extent at least, as they are in themselves, and not merely as they are relative to a knower. The explanation of how such knowledge is possible has been given in terms of the relation of identity, i.e., the content of the universal concept is identical with the essence individualized in nature. For example, a concept such as "man" is a relation of identity between a "what" (an essence) and individual men. The concept is said to be a "formal sign" because its whole nature lies in its "intending" something other than itself.

The distinction between formal sign and other kinds of signs may be understood by considering the chain of significations leading to the concept of man. A certain sound or group of marks on paper signifies the word "man." The word is a logical term because it signifies the concept "man." What does the concept "man" signify? It signifies a "what," an essence that real existents have. This essence is the "comprehension" of "man," comprising such intelligible elements as substance, material, living, sentient, and rational. In short, man is a rational animal. The concept is said to signify primarily the essence and secondarily the real individuals identified with the essence. For the concept as a formal sign is an "intention" and must signify something other than itself. A concept must always be *of* something. As a formal sign, and in contrast to an instrumental sign, its whole nature lies in "intending." An instrumental sign such as "a cloudy sky" may mean "rain." But one must first know *what* a cloudy sky is to know what it means. It has a nature independent of its cognitive function. A concept has no nature except its cognitive function of "intending." Hence, we know man through the relation of identity, which is the intending relation, and only afterward, and reflexively, do we learn what the formal sign is which is the concept. We know man as a real substantial being by means of the concept. Only after a great deal of reflection do we know the concept *qua* concept.

We can now state the nature of the kind of knowledge which logic is. As purely formal, logic is the science of the mutual relations which intentional forms have. Concepts, propositions, and syllogisms are studied chiefly in relation to their mutual relations and in abstraction from content and from the application of concepts. "Material logic" is concerned with the same intentions, not as such and in their mutual relations, but in relation to their content. In purely formal logic one is dealing merely with second intentions as such, while in material logic one is concerned with intentions in relation to *what* they intend.

Logic and metaphysics. The term "epistemology," and the "subject" it refers to, are both rather recent notions. Historically the term can almost be identified with the attempt to explain how knowledge is possible on a nonmetaphysical basis. It is modern subjectivism's substitute for metaphysics. Since this is actually impossible, the realist would say that such epistemology is simply bad metaphysics. If "epistemology" means anything more than this, then it would seem to be the same thing as "material logic."

We can now better understand why "logic" and "intentional logic" are the same, and why something like recent "mathematical logic" cannot be identified properly with logic. It is axiomatic that a conception of the nature of logic rests upon metaphysical premises, implicitly or explicitly, unconsciously or consciously. Second, a logic, to be worthy of the name, must meet this test: the metaphysics implied by a logic must be capable of explaining and justifying it.

The axiom can be verbally denied. However, this does not change the fact. Mathematical logic usually (not always) rests upon a nominalistic metaphysics, intentional logic upon realism. Whether one takes essences to be real, or denies them to be real, in either case one is "talking" metaphysics. Metaphysics is not avoided by the act of denying a metaphysical proposition. Assertions and denials are still in the same context of knowledge. Whether one asserts that God exists or does not exist, it is still metaphysics in both cases, not logic, seismology, or economics. The denial of this would make communication impossible.

Furthermore, what is true theoretically is the case historically. One hardly needs to press this point if one considers history from Aristotle down through Hegel to Russell. (1) When we say that logic presupposes metaphysics we are thinking of the three main positions possible: nominalism, realism, and idealism. We are not referring to any one specific variation out of an indefinite number of possible ones to be found in (say) the first. (2) Again, what is axiomatic is independent of, or, alternatively, common to, any and all metaphysics. In other words, the axiom is not peculiar to realism; hence, we are not begging the question. (3) Finally, when we use "metaphysics" in this context we are not identifying the term with "rational metaphysics." A proposition is metaphysical whether it is "reasonable" or not. In fact it has to be that first in order to be either rational or irrational. A person is "talking" astronomy whether he says that the distance from the earth to the moon is 240,000 miles, 236,000 miles, or six inches. The type of proposition is not determined by the correctness of the distance. The type of proposition must be determined independently in order that one can know its reasonableness. And so the fundamental propositions of nominalism are metaphysical, whether or not they are amenable to reason.

The term "presuppose" is ambiguous. Sometimes "*A* presupposes *B*" means "*A* implies *B*," at other times "*B* implies *A*," depending upon the kind of knowledge considered. If a theorem in a mathematical system presupposes postulates we do not mean that the theorem implies the postulates, but rather that the postulates imply the theorem. On the other hand, when we say that physics presupposes mathematics, we mean that knowledge of physics implies knowledge of mathematics. Even so, we must be careful; for we do not mean that the truth of physics is evidence for the truth of mathematics, but that if there are certain truths in physics then there must be certain propositions that are mathematically true.

Now the relation of logic to metaphysics is at least analogous to the second of the two examples. This is not the whole story, as we shall see. At the moment we can say that intentional logic and mathematical logic have this in common, that they both have metaphysical implications. When we say that logic presupposes metaphysics we mean that if a logical position is taken as true, then of necessity one must assert a certain metaphysical position as true. Logic that is intentional presupposes or implies hylomorphism. However, logic does not enter constitutively into the proof of a metaphysical proposition, but is rather a necessary instrument for the organization of evidence bearing upon such proof. Intentional logic does not prove hylomorphism, nor does mathematical logic prove nominalism. The evidence for either hylomorphism or nominalism must be independent of logic, although the bearing of such evidence upon a metaphysical proposition will be demonstrated logically. However, there is a sense in which intentional logic implies hylomorphism because it implies the reality of essences. Also, most of what goes under the name of mathematical logic usually implies nominalism because it implies the denial of the reality of essences.[4] However, the way each presupposes the other is not the same. This will be explained in the next section, in which there is an analysis of three meanings of "presupposition."

It may appear as if we had an option as to "logics." But such an option exists only from the standpoint of arbitrary "will" or "feeling." If so, then we may expect one position or the other to fail to pass a most reasonable test, namely: Can the logic which presupposes a metaphysics be the instrument by which the truth of the metaphysics is known? With this test in mind let us examine the problem again.

But first let us clarify the term "nominalism." Both realism and nominalism assert the existence of individuals. What is unique to nominalism is the denial of the objectivity of essences. It is this that produces the most radical philosophical cleavage. The difference between the ideal-realism of Platonism and the moderate realism of Aristotle is chiefly concerned with the mode of existence or being of essence. As to this difference we shall beg the question at present.

What is the relation between realistic metaphysics and intentional logic? We can reason as follows. If realism is true, essences are objective; if there are essences, then there are formal signs; if there are formal signs, then knowledge of things is possible through the instrumentality of intentional logic. We can also reason that if things can be known through the instrumentality of intentional logic, then there must be formal signs; if there are formal signs, then there are essences; if there are essences, then realism is true (at least true in this respect). Realism and intentional logic seem to be mutually implicatory. But this must not be misunderstood. If there is no evidence for either *A* or *B*, then it is fruitless to show that they are mutually implicatory, at the same time attempting to use each as evidence of the other. This is not the case with realism and intentional logic.

In the first place, the evidence for realism is quite independent of intentional logic, although such evidence cannot be "handled" without such logic. Second, in saying that there is a mutual implication two things are meant. (1) "Intentional logic implies realism" means that if realism is false, then intentional logic is false. It is not meant that realism is "deducible from" intentional logic. (2) "Realism implies intentional logic" means that if intentional logic is false, then realism is also false. But in addition it means that intentional logic is "deducible from" realism. The ground for this is the dual mode of existence a form may have, as essence and as intentional form. Intentional logic is necessary but not sufficient as evidence for realism. But realism is both necessary and sufficient as evidence for intentional logic.

Strictly speaking, the last proposition is true only of intentional logic as "formal," not as "material." The correct application of logic in various kinds of knowledge is not deducible from metaphysics, for the nature of the kind of knowledge itself is a determining factor. It is also to be understood that we are talking about the ultimate justification of intentional logic. The latter is directly warranted by its ability to disclose the real. It is only on reflection, when examining the nature of the instrument, that we see why intentional forms are the means by which we know the non-intentional.

Let us now turn to the relation of nominalism to mathematical logic. We can certainly reason that if mathematical logic is true, there are only instrumental signs and no formal signs; hence, no essences; therefore, nominalism. But if we begin with nominalism and infer no essences or formal signs, we can assert that there are only instrumental signs. But there we stop. We cannot say that mathematical logic follows necessarily from there being only instrumental signs. Some other "logic" might be compatible with nominalism. Nominalism is necessary, but not sufficient, for mathematical logic.

What does this mean? It means that nominalism implies no one logic, but allows alternative ones. For example, instead of a mathematical logic one might, consistently with nominalism, hold to some kind of voluntaristic logic. Each logic implies nominalism in the sense that it could not be true if nominalism were not true. And yet from the standpoint of nominalism all that can be said is that it is neutral with respect to any one logic as against the other, but is compatible with all of them. In fact the neutrality of nominalism is such that it is compatible with no logic at all, with complete skepticism.

If there are only instrumental signs, and essences are not real, then one might identify mathematical logic with logic. But one would not be inconsistent at all to argue that if we can't know the thing but only the sign of the thing, then no knowledge is possible, not even logical knowledge. It is interesting to observe that such skepticism could not follow from realism, nor has anyone ever thought so. But in the case of nominalism, not only is skepticism compatible with it, but historically it has been so argued.

It seems, then, that while almost any "logic," or none at all, is compatible with nominalism, only intentional logic is incompatible with it. Now let us see what happens if we ask what the evidence is for the truth of nominalism. Whatever the evidence may be, which among the alternative logics is the instrument by which the truth of nominalism may be made known? The very asking of the question gives the answer. It would seem that there can be no evidence for nominalism. Nominalism is, then, a metaphysical *postulate* which allows, but cannot explain or justify, various logics; and further, there is no way of knowing which logic could be an instrument in knowing the truth of nominalism, if evidence for its truth were possible.

Mathematical logic, then, fails completely the test for a logic. It not only implies a metaphysical position (nominalism) which can neither explain nor justify it; but in so implying, it is in effect demanding a metaphysical position of which it cannot be an instrument for knowing its truth.

"Mathematical logic" is, then, misnamed. Some of what goes under that name certainly *is* mathematics, but perhaps the subject matter might better be spoken of as the "logic of mathematics." Our conclusion was arrived at through considering the relation of logic to metaphysics, rather than through an examination of mathematical logic itself. Logic must be "intentional," otherwise it is not logic. To substitute a nonintentional system for intentional logic is to substitute real relations for logical relations, and is equivalent to eliminating logic itself.

If logic is eliminated, then rational metaphysics is likewise eliminated and we cannot know the real.

The Analysis of "Presupposition"

College and university catalogues are filled with innumerable categories presumably representing kinds of knowledge. Since their number is apparently limited only by the imagination of their creators it is reasonable to ask for the basis for the compounding of categories. One might speak of the "chemistry of knowledge," for certain kinds of knowledge are elemental, and other kinds of knowledge are compounds, being constituted by the elemental kinds. And perhaps there are "affinities" and "valences." Are history and sociology both elemental? Or is the former an element of the latter as a compound? Is natural science elemental or is it compounded of one part of experimental science and one part of metaphysics (cosmology)? Mathematics and experimental science seem to have an affinity; but can, say, history and mathematics be compounded? Apparently not.

The "chemistry of knowledge" is analogically a quite imperfect notion and can be dangerous and misleading. It can, however, call attention to the fact that not all kinds of knowledge are on the same co-ordinate level of classification, regardless of the principle of division. As we shall see, experimental science is a knowledge "element," moral or social science is a "compound." On the other hand, something like "home economics" is a "mixture." Classification of knowledge can be on a "natural" or "artificial" basis. The former is on the basis of "subject matter," the kind or aspect of reality studied. The basis of the latter can be anything, depending wholly upon the utilitarian purposes of the classifier. Home economics or domestic science is a "mixture," an example of artificial classification.

When the two kinds of classification are confused, what usually occurs is the reduction of all classifications to the artificial. In fact this usually means the ordering of knowledge for administrative or bureaucratic purposes. The separation, and not merely the distinction, of sociology from ethics in higher education is not natural. It is to deny the *nature* of ethics as a kind of knowledge. There is no difference whatever in principle between this and, say, the Nazis classifying Jews as subhuman. In each case certain "natures" are denied in the name of utilitarian purposes. In the one we have "intellectual nihilism"; in the other a kind of "political nihilism."

In the remainder of this chapter the fundamental kinds of knowledge will be reviewed. Since kinds of knowledge are said to be related in certain ways by "presupposing" each other, a clarification of this notion will first be necessary.

Some meanings of "presupposition." The meaning of "presuppose" is notoriously vague. Let us consider some examples. When we say that a theorem in a mathematical system presupposes a certain axiom, what is meant is that the axioms imply or "prove" the theorem, i.e., the axioms are evidence for the theorems. But when we say that communication presupposes the principle of contradiction we do not mean that communication implies, in the sense of "proves," the logical principle. Communication may be a sign of the truth of the principle, but it hardly constitutes evidence for its truth. Now implication is there in both cases, but there seems to be a difference even though both may be put in the form of "if-then" propositions —"if the axioms, then the theorems"; and "if communication, then the principle of contradiction."

Again, consider the three propositions: "physics (experimental) presupposes mathematics," "physics presupposes metaphysics," and "physics presupposes facts." Do we mean that propositions in physics imply the truth of certain facts, or that the certain facts imply the truth of the propositions in physics? Both alternatives sound reasonable, but we hardly mean both. Or do we? But in saying physics presupposes mathematics, although we mean that knowledge of physics depends in some sense upon mathematical knowledge, we do not mean that propositions of physics imply, in the sense of "prove" or "determine," the truth of mathematical propositions. The same may be said for the statement that "physics presupposes metaphysics," although, as we shall see, even here the term "presupposes" has a different meaning; that is, the relation of physics to mathematics is not the same as the relation of physics to metaphysics. Thus far it is evident that when we express a statement in the form of "*B* presupposes *A*," the meaning of it may be unclear.

Which meaning of "presuppose" can be meant in any given case depends in part upon what the nature of *B* and *A* is. For the problem at hand we are concerned with them only insofar as they stand for kinds of knowledge. If *A*, *B*, and *C* stand for kinds of knowledge, then specific propositions of each may be represented respectively by a_1, a_2, . . . ; b_1, b_2, . . . ; c_1, c_2, . . . Formally there are these four possibilities, accordingly as reference is to "some propositions" or to a specific proposition.

(1) The truth of b_1 presupposes the truth of a_1.

(2) The truth of b_1, b_2, . . . —meaning "some" (indifferently) but not all propositions of *B*—presupposes the truth of a_1.

(3) The truth of b_1 presupposes the truth of a_1, a_2, . . . —meaning "some" (indifferently) but not all propositions of *A*.

(4) The truth of b_1, b_2, . . . presupposes the truth of a_1, a_2, . . .

To what does the "some" in (2) refer? If it refers merely to b_1, *plus* one or more other propositions, then the difference between (2) and (1) in this respect would only be numerical, and this would not suffice to distinguish between two meanings of "presupposition." The "some" is "indifferent" only with respect to which propositions of type *B* knowledge are actually true if a_1 is true. The truth of b_3 and b_4 may presuppose a_2; and a_1 makes possible the truth of b_1 and b_2, but does not determine which is true. "Type *A* knowledge is regulative of type *B* knowledge" means that the actual truth of a proposition of *A* allows the possibility of asserting the truth of this or that proposition of *B*. And by "this" or "that" is not meant just "any," but rather the "some" that are relevant to the "regulative" proposition.

In (3) the "some" refers to a group of propositions of *A*, all of which are actually, and not merely possibly, true. This interpretation is necessary if (3) is to have any distinctive meaning. Otherwise all that is meant is that the actual truth of a proposition in one kind of knowledge presupposes the possibility of truth in another kind. While this is correct, it is a general proposition about the nature of truth and knowledge, and does not offer any distinct meaning of "presupposition." What can be said about any kind of knowledge in relation to any other cannot suffice to distinguish a specific relation between any two kinds.

In (2), while a specific "some" of the propositions of *B* is referred to, the specificity being determined by a_1, the proposition a_1 is indifferent not to the possible truth but only to whether this or that member of the "some" group is actually true or false. In (3), while a specific "some" of the propositions of *A* is referred to, the proposition b_1 is indifferent neither to the possible nor actual truth of the members of the "some" group, but only to this or that member of the "some" group which is actually true. In this case type *A* knowledge is instrumental to type *B* knowledge. The (3) and (4) can be combined, for the latter is but a weaker form of the former. That is, the difference between the two is essentially numerical, whether reference is to b_1 or to b_1 and b_2. . . . There are, then, three possibilities, representing what we shall call the relations of "constitutive of," "regulative of," and "instrumental to."

In the relation, type *A* knowledge is instrumental to type *B* knowledge, meaning that if a specific proposition (b_1) of *B* is true, then some propositions (a_1, a_2, . . .) of *A* are true, the "some" may be general or restricted. If general, then the "some" may be "any." In this case "any" means, not "all," but (indifferently) any one proposition. If limited or restricted, then a specific "some" (a_1 . . . a_{10}) is meant as against some other "some" (a_{11} . . . a_{20}). In the regulative relation the "some" is always restricted. As we shall see later, when we say mathematics is instrumental to experimental science the restricted relation is meant. When we say that historical propositions are instrumental to metaphysics it is the general relation that is meant.

One kind of knowledge cannot be partly instrumental to, or partly regulative of, some other kinds of knowledge. In either case it is wholly so, or not at all. But one kind of knowledge may be partly constitutive as evidence of another kind. There is only one case, as we shall see, of one kind of proposition being wholly constitutive as evidence of another kind. The following summary statement of the three meanings of "presuppositions" may now be stated. Examples will be given, but their explanation will be found in subsequent chapters.

(1) "Type *B* knowledge presupposes type *A* knowledge" means that *"A* is partially *constitutive* as evidence of *B"* if the truth of some specific proposition of *B* requires the assertion of some specific proposition of *A*. (If the converse is also true, then "wholly constitutive" is defined.) Example: Some propositions of metaphysics are constitutive of the philosophy of human nature.

(2) "Type *B* knowledge presupposes type *A* knowledge" means that *"A* is *regulative* of *B"* if the truth of some (indifferently chosen) propositions of *B* requires the truth of some specific proposition of *A*. Example: Some propositions of metaphysics are regulative of the experimental sciences.

(3) "Type *B* knowledge presupposes type *A* knowledge" means that *"A* is *instrumental* to *B"* if the truth of some specific proposition of *B* requires the truth of some (indifferently) propositions of *A*. Example: Some propositions of the experimental sciences are instrumental to metaphysics.

Kinds of Knowledge

A kind of knowledge is to be understood through natural, not artificial classification. That is, a kind of knowledge is to be understood in terms of its subject matter. The use that is made of knowledge is altogether another matter. Unless a kind of knowledge had a *nature* independent of its use, it could not be used. There is a place for "utility," and there is the "practical" and a "pragmatic" element in knowledge. But the modern pragmatic naturalist, for the most part, has not been concerned with "knowing" but with acting or doing. With but few exceptions, equipped but with an "attitude" (naturalistic and anti-theistic) and a "method" (something called "scientific"), he sallies forth to conquer nature, i.e., adjust to the environment; and conversely.[5] Fundamental kinds of subject matter are concerned with fundamental kinds of being, or with its modes or aspects. In this respect metaphysics is in a peculiar position relative to other kinds of knowledge. Yet, not only is this as it should be, but it could not be otherwise, for that knowledge which is *about* the nature of knowledge is itself one kind of knowledge among others.

We have given reasons for believing that moderate realism is the most *adequate* metaphysical position to account for the nature and kinds of knowledge. This adequacy, in itself, is not sufficient for demonstrating the truth of realism. Rather it is one *sign,* among others, of its truth. But unless the truth of realism could be demonstrated independently, it could not serve its purpose in the classification of knowledge. Kinds of knowledge should have something to do with kinds of being. Hence, we have spoken of "contexts" and "domains" of knowledge. Of course, these are mental, not real, entities. But they do have a "foundation in things." If they did not, then they would be *nothing but* mental fictions, and would represent nothing real but only human purposes willed in abstraction from the rational.

There is theoretical and practical knowledge. The practical is synthetic, i.e., composed of kinds of knowledge, integrated. The theoretical may be either autonomous or synthetic. An autonomous kind of knowledge is that which is not the product of the integration of two or more kinds of knowledge. Synthetic knowledge is constituted by kinds of autonomous knowledge. Since in common speech an autonomous kind of knowledge more often than not is called by the same name as a synthetic kind of knowledge, there is a problem of terminology in connection with the analyses of the following chapters. The three following considerations are to be kept in mind.

(1) The order of knowledge and the order of being should not be confused, and it is our hope that we shall not do so. Sometimes the same term will refer, at different times, to each. For example, the "ontological" may refer to a context of knowledge or to the aspect of being which is the foundation. In any given

case the specific meaning should be disclosed by the universe of discourse.

(2) When a kind of knowledge is thought of in and for itself, and hence in abstraction from the ontological, then the knowledge is considered as "positive." It is in this sense that a nonontological kind of knowledge is autonomous.

(3) When a nonontological kind of knowledge is integrated with the ontological we have a synthetic kind of knowledge. Historically an autonomous and a synthetic kind of knowledge have often been called by the same name. The term "mathematics" may be the name for the study of quantity *qua* quantity or of quantitative being. The first is mathematics in its positive and autonomous sense; the second is synthetic and is the philosophy of mathematics. Again, the specific meaning will often be determined by the context of the discourse.

How may the various contexts be determined? And why is a context *what* it is? It may seem that the most obvious way to find the answer is to make an empirical or phenomenological description of what men are doing when they are working in their special fields of knowledge. We can observe, for example, experimental scientists and theologians at work and discover what kind of "things" they are talking about. Presumably we would then know what experimental science and theology are. In the same manner it would seem that we could find out what home economics, civil engineering, etc., are. The Christian theologian is concerned, for example, with such propositions and their implications as are found in the Apostles' Creed. On examination it will be observed that the propositions are not generalizations. And although descriptive of uniqueness they seem to be different from the kinds of propositions the historian seeks. On the other hand, the experimental scientist never seems to be interested in any particular thing except as a member of a class.

And so on. One could go to some length with such observations. And yet a little thought will reveal that, however helpful and necessary such descriptions are, in themselves they can never give us the answer we wish. We cannot observe a scientist at work and know what science is, as we might observe the behavior of a wasp in order to know what it is. And the reason is this, that we have first to know what experimental science is in order to know when the scientist is working as a scientist, and when he is not; when he is talking science and when he is not. Presumably the wasp always works as a wasp. Otherwise the question is begged, or we fall into the sophistry of saying that experimental science is simply that which the experimental scientist does.

A biologist may talk about living matter, the scientific method, and biology. The first is the subject matter of biology; the second is about a method used in studying the subject matter. One and the same man talks about living matter and a method, but the subject matter is quite different in the two cases. He may be an authority on the first, and not on the second. For it does not at all follow from the fact that he uses a method that he knows the method quite as well as the subject matter which is studied by the method. Of course, he may. But if so, it is because he knows logic as well as biology. On the other hand, in the third case he is talking about a kind of knowledge called biology. He is not talking as a biologist primarily, but perhaps as a philosopher. But one could not know all of this, in fact one could not even make these distinctions, if kinds of knowledge could not be distinguished independent of the oral and social behavior of a person. And to confuse a proposition about living matter with one about biology as a kind of knowledge, as if the evidence were the same, or as if an authority on the first was *by that fact* an authority on the second, would be simply to confuse first and second intentions, or in positivist terminology, an object language with a meta-language.

It is in terms of a metaphysics that the subject matter of the elemental and fundamental disciplines must be determined. A factual description of what the practitioner of a discipline does has two functions. First, it is instrumental to the metaphysical problem. Historically man did not begin with clearly defined subject matters. The latter emerged from a confused whole. And even today were it not for the fact that in some manner or other such emergent disciplines exist there would be no problem of the metaphysics of knowledge. However, a factual description of these existing disciplines, so far from solving the problem of the order of knowledge, really presents or creates a problem.

Second, a factual description based upon observation of what the various practitioners of fields of knowledge do provides a check upon any metaphysical analysis. For example, it would be a sign of metaphysical inadequacy, and an unfortunate kind of *a priorism,* if one were to insist that experimental science is not concerned with quantitative measurement or with moving things. Not only would there be an irresponsible use of "names," but if a metaphysical analysis literally has nothing to do with what a practitioner of a kind of knowledge does, then so much the worse for the metaphysics in question.

The phenomenological context. Man is a creature who knows, acts, and makes, as well as experiences. He wishes to know "things"; what he makes are artifacts. Artifacts and things are both phenomenological. They appear, have space and/or time characteristics. But an artifact lacks a private nature independent of the knower and maker. Things have this private nature, and we may speak of it as the ontological aspect of things in contradistinction to the phenomenological. These are two contexts with which we are already familiar. There is also a "mathematical" context.

Within the phenomenological context there are two domains, history and experimental science. Both are positive disciplines, since they are considered in themselves and as autonomous. The first seeks the singular proposition; the second, the generalization. It is "signate matter" that defines the possibility of history. Since there can be no science of particulars or individuals as such, history is not a science in the sense in which other kinds of knowledge are. It is "common sensible matter" which makes possible generalizations and experimental science. Since neither signate nor common sensible matter can exist without the other, the context of history and experimental science is the same. As domains they are distinguished by the type of proposition sought. In historical knowledge generalizations function as means to the end of discovering true historical propositions. In experimental science historical propositions function as means to the end of arriving at true generalizations.

The mathematical context. It is "intelligible matter" that makes possible mathematical knowledge, and hence distinguishes another context. Why should signate and common matter distinguish domains, and intelligible matter a context? The reason is that intelligible matter can have a mental existence in abstraction from signate and common matter. The range of possible mathematical forms in man's imagination is much wider than the actual forms which exist in common and signate matter. The latter are limitations upon the former. The mathematical context has only one domain, the general, and which is identical with the context itself. For this reason the context may be called "formal," provided of course that one understands that the kind of forms considered are only those ordered to intelligible matter.

The ontological context. The ontological context is composed of two domains, the metaphysical and the theological, depending upon whether the general (universal) or the singular and unique is sought. Whether or not there are theological truths is not in question here. Even if one were to deny that there are any such truths, it would be necessary to be clear about the kind of proposition and the kind of "knowledge" that is being denied. There is a difference between saying that "quality is a function of quantity" and "the Father and the Son are of one substance." The first is general; the second is singular, which we shall speak of as "descriptive of uniqueness." But the content of such singularity is quite different from that of an historical proposition, for God is not one thing among others. If the theological is denied, then particularity is confined to the spatial-temporal. And conversely.

Attention is to be called again to the kind of propositions composing the Apostles' Creed, which is a good example of what some theologians do when they are working as theologians. They are not primarily value judgments, historical propositions, generalizations, or even general or universal propositions about being—except in the sense that for certain purposes a singular can be taken as universal. The term "God" is equivocal, sometimes being the subject of a metaphysical proposition, sometimes of a theological proposition. In the first case are included all propositions derived through reasoning upon evidence given naturally in human experience. In the second case are included all of those propositions for which the evidence is divine revelation. The Christian would prefer to speak of these as truths of revelation rather than revealed truths. A theological proposition is, then, strictly speaking, a truth of revelation. "Natural theology" is really metaphysics; it is not theology based upon revelation.

Whether the domain of a proposition is metaphysical or theological in any given case is sometimes difficult to determine. Nevertheless the distinction remains and clear-cut cases of each can be given. To speak of God as the cause of the world is metaphysics, for "God" is taken merely conceptually. The evidence for God's existence must be independent of revelation. On the other hand, to speak of God as one member of the Trinity is strictly theological. Such uniqueness could not be known except through divine revelation. The being of God is the same, but the source of knowledge is different. If there is some evidence metaphysically for the existence of God, then there is some ground (not sufficient evidence) for faith in a truth of revelation such as the doctrine of the Trinity. But there is no reason why one should have faith in a doctrine *about* God if there is no reason at all to believe *that* he exists. From the standpoint of the order of being the theological has priority over the metaphysical, i.e., the God who is the cause of the world is first the God of the Trinity. From the standpoint of the order of knowledge the converse is true. The modern world may be said to have begun with a denial of this, and with the assumption that one can have the theological without the metaphysical. This soon turned into its opposite, and so by the eighteenth century we have metaphysics without theology. The twentieth century is witness to the logical conclusion of the process—neither metaphysics nor theology, but the triumph of positivism and subjectivism.

Because the strictly theological proposition is singular and ontological, it does not necessarily follow that an extreme Platonic interpretation is correct. That is, a theological proposition may have a phenomenological reference, and a historical proposition may have an ontological (theological) reference. For example, a miracle may take place in space and time, the uniqueness of which may be described in terms of a historical proposition. If it is true that through supernatural power Christ healed a certain person—and whether it is true or not is irrelevant for the present—then this is at least a historical fact, expressible in a historical proposition. But it is also a theological proposition, for it is a historical proposition with an ontological reference. Metaphysically we would say that the primary cause is referred to directly, not secondary causes. From the standpoint of knowledge the evidence sufficient to prove or make plausible the historical proposition would be necessary although not sufficient to prove the theological proposition, i.e., the same historical proposition with an ontological reference.

The synthetic context. An autonomous, theoretical science is obtained by abstracting a mode or kind of being from being. The autonomy exists only in the order of knowledge. In the order of being a mode is completely dependent. When history, experimental science, and mathematics are thus autonomous they are "positive" disciplines. When the contents of these disciplines are considered as they *really* are, i.e., in relation to being, then we have the "philosophy" of these subjects—the philosophy of history, the philosophy of nature (which is *natural* science), the philosophy of mathematics. As has been pointed out, the name of a discipline is often used equivocally, e.g., "natural science" sometimes meaning the "philosophy of nature," and other times meaning "experimental science." Even in this volume often the specific meaning of the name of a kind of knowledge will have to be grasped by the context of discourse.

The "philosophy" of a discipline defines a theoretical, synthetic context. This means that the mathematical and the phenomenological domains are integrated with the ontological. The ontological is not only that *with which* the positive disciplines are integrated, but also is that *by which* they are integrated. The last fact is important. First, if it were not so, then an infinite number of kinds of knowledge would be necessary;

$n + 1$ to integrate n kinds of knowledge, $n + 2$ to integrate $n + 1$, etc. But this would be equivalent to the impossibility of any integration. A corollary would be that the impossibility of metaphysics is equivalent to the impossibility of integration of knowledge, or any order of knowledge at all. Second, the ontological domains are not positive sciences, and hence nothing could integrate them.

There is nothing mysterious about the notion of integrated knowledge, or that of a synthetic context. All that one must understand is how one obtains the autonomous, positive sciences. Chronologically, and psychologically, the synthetic contexts are prior. Inquiries are made about *nature, natural* things, the *natures* of things; in other words, about *changing* being. The emphasis may be on change or on being. Historically, as well as psychologically, it has been on the latter. However, a division of labor allows the mode to be mentally abstracted in order that the details may be explored. It was then that "experimental science" emerged. Experimental science is theoretical and autonomous because the details are just what they are. But what has been separated for a purpose must be put together again. This is the synthesis of the ontological with the phenomenological, of metaphysics with experimental science. And now we understand not merely change *qua* change, or being *qua* being, but changing being—in short, *natural things*. We now have natural science. We begin and end with questions of natural science. Experimental science is that which emerges in the process.

And so with mathematics. We begin with an inquiry into quantitative being, through analysis consider quantity *qua* quantity, and through integration with metaphysics (being) return to quantitative being. As autonomous and independent of the metaphysical, mathematics is "positive" and concerned with quantity *qua* quantity. Mathematics means the "philosophy of mathematics" when reference is to the synthetic context, that of quantitative being.

Wherein lies the autonomy of a science? A science is autonomous if it arises directly from experience without the *constitutive* mediation of any other kind of knowledge. The term "constitutive" is important, for another kind of knowledge may be "regulative of" or "instrumental to" an autonomous science. For human beings there are only two sources of experience, sense and divine revelation. The latter is the source of theological propositions, if it is admitted that they are possible. Sense experience is the basis of all historical propositions, whether they be derived from immediate experience as in experimental science or by witness as in history. Of course, generalizations are not sensed, but they are, as we shall see, *wholly* constituted by propositions (historical) that are based on sense. The autonomy of both mathematics and metaphysics lies in the fact that they are obtained through abstraction from sense experience. The denial of this makes an unintelligible mystery of the problem of how sense and intellect can ever get together. The mystery is only deepened by appeal to such a notion as "isomorphism," which is of course a perfectly valid concept in any special science concerned with instrumental signs. It is wise to relegate mystery to the theological where it belongs. When this is not done its locus is simply shifted elsewhere, thus creating the modern alternatives either of an anti-intellectualistic, formalistic *a priorism* or of a doctrine of "created truth," thus confusing knowing with making and fact with artifact.

The synthetic context of logic. Is logic a theoretical or a practical synthetic knowledge? The answer depends partly upon how the term "practical" is to be used. For historical reasons the term as here used is confined to knowledge of acting and making. Of course logic is an instrument in knowing, but knowing logic is still knowing and not acting or making. It is true that logic may be said to be practical, to be useful, in knowing. But when the term acquires such a broad meaning its distinction from the theoretical breaks down. Mathematics is practical and useful in knowing about the physical world, but it is not for that reason a practical, as opposed to a theoretical, science.

As synthetic the object of logic is intentional being; and "logic" means "material logic" as well as "formal logic." What is it that is integrated? It is metaphysics and strictly "formal" logic. It is possible, for a limited purpose, to abstract intentionality from being and consider intentionality *qua* intentionality.

This is logic in a positive sense, and is usually what is called "formal logic," that which is studied somewhat mechanically and in abstraction from what is intended, and from all metaphysical considerations. When *what* is intended is considered, i.e., the kind or mode of being, the "matter" referred to, then we have what is called "material logic."

One may have a questioning feeling about this analysis. If there is a positive side to logic, why has it not developed in its autonomy as has mathematics and experimental science? Insofar as logic has some semblance of identity over a period of two thousand years, it seems to be directly based upon metaphysics, and hence to have no autonomy. Insofar as it seems to have acquired autonomy and become a positive science, it seems to have little to do with traditional logic—and this in spite of the fact that recent logic is said to include, and not repudiate, whatever contribution Aristotle made. Is there not a difference between the periods from Aristotle to Leibnitz and that from Leibnitz to Carnap and Quine? Furthermore, if logic as positive is concerned with intentionality *qua* intentionality, then why is it that recent logic seems to pay little if any attention to it? In short, mathematics as positive still seems to be concerned with quantity, and experimental science with motion; but logic as positive is no longer concerned with intentionality. Is there not something wrong with our analysis of the nature of logic?

Part of the answer perhaps lies in the proper use of a name. Because of the chaos that has existed in the order of knowledge there has been unclarity about the nature and limits of subject matters, and what name should go with what subject matter. Sometimes "logic" is a name given to what is really the "philosophy of mathematics." At other times it is identified with "inductive techniques," "system construction involving real relations," "grammar," or "linguistic analysis." The confusion has been concomitant with the decline of metaphysics and the rise of positivism. In the absence of an order of knowledge about all one can do is arbitrarily take one's pick among the lot. Otherwise logic must be delimited and defined, as we have attempted to do, so that it has a nature of its own. It has already been pointed out that to identify logic with general system structure or construction in terms of real relations is simply to misuse a term in addition to denying the existence of logic as knowledge.

However, logic as positive does present a peculiar problem, but one which may be understood if we realize that "positive" is a matter of degree. Or, we might say that not every positive science is equally positive. This may be seen by examining metaphysics and each synthetic science. Metaphysics is autonomous but not positive, for it is concerned with being, not anything in abstraction from being. It is not an integrated science, but rather is that by which another science is integrated. The other synthetic sciences all have a metaphysical part, but they are more or less metaphysical—not of course in the order of being, but in the order of knowledge. The order of more or less would be represented by logic, natural science (or the philosophy of nature), and the philosophy of mathematics. Logic is chiefly metaphysical; its autonomous side is not very important. The philosophy of nature, on the contrary, is composed essentially of equal mixtures of metaphysics and experimental science. On the other hand, what appears to be of chief importance in the philosophy of mathematics is the mathematics itself. It is for these reasons that historically logic has always been "close" to metaphysics, experimental science has tended to clash with metaphysics, while mathematics has always *seemed* to be so independent of metaphysics.

When logic is taken as positive there is little of importance that can be said, and this is in contrast to something like, say, mathematics. The principle of contradiction, for example, can be abstracted from its metaphysical foundation; and as such it becomes just a principle which seems, strangely enough, to be necessary to intelligible discourse. All of which is true, of course. To understand why it is so, one must turn to metaphysics. Otherwise, it becomes a mystery why what *is* so *must* be so. At this point, without metaphysics, there is the temptation to "speculate." The consequence is that it will occur to one person that perhaps the principle is not necessary at all, and that there are "alternative logics" to be chosen according to convenience; to another person that the principle is a "law of thought," that by its "structure" the mind must think with it; etc. In the latter case "speculation" is simply the unfruitful exercise of making a metaphysics out of logic as positive. This is Hegelianism. After Hegelianism comes cynicism and despair. The end result is the contemporary scene in which logic as intentional, i.e., logic in the sense in which it has a *nature,* has practically vanished, not only in the professional journals but also in the educational system.

Other illustrations can be given of the positive side of logic. The form of the syllogism *can* be—whether it ought to be or not—interpreted as a transitive relation. The mechanics of the syllogism as taught in the classroom is also representative of the positive side of logic; and as every teacher knows, a good deal can be learned without the necessity of introducing the metaphysical.

But therein lies a danger, that of reducing logic to a formal science such as mathematics. The peculiar nature of logic lies in the fact that it is concerned with knowing about knowing itself. Hence its formal nature lies in the fact that it is concerned with formal signs, not instrumental signs. Now an instrumental sign has a nature over and above its intending, while the whole nature of a formal sign lies in its intending. For this reason the formal nature of intentional signs is quite different from the formal nature of nonintentional signs. Since in mathematics the forms are nonintentional, the positive aspect of mathematics becomes very important and useful. On the other hand, in logic, since the whole being of intentional forms lies in their intending, consideration of them in-and-for-themselves is of little importance and not very useful, although, of course, it can be done. But, once again, in so doing there is the danger that logical relations are reduced to real relations, second intentions to first intentions. But is there not a contradiction? Have we not said that logic as a synthetic science is concerned with intentional being, whereas logic as positive is concerned with intentionality *qua* intentionality (in abstraction from being), and at the same time that logic as merely positive tends to lose its intentional character? No, there is no contradiction; rather a paradox, the kind attending any positive science. In metaphysics there is abstraction in order to obtain being, and in a positive science to obtain a mode or kind. Since being must be interpreted analogically, that which is abstracted from being is also being. And yet to the extent that anything is conceived as other than being, or in abstraction from being, it becomes (in knowledge) nonbeing. And so intentionality remains such only in intentional *being*. The moment one attempts to grasp it in and for itself, intentionality *qua* intentionality, then one loses it; one grasps only the nonintentional.

The paradox is not peculiar to logic, but characterizes all positive science. In natural science one abstracts the mobile from mobile being in order to understand the mobile *qua* mobile, which is experimental science. Yet in the very process of grasping motion in this manner one tends to lose it, recapturing it only by a return to metaphysics. When the return is not made, but rather a metaphysics is created out of the positive science, then the science becomes art. The "motion" of making the world in idea is confused with the motion of the world.

In mathematics as a synthetic science, i.e., the philosophy of mathematics, the same thing occurs. When one attempts to grasp quantity *qua* quantity, and the relation of quantity to being is forgotten, then what one obtains are "relational structures," and mathematics ceases to be concerned with understanding intelligible matter and becomes identified with the art of "system construction."

The synthetic context of value. The context of value is concerned with knowledge about acting and making, together with the experiences ordered to them. Such knowledge is "practical." Aesthetics has to do with making, and hence with the arts. The moral and religious sciences are concerned with acting. Since the religious implies a theological factor, and theology is to be left to a subsequent study, the analysis will be confined to the moral and the arts.

It has been pointed out that there is (1) theoretical, autonomous knowledge; (2) theoretical, synthetic knowledge; (3) practical, synthetic knowledge. The context of the latter is that of "value." The "practical" cannot be "autonomous." The denial of this reduces evaluations either to generalizations or to ontological propositions. Practical propositions are neither.

Evaluations may be singular or general, depending upon the nature of the minor premise in the "practical syllogism." Examples of such propositions are: "Beethoven's Eighth Symphony is more beautiful than Berlioz' *Symphonie Fantastique*"; "The American youth of today are morally better than the youth of twenty years ago." These propositions are of a type different from such propositions as, "Sheep are cloven-footed," "This is a red book," or "Caesar crossed the Rubicon," which are phenomenological propositions. (While a sentence in which "this" is indeterminate is literally an incomplete proposition, for the purpose of economy it may so remain with the understanding that some definite reference is always assumed.) For the understanding of evaluations an ontological reference is necessary. On the other hand, for the understanding of the proposition "This is a book," the ontological does not seem to be necessary. There is certainly a great deal of difference between the proposition stated about American youth and a similar proposition with a couple of words changed, namely, "The American youth of today are taller than the youth of twenty years ago." Not only is the nature of the evidence to which appeal is made quite different in the two propositions, but also the manner in which the truth or falsity of two propositions is discovered is quite different.

Knowing, doing (acting), and making are human activities, but they are not the same. The practical disciplines—religious, moral and artistic—are concerned with the latter two. Yet knowing about acting is knowing, and not acting; and knowing about making is knowing and not making. The distinction between acting and making arises because there are only two things one can perfect: one's own nature (or another's) or the nature of a "thing." The one is a "fact," the other an "artifact." In the former, one "acts"; in the latter, one "makes." In acting the good of the self is ultimate; in making it is the good of the work or object. In the latter we have art; in the former we have the moral and religious sciences as practical disciplines. If the theological is not admitted, then the moral is absolute. For illustrative purposes only we shall limit ourselves to art and the moral sciences.

Although acting and making are both practical, in contrast to knowing, they are not the same for the reasons that have been given. To break down the distinction is to destroy both art and morality. The phrase "making or remaking human nature" can be misleading. A child is potentially a man independently of anyone's purpose. On the other hand, a piece of marble is potentially—what? As an art object it is potentially a statue or wall-paneling. Independent of the mind of the artist it is either or both or neither. In perfecting human nature the end is given; in perfecting a work of art the end is humanly determined.

3

Knowledge as Practical: The Arts and the Moral Sciences

The distinction between knowing and making or producing presupposes the distinction between fact and artifact; and conversely. Objects may be made for either one of two reasons, for their immediate value (aesthetic) or for use value. The first defines what are called the "fine arts"; the latter, the "use arts," or what may be called the "technological arts." Music, poetry, literature, painting and sculpture are clearly examples of fine arts; engineering, industrial arts, and agriculture are essentially use arts. The former are ends-in-themselves *qua* art. The latter, even as arts, have their value chiefly as instrumental in the production of goods. Architecture is a mixture of both. Also, instrumental to even the use arts are the arts of "acquiring," e.g., mining.

It is sometimes said that in art the interest is not so much in "knowing" as in "knowing how." Properly interpreted this is correct. A practical discipline is knowledge because it is a discipline. Yet the discipline may or may not offer the intrinsic values that come from knowing *qua* knowing. There is a sense in which any kind of knowledge may be said to be practical. But the present context requires a more specific meaning of the term. Also, the term "know-how" is equivocal.

Art and Knowledge

In order to understand the nature of practical knowledge in general, and specifically the nature of art as knowledge, we must answer three questions. First, how does the theoretical or intellectual element enter into art? Second, are there many art disciplines, or only one? Third, are there many practical disciplines, e.g., art, morality, religion, or only one? The third question will be answered when we consider the moral sciences.

How the intellectual element enters into art. Any work of art must be constituted by a sensuous and an intellectual element. All art is making, but not all making is art. An ink blotter that is framed and hung on a wall is man-made, but it is not for that reason an art object. On the other hand, on the level of pure idea the most that man can do is to discover and contemplate. If man becomes "creative," what he produces is either falsehood, the contradictory, or myth in the Greek and Roman sense. Although it is true *that* both the sensuous and the intellectual elements are necessary for an art object, just *what* the nature of either may be depends upon the object; and this, in turn—as it does not for a *natural* thing—depends upon the imagination of the artist.

In the fine arts there is a distinction between the maker and the experiencer; in the use arts, between the maker and the user. They may or may not be the same person. People other than the maker enjoy a poem and use an automobile. The term "use" is equivocal, for by "good use" we may mean an appraisal of the art of driving an automobile or the morality of its purpose in being driven. With these distinctions in mind let us consider the intellectual element in the technological arts.

We have spoken of the arts of using and acquiring. The latter is subordinate to the former. Mining iron is for the purpose of obtaining the raw material which is formed into objects. The principles that enter constitutively into the formation of the object are those of experimental science. It is for this reason that the use arts are called "applied sciences." The purpose for which the object is made functions only as a regulative factor. We must distinguish, then, between (1) the purpose for which an object is made; (2) the purpose for which it is used; (3) the theoretical principles used in making the object; (4) the application of the principles to form the object; (5) the art, skill, the "know-how," in molding the raw materials into the object; (6) the art of, or skill in, using the object made.

To illustrate: (1) the purpose for which a bridge is made is for economy of transportation and communication. The value is economic, although it may be more than that. In itself such a value is a "social" or moral good.

(2) The specific purpose for which it is used depends upon the purpose of the transportation. It might be built for a commercial purpose; or in wartime to enhance or withstand a tyranny. Again, the kind of knowledge that is relevant here in judgment is that of a moral science.

(3) Although aesthetic principles may be regulative the principles used in making the bridge are those of mathematics and the experimental sciences. These are theoretical and autonomous, and are not practical except derivatively. They can only be practical in *use* because they are theoretical in *nature*. Insofar as physics is an "engineering subject," engineering is a science and not an art. The engineer must know physics in order to know how to make the bridge. But the nature of physics as knowledge has nothing to do with bridges. The "know-how" is the art, and this leads us to (4) and (5).

(4) The engineer applies theoretical principles in order to make bridges "in general," possible bridges in imagination. This kind of "know-how" requires an explicit intellectual or theoretical element. The physics of the "forms" and "plans" are not determined by the raw material. But what "form" or "plan" is selected may be determined partly by the nature of the raw material. Here the nature of the raw material performs a regulative function in relation to the mathematical and physical forms—a function only possible in an art object, never in a natural thing.

(5) The ultimate aim of engineering is to build this or that bridge, not bridges in general. For this another kind of "know-how" is necessary. It is the kind which is based upon experience, in which the theoretical element is only implicit, or may be absent. It is called "skill," and can only be acquired by "practice" in making an *actual* object. A skill consists in movements and manipulations based upon rules and precepts which can be communicated orally, in writing or by imitation. It is the "know-how" of the foreman on the job, and is the technological

equivalent of the moral virtue of prudence. *It is the art of dealing with the particular* qua *particular.* Since there is no science of the particular as such, it is that which cannot be acquired merely in the engineering school. However, this kind of skill is not a substitute for (4), but is something in addition. When it is a substitute we have the purely "empirical" and pragmatic, e.g., the electrician rather than the electrical engineer. The savage skillfully builds a canoe. He knows how because of "experience." He knows that for speed it should be this shape rather than that. But he never knows why. To say that it "works" is to beg the question. Of course it does! But it is the shape that *explains* the working; and not conversely.

(6) There is finally the art of using the bridge after it is built. The efficient, social use of a bridge is a "traffic problem."

In the light of these distinctions we may avoid the confusion between (*a*) what constitutes engineering as a practical discipline; (*b*) what the engineer *qua* engineer must know; (*c*) what knowledge it is desirable for a man who is an engineer to have. Also, we can better understand and interpret a paragraph such as the following:

> Contrary to the popular conception, the calculation of stresses and sections, the designing of members and details, and the supervision of their erection are not the only things a bridge engineer has to do. In addition, he has to conceive a project, develop it, verify and demonstrate its economic justification, battle opposition and secure authorization, wrestle with the problems of legislation and financing, determine the best location from both engineering and city-planning considerations, determine the best type and lay out for economy, efficiency, and durability, plan approaches and connections for maximum convenience and safety of traffic, design the form, lines, and proportions of the structure for beauty as well as for strength, select and specify the best materials for the work, prepare construction contracts and specifications, deal with public officials, property owners, clients, contractors, and material men, present recommendations and reports in a clear and convincing style, and—above all—have a sound and comprehensive grasp of the civic and social import and influence of his plan.[1]

When properly conceived, engineering, and all technology, is ordered to moral and/or aesthetic ends. To the degree that an educational program does not recognize this, it is unsatisfactory. The contemporary danger is to suppose that technology determines these ends; rather it must partly be determined by them.

In technology there are always three factors: (1) the raw material that is to be made into an object; (2) the theoretical principles in terms of which this is done; (3) the problem of "means," which is knowing how to shape the raw material in the light of the principles. A practical science is one defined by the fact that it is concerned with the problem of "means." The intellectual element constituting the means will be the experimental science. The raw material will exert a regulative function in determining the means, i.e., limiting the possible kinds of bridges given a certain material, say, wood or steel.

What is the difference between technology and theoretical science? Whereas the "material" is instrumental to the *knowing* of theoretical principles, the latter are instrumental in *knowing how* to *make* an object *for a purpose*. The last three words are important. In "knowing," the purpose is given, namely, truth. It is not relative to man's interest. On the other hand, in the use arts interest is relevant, for the correct "knowing how" can never be determined in abstraction from alternative purposes. While something may be made for the purpose of making something else, ultimately the purpose of making is for the sake of some kind of value.

When we consider technology as knowledge we must distinguish what it is "in and for itself," and what it is "for another." This distinction holds for any kind of knowledge except the ontological. A technological problem may be determined by its own requirements or by moral requirements. In the former sense technology will be called "positive"; in the latter, a "practical moral science." From a purely positive standpoint in technology an object is "made well," and hence is "good," if it is useful and efficient for the purpose for which it was made. Whether or not the purpose itself is good or evil is irrelevant. Technology *qua* technology, i.e., in its positive sense, is morally neutral. Therefore the kinds of knowledge which constitute technology are mathematics and the experimental sciences plus skills. The various skills make it an art; the former make it a science. But its specific essence lies in its nature as an art, for it shares with nontechnological knowledge its character as experimental science.

The practical aspect of technology consists of skills, those required to apply principles in order to create an object. But "practical" is a predicate that may apply to technology itself as positive. As such it is a means for moral (social) and/or religious ends or purposes. In this sense technology may be said to be a social science. It is also correct, and even more exact, to say that it is subordinate to moral values. Moral truths do not constitute technology as positive, but they do constitute technology when it is conceived as a social science. Technology as positive is subordinate to technology as a social science, and the latter may be said to include the former. But it is theoretically impossible, and hence nonsense to say, that technology as positive wholly determines technology as a social science. No "use art" determines the purpose for which the art itself is to be used. *What* object is to be made depends upon the purpose for which it is to be used. Since this depends upon personal and social values, which in turn presuppose the ontological, technology, in all its forms, and as a social science and not merely as positive, is constituted by an ontological element. As positive it is constituted only by mathematics and the natural sciences. Skills constitute the "know-how" of technology as positive, but relative to social science technology is itself the "know-how." As such it is strictly on the level of moral "means."

The principles may be summarized as follows:

(1) As positive, as a means, technology is a part of social science.

(2) As a means technology serves either good or evil ends. The end itself is not determined by technology as positive.

(3) If the end is given, technology provides the "know-how."

(4) The object *made* is determined, from the standpoint of knowledge, by both the phenomenological and ontological—

just as is the object *known*. The difference is this, that the object made has no private nature, no "insides." Therefore the ontology of the object made is dictated or conferred by the mind, whereas the ontology of the object known is dictated by the nature of the object. This explains the sense in which a use art is relative to human purposes. When knowing is confused with making, a relativism which is also a nihilism is the consequence. Natural science or the philosophy of nature is reduced to art.

(5) What is ontologically true is not a problem of a use art as such. In a civilization technology may be a *sign* of prevailing metaphysical ideas. It does not determine, but rather is determined by, them. For example, in a materialistic civilization in which the sin of pride becomes a virtue, automobiles may be made with more chrome than is necessary. It is likely that automobiles would be made differently if the virtue of humility were taken seriously. Even razor blades would probably be made differently.

(6) What a use art *qua* use art ought to be is a judgment *of* art *by* morality and religion; it is not a judgment of the *object made* in terms of the use art itself.

(7) Technology transcends the practical as "skills" only when it becomes practical as a means for realizing ends having to do with "doing," not merely making.

The fine arts and knowledge. In the use arts something is not made in order to know it, but rather to use it. But knowledge is necessary in order to know how to make it. In the fine arts, too, something is not made merely in order to know it. Here the purpose is aesthetic feeling, feeling having a certain quality. Although feeling is relevant in the distinction between knowing and making, it is not the main factor in distinguishing between human and animal making. Both animals and humans feel. But animals do not make poems or paintings; nor do they obtain the quality of feeling that comes from contemplating them. The reason is that while humans and animals both feel, only humans have an intellect. In man the relation between feeling and intellect is such that what is felt depends partly upon what man knows.

As in the use arts there was a distinction between "maker" and "user," so in the fine arts there is a distinction between "maker" and "experiencer," or between "making" and "experiencing." Experiencing, in turn, has two aspects, contemplation and criticism. Since in art (when the term is unqualified, reference will be to "fine art") there are always the sensuous and intellectual elements, principles, means, and raw material must always be distinguished. The means consist not only of skills, but also of the kinds of knowledge in the phenomenological context, e.g., knowledge of the scientific theory of color mixture in painting. The principles are aesthetic, and they include, whatever else, ontological knowledge. For art imitates nature by means of the "image" or "ikon," although not in the sense of "reporting." The ontological element in art is necessary because it is also part of a natural thing imitated. But since art is not "reporting," the aim is not merely to make an object, but to make a beautiful object. Now either there can or cannot be knowledge about the beautiful. If there cannot be, then art is merely a name for a kind of "activity." "Art criticism" is merely a misleading name for autobiographical monologues consisting essentially of historical propositions. One does not talk about the object, but about oneself. The object becomes merely the *occasion* for autobiographical utterances. This, in effect, reduces art to something else, and may be called "art nihilism."

If there can be knowledge about the beautiful, then what kind of knowledge is it? Realistically beauty is a transcendental category, certainly not one of the predicaments. And like any other transcendental it must be understood in terms of the doctrine of analogy. In any case, beauty is something directly experienced, whether one takes it as does Aquinas, as that which gives pleasure on sight, or more naturalistically as a feeling "sought or entertained for itself, and simply 'tasted'." [2]

The ontological may enter into art in two ways, through form and content—but not in the same manner, for it is regulative of the latter and constitutive of the former. For example, a picture of Christ being crucified is not necessarily a good work of art because ontologically true. On the other hand, a painting of Christ in a night club conga line would *not* be a good work of art because ontologically false. The ontological limits what can be art.

The ontological enters constitutively into art through "form." As a transcendental, beauty is a unity; but it has many meanings, and hence subordinate expressions, when its being is diffused, e.g., pattern, design, harmony, novelty, freshness, economy, unity, range, depth. It is for this reason that there can be a philosophy of the beautiful, aesthetics, in a sense in which there can be no philosophy of technology or of the use arts. The phenomenological disciplines, experimental science and history, are *used* in fine art, and hence are on the level of "means." They are instrumental to the "making." The ontological enters into art on the level of ultimate principles.

Whereas making in technology is for use, in the fine arts it is for immediate value. Hence, art is practical only in a single sense. Technology is doubly practical. As positive and relatively autonomous it is applied (practical) science. But technology is also itself a means to a kind of good, and hence is subordinated to the moral sciences which, in turn, are partly constituted by the ontological. On the other hand, fine art is practical only on the level of its own means. But the purpose for which an art object is made is not a practical one. The purpose is an end in itself, aesthetic value. Aesthetics as a discipline, as a kind of knowledge, is theoretical and not practical; it is a branch of special metaphysics. In art the phenomenological and ontological disciplines are brought together. Whereas in a synthetic theoretical discipline such as the philosophy of nature the phenomenological and ontological disciplines are brought together for the purpose of *knowing* a *natural* thing, in a practical synthetic discipline such as art it is for the purpose of *making* a *beautiful* thing. "Knowing" is present in both the theoretical and practical synthesis. In the former the purpose is knowing *qua* knowing, and feeling is derivative. In the latter feeling is primary, and in art at its height it is true to say—if properly interpreted—that one knows *through* aesthetic feeling. The error to be avoided here is that of conceiving as separate what is distinguishable. In man intellect and feeling do not lie in juxtaposition.

In "making" the ontological may be only implicit. That is, the artist does not have to be aware of the theoretical elements. It is for this reason that the artist may be quite surprised to learn how much "philosophy" the critic may find in his work. In that form of experiencing called "criticism" the ontological is explicit. We are here speaking of the ontological as constitutive. As regulative it may be explicit for the artist. He will not wipe his brush on a canvas and frame it. This is done, of course, but it is not art—no more than is the sing-song gibberish of an idiot to be called poetry.

It is not the purpose of this study to solve problems concerned with art. Rather it is to show the nature of the kind of knowledge which art is, the kinds of knowledge which constitute it. It has been sufficient to point out that the ontological enters regulatively into art in its content, constitutively in its form. Just how it does so in any given medium is another matter, one which would require considerable analysis.

There are two fundamental errors to be avoided in understanding the nature of art as knowledge. In the one the ontological is denied; in the other it is admitted but its function is misconceived. If the ontological is denied, then art becomes "the expression of the personality," or some such thing. Since the only kinds of knowledge now relevant are phenomenological, art criticism reduces to singular propositions and generalizations. The former often consists in personal biography and autobiography, together with historical gossip about "influences." Of course history, psychology, and sociology are not at all irrelevant to art, but they are not sufficient to understand it. When they are taken to be so, aesthetics, which is essentially a theoretical metaphysical discipline, is reduced to psychology. Communication breaks down because people no longer talk intelligibly about the art object. The object becomes simply the occasion for people indulging in monologues about themselves.

The other error does not eliminate the ontological in art. It merely misconceives the nature and function of art. Art is thought of, not as the synthetic practical discipline which it is, but as a theoretical discipline on the same co-ordinate level as experimental science and metaphysics. In fact art becomes their rival; not, however, in the sense of being a substitute for them, but in the sense of supplementing them. The function of art is to reveal truths inaccessible to the mere scientist or philosopher. This poses a fatal dilemma. If art ceases to be a "making" and becomes essentially "knowing," then the unique nature of art is destroyed. On the other hand, if it is still conceived of as a "making," then to make it supplement the theoretical disciplines in "knowing" is in effect to reduce knowing to making. Science and philosophy are modes of making the world; art is another mode.

A final question may be raised. If moral science and fine art are both synthetic practical disciplines, and the aesthetic is an end in itself, then would it not follow that there is a lack of relation between the two? Either that, or one is subordinate to the other. None of these alternatives seems satisfactory; yet they seem exhaustive. We seem to be faced either with a moralistic view of art, or with an "art for art's sake" doctrine. To subordinate art directly to morals would be to deny the aesthetic as an end in itself. To subordinate morality to art, or to hold an "art for art's sake" doctrine is equivalent to the reduction of morality to art. The "beautiful" is exhaustive of the "good." The latter becomes but a mode of the former.

It is true that these alternatives are unsatisfactory. But they are not exhaustive if beauty is understood realistically (not necessarily Platonically) as a transcendental. The understanding of moral and aesthetic value, beginning with particular experiences, culminates finally in general metaphysics. As transcendentals "good" and "beauty" are distinct yet related. It will then be seen that both the moral and aesthetic "ought" are concerned with the relation of "conformity." Both an act and an object of fine art are good and beautiful to the degree that they conform to the "ultimate nature of things," being—not to the degree that they conform to "use purposes" (e.g., advertising), government regulations, the will of a political party, social or box office approval, or the caprice of the doer or artist. Phenomenologically, morality and art are relatively independent and autonomous. They are related transcendentally. And that is to say that neither morality nor art is merely a means to the other. In contrast, use art or technology is not related transcendentally to morality, but rather is directly subordinated to the moral. The significance of technology as a positive discipline is exhausted in its character as a "means."

The three unsatisfactory alternatives as regards the relation between art and morality arise because beauty and good are not conceived as transcendentals which must be interpreted analogously. Neither one constitutes a genus to which the other is a species, e.g., as "animal" is to "dog.'

The Moral or Social Sciences

The relation between a kind of knowledge and an institutional entity called a department in a college or university which presumes to teach the knowledge is sometimes obscure. If there is a confusion of "names," it is because of confusion as to the nature of the knowledge to be taught. There is a sense in which social science is both "one" and "many." A plurality of social sciences are generated depending upon what is studied in a complex society, e.g., problems of government and state, problems of law, problems concerned with the production and distribution of wealth. Social science is "one" because of a unity of method in the various social sciences, and because of the fact that a problem in any one cannot be completely separated from a problem in another.

The nature of some social sciences. Law is a social science because the purpose of law is to make use of historical and sociological knowledge so that in the light of ethical principles certain social problems may be dealt with. To put the matter in another way, in law there is the use of legal techniques in the application of ethics to specific social problems with the help of historical and sociological knowledge. In abstraction from historical and sociological knowledge law becomes relatively unrelated and irrelevant to the constantly changing social order. Law becomes "unscientific." This is the case when law becomes purely deductive and there is argument from precedent alone. There is an apparent rigor that is obtained through sacrifice of the inductive element. The very act, however, that formalizes law also perverts it. On the other hand, if the normative element is overlooked in the legal process—whether in the making or application of laws—then however scientific law may be, it cannot be very moral. It degenerates into a type of studied opportunism. This kind of perversion is implied in the comment of the sophisticated cynic to the effect that "law is what lawyers do." It is also the foundation of much of the so-called legal education in which a law school becomes nothing more than a tutoring agency to prepare students to "get by" the state examinations. Such "education" is always dignified by being called "practical." It so happens, however, that there is a dialectic of error such that the "many" become "one," so that when law avoids the ethical it also becomes unscientific. The practical becomes very impractical.

Regardless of how "government" and "political science" are taught in "departments," insofar as they are disciplines they must be social sciences. Since for certain purposes it is possible to study almost anything scientifically, these subjects may and can be treated descriptively, i.e., historically and comparatively. But this specific purpose must finally be instrumental to the normative. One discovers what a state and a government are in order better to determine what they ought to be, what they ought to do. He who attempts to avoid ethical issues never succeeds in doing so. He only avoids thinking about them.

Economics is a social science concerned with the application of ethical principles to the various problems having to do with the production and distribution of wealth. It, too, has a "scientific" or positive aspect, and for certain purposes and in the solution of certain problems, this is sufficient. On the other hand, if the normative side of economics is neglected, then it becomes a pseudo-science which in practice becomes a dogmatic effort to justify the particular interests of a group or class. This is its status in all those institutions of higher learning—and there are exceptions—where economics is taught merely descriptively, or where it is taught as a "practical" subject, the chief purpose being the training of students "so that they can go out into the business world and make a success." Because of the prestige which a certain metaphysical interpretation of science had in the eighteenth century, there were those who attempted to interpret economics as a purely natural science. The consequences in practice of the belief that no ethical principles must be allowed to interfere with the "natural laws" of economics have turned out to be what those thinkers who were not paralyzed by the shock of modern science predicted. The Western world in the twentieth century has reaped what was sown. The very attempt to make economics what it cannot possibly be also allowed economic man to rationalize and justify his escape from moral responsibility. No one is to blame for economic evil. It results from business cycles, the natural laws of economics, the sinfulness of man; all of which, of course, is true. But the tragedy of this pseudo-scientific sophistry is that when criticism is directed at persons and institutions, rather than at impersonal forces, it is those people of heightened moral consciousness who wish to "interfere" in the name of ethical principles who are condemned the most as responsible for retarding "economic recovery" and progress. Economic morality is then interpreted as "playing the game" according to the "laws" which have nothing to do with morality.[3]

Social science without experimental science is impractical; without ethics it is not very "social" in a human sense. It is slowly and painfully being recognized in theory that economics, to the extent that it is rational, must be ethical. When this is recognized in practice, then there will be a reorganization of those "schools of commerce" which dignify their non-normative curriculum by the simple expediency of requiring a course in "business ethics"—in which the ethical is either reflexive of, or merely regulative of, business. A case can be made to the effect that the state should only have a regulative function in relation to private business. However, the ethical should be constitutive.

A word should be said about "history" as found in the curriculum of higher education. In college catalogues history is often found classified as one of the social sciences. If the structure of human knowledge were finally to be determined by college catalogues, there would be no problem. Fortunately, this is not the case. History is not a social science for several reasons. In the first place, in historical research the normative element, which partly defines a social science, is regulative rather than constitutive. This proposition requires interpretation in order to avoid misunderstanding. It is recognized that the normative element is indirectly present in historical research and historical writing. Both are in fact highly selective in choice of material. Written history consists of that which the historian believes to be of importance, and this implies evaluation. However, the evaluation as such does not determine the truth of the historical proposition. If it is true that George Washington was the first president of the United States, then no evaluation of any kind can determine or change the fact. In the social sciences the evaluational factor, through the metaphysical, enters as *content,* and partly determines the truth of that content. In any social science problem the answer to the question as to "what ought to be done" is determined by ethical criteria together with the nature of the circumstances which created the problem and which are to be changed. With respect to history it is one thing to say that data are selected through evaluation, and quite another thing to say that such evaluation constitutes or determines the truth of that which is selected. One can evaluate history, also. That is, one may appraise events that have happened. But through evaluation one cannot make an event happen that did not happen. But through creative and practical action one may make something "come" true that ought to happen. To "judge" history one must first have the history. Appraisal is the problem of the philosophy of history.

In the second place, history is not a social science because it is not a science seeking the "general" or "universal." This is again the function of the philosophy of history. When it is said that we ought to learn "lessons" from history and conduct ourselves accordingly in the future, it is still not history that is being "applied." The lessons learned and used are sociological, derived from the study of written history, and not from the study of that data alone from which written history is derived.

To put it in another way, the lessons learned are not arrived at by means of the historical method but rather by studying *that which has been obtained by the historical method.*

History does have a relation to social science. Some generalizations about past events are necessary in order that social science may have something more than guess work. It is history that provides the data from which generalizations arise. History, therefore, is instrumental to all of the social sciences. While not itself a social science, historical knowledge is necessary in the solution of social science problems. This instrumental relation which history has to social science does not make history a social science. Mathematics may be instrumental to the natural sciences, but this fact does not make mathematics a natural science. Nor can it be argued that social science is "about people"; and so is history; therefore, history is a social science. By means of this combination of poor logic and arbitrary definition history can be "proved" to be a social science—which apparently is the only justification for the classification to be found in some college catalogues.

The use of the term "social science" instead of "moral science" is a concession to contemporary terminology. It is, of course, true that in social science both ethics and science are "applied." But which is used for the sake of the other? It is science which is instrumental to ethical ends. Experimental techniques are used in order efficaciously to apply ethics or realize moral ends. Hence, what social science stands for could even more accurately be designated by such a term as "moral science."

The social sciences and the ethical. In contradistinction to the arts the social sciences are concerned chiefly with the ethical ends and their relations to social change. In distinguishing between the arts and the social sciences it is not to be implied that they have nothing in common or that ultimately aesthetic and ethical ends can be completely separated. The basis of the distinction rests simply on the fact that aesthetic and moral values are not identical in nature, that neither one can be reduced to the other, and that the nature of art and social problems are not the same.

Because of the close relation between the practical disciplines, and because of the very fact that they are practical, it follows that from the standpoint of the nature of knowledge what determines whether a problem belongs to one rather than another is the nature of the end sought. A problem in one of the practical disciplines may require a prior solution of some problem in one of the other. If a problem be that of the elimination of slums and the planning of new houses, there is a social problem. In solving such a problem one may call upon the help of artists. In an architectural problem certain technological problems may arise. In this case technology is instrumental in the solving of a problem of art, while the problem in art is instrumental in the solving of a social problem. The moral is concerned with the "doing" which perfects man's nature. Art is concerned with "making." But ultimately even "making" in any art, "fine" or "use," is for the purpose of perfecting man's nature, although the way they do it is not the same.

We have already mentioned that the term "social science" is a concession to contemporary terminology, and that a more accurate term would be "applied ethics" or "moral science." It is not an accident that the first term is the more familiar. An investigation into the history of the idea would lead one to the influence of a century of positivism and naturalism on Western thought and, in particular, American thought. If the term "science" is used, then for the sake of clarity it ought to be qualified by an adjective, e.g., "normative." It will be understood here that "social science" is equivalent to "normative social science" or "moral science."

One type of problem is that of attempting to find true general propositions describing social phenomena that are now occurring or have occurred in the past. Another type of problem is to describe some particular social situation as it now exists, evaluate it, and then in terms of the logic of means and ends plan carefully what ought to be done about it. These two types of problems are not at all the same in the type of question asked or in the nature of the evidence that is relevant. To call both types of problems "scientific," and to say nothing more, leads only to confusion. The first type of problem is scientific in the sense in which any problem in the natural sciences is scientific.

The second problem is not scientific in that sense at all. To describe what is in fact the case is one thing, to attempt to state what ought to be the case is something quite different. Only by some kind of *a priorism* in the worse sense of the word can the former meaning be reduced to the latter. The illogic which would allow such a reduction would also allow for the arbitrary reduction of almost anything to anything else.

The social sciences are of necessity concerned with evaluation on an instrumental level. They have to do not merely with factual situations, but also with ethical principles; not the discovery of the latter, but their application. For ethical principles to be efficacious they must be applied. Hence the social sciences are concerned with the applications of ethical principles to constantly changing factual situations. This is not to separate theory from practice. Rather it is to distinguish that which must be distinguished in order to avoid confusion. The manner in which ethical principles are established is not the same as that in which facts are discovered, and the way in which ethical principles are applied constitutes another kind of problem. One is not reasoning merely factually or purely normatively. The reasoning is essentially instrumental, dealing with means in relation to circumstances *in the light of ethical principles.* On the instrumental level of the social sciences ends which have time components, and hence are subject to change, are determined by existential circumstances in relation to ethical ends and principles. On the normative level, which is that of theoretical ethics, ends are determined metaphysically.

A few examples will illustrate the principles just stated. The concept of democracy implies some ends which do have, and some ends which do not have, time components. Democracy may imply, at a given time and place in history, a particular theory of property in the means of production. This end has a time component. That is, the end, being also a means to certain ends which are not subject to change in the same respect, may be "practical" only for a certain historical epoch. Whether or not the property relations can remain a practical instrument through technological and social change is a matter to be tested. Otherwise, instead of being an end with a time component, and hence a means to still further ends, it becomes an absolute end in itself. A certain pattern of property relations is moral on the level of "means." The principles of justice are not on the same level. They do not change with change of circumstances. One should not relativize what is not relative to circumstances. Nor should one absolutize the relative. To absolutize that which by its very nature cannot be absolute is certainly "unscientific." This principle remains true, although its truth alone does not guarantee against its misapplication. On the other hand, if the concept of democracy were to be defined totally in terms of temporal ends, then there could be no rational ground for change of ends. Change is never absolute; there must be some continuity. It is recognized that social change may in fact occur haphazardly and chaotically. But insofar as reason plays a part, social change is guided by principles which are not themselves in constant flux. And these are metaphysical factors.

In the case of democracy, one of the central ideas would be that of freedom. Freedom is not something that is good here and there, now and then. Human freedom is an ethical demand, and the method by which this truth is established is the normative reasoning that is peculiar to theoretical ethics as a discipline. To put it in another way, the evidence relevant to the proof or disproof of the necessity of freedom is never sufficiently supplied by existential (meaning "social") circumstances alone. Human freedom—the interpretation and analysis of the idea is not required for our present purpose—is an ethical idea in terms of which particular expressions of freedom may be evaluated. It may be very scientific to analyze carefully existential circumstances and in terms of the logic of means and ends determine what is necessary in order to enhance the growth of human freedom. But it is false, if not meaningless, to say that experimental science alone can determine whether the growth of human freedom is a worthy ideal. Herein lies the error of the pragmatist or instrumentalist with a positivistic tinge who puts a halo around the word "science."

The attempt to make ethics an experimental science is equivalent to the reduction of evaluations to generalizations. It is equivalent to the reduction of ethics to applied ethics or social science. The absurdity lies in the fact that if this is done there is really nothing to apply. To say that the scientific principles of sociology, as a descriptive science, are what are to be applied is no answer. There is nothing in the scientific principles or "laws" by themselves to tell how they ought to be applied, or what ends and values they should seek to enhance.

In practice the attempt to reduce ethics to social science, instead of recognizing that social science must have an ethical foundation, leads to one or the other of two unsatisfactory consequences. In the one case, if ethics is neglected entirely, social science degenerates into a "systematic" presentation of an ethical nihilism, buttressed perhaps by certain platitudes, personal prejudices and bits of wisdom that seem "obvious" to the author. In the other case ethical principles are not absent. They are present, but always as something which it is presumed to be futile to discuss. An example of this type of anti-intellectualism in the name of science is to be found in a paragraph by Stuart Chase. Mr. Chase writes, "In the past I have cherished the hope that science might displace traditional ethics by shifting the criteria of value to human survival. What makes for survival is 'good'; what opposes it is 'evil.' How can we know which choice in a specific situation makes for survival? Ask the biologist, the anthropologist, the physician, the psychologist . . ."[4]

In the first sentence Mr. Chase demonstrates that he has a complete misconception of the nature of both natural science and ethics. In shifting from one criterion of value to another, say, human survival, one is not shifting from ethics to natural science. The shift takes place on the level of ethics. Of course, after the shift takes place, then comes the application to "a specific situation." This is the level of the particular evaluation, the instrumental, in short, the level of social science. "What makes for survival is good" means "what is instrumental to human survival is good." Most certainly at this point we should go to the anthropologist, the biologist, etc. Only by an application of the techniques of the experimental method to causal relationships can the desired effect be known and obtained. But what has this to do with displacing ethics by "science"? Nothing whatsoever. It has never been the function of theoretical ethics to determine what choice should be made in a specific situation. Its function is to determine the principles by which wise choices may be made. It is not the function of social science *qua* science to determine the ultimate ethical principles and ends which are to be applied. Its function is to apply ethical principles to specific situations by making use of any and all aids that the sciences can possibly furnish. Mr. Chase does not get rid of ethics or displace it by "science." He simply accepts a particular naturalistic, ethical criterion as a dogma and wishes to be scientific about its application. *If* human survival is assumed as an ethical criterion, then . . . But how do we eliminate the "if"? How do we choose that criterion among others? To answer that one must indulge in the normative reasoning of ethics. The biological and medical sciences, as sciences, do not and cannot give the answer.

At this point we may mention two other arguments that are often given by social scientists who refuse to admit that social science must be applied ethics, that it has a normative factor in a sense in which natural science does not. It is said that the ends social science has to work with are those which have time components, those which are "concrete" and applicable at given times and places. If there are any so-called ethical principles or ends over and above these concrete ends, they are so general and vague as to lack significance, and for practical purposes are meaningless. There is a measure of truth in the first part, but the conclusion does not follow. It is futile to condemn ethics for not doing something it can't do. Generality cannot always be equated with vagueness. It is not the function of ethics to deduce the "concrete" and "practical," since the nature of such means must of necessity be partly determined by social circumstances. It is the function of ethics to be general. It is the function of social science to relate the ethical to specific circumstances.

There is another instrumentalist argument in which it is said that there are no ends in which there are not time components, that all so-called ends and principles are subject to change, that there are no timeless ethical truths, and hence there is no normative, but only instrumental reasoning. Perhaps this is not so much another argument as an inference from the one just considered. The point is that insofar as ethical principles have clarity and concreteness they are subject to change; to the degree that they are not subject to change they are so vague and general that they cannot serve the function claimed for them, namely, that of prescription or guidance. Ethical "truths" that are supposed to be timeless are really tautologies. For example, the sentence "Murder is immoral" is true, but it says nothing, for "murder" means "morally unjustified killing." What one is really saying is, "Murder is immoral because it is not morally justified."

An adequate answer would take us beyond the scope of this work. A few remarks will suffice to show that such an argument is not fatal to our thesis. What the instrumentalist says is true, but it hardly proves what he believes it does. He has chosen his examples and he has proven his point for that example and similar ones. The ethical problem still remains after the logical exercises. What are the principles in terms of which killing may be judged to be moral or not? Any set of social circumstances alone cannot give the answer. Facts alone can never be morally coercive. The denial of this is equivalent to the denial of any and all meaning to morality. Nor does it help very much to say that while all ends must have time components and are merely instrumental, for "practical purposes" some ends are taken *as if* they were noninstrumental for a historical epoch, or for a group of people for a certain given period. Of course this is true as a description of what in fact is sometimes done. But why? On what rational grounds can some ends be taken as if they were noninstrumental? What is the principle which can serve as a criterion for choosing between competing instrumental ends, that end which is to be taken *as if* it were something else than what it is. If an answer is given, then *that* principle cannot be instrumental even in an "as if" sense. If no answer is given, then the arbitrariness and irrationality that characterize all ethical nihilism are not avoided.

Finally, the instrumentalist who denies theoretical ethics as a discipline over and above social science, or who wishes to reduce ethics to social science, will point out that while it is true that in any system of ethics in the history of thought ethical ends have been taken as noninstrumental *in that system,* it is a historical fact that there have been different systems, and that the systems themselves have been modified in change. In short, all ethical ideas change, and hence by definition are instrumental. Historical facts, of course, are not to be denied. The conclusion is questionable for two reasons. In the first place, two kinds of change are confused. There may be a change in instrumental ends because they no longer serve as effective means to the realization of ethical values. There is also the change that comes in ethical ideas as the result of increased understanding. The ideal of brotherly love is not an ideal whose validity depends on time and place. A particular expression of love may change. Philanthropy might be the expression of love at one time, the expression of hate at another. But in order that particular expressions of love may have some common unity, there must be some general meaning of love. And this meaning may "grow." However the change is not from love to nonlove as an ideal, and no social circumstances could possibly force such a change from a rational standpoint.

The case is different with instrumental ends. Circumstances may determine that from a rational viewpoint a change from, say, philanthropy to nonphilanthropy, and hence some other means, in certain given circumstances, is necessary. In the second place, one cannot argue directly from historical relativity to ethical relativity for the reason that the evidence necessary to prove historical relativity is not sufficient to prove the latter. Even the nature of the evidence in the two cases is not identical. It is often the case that ethical relativity is assumed and not argued, and examples of historical relativity are offered as proof of ethical relativity, when really all that one has done is to *illustrate* what is assumed. The concept of ethical relativity is *compatible with* historical relativity, but this does not mean that the former is implied by the latter.

The social sciences, then, are not merely ethical or scientific. They are both. They are hybrids, practical synthetic disciplines. Without the techniques of the experimental method, together with the generalizations of common experience, there would be no rational way to apply ethical principles. On the other hand, if social science pretends to have no connection with normative reasoning, then in the attempt to be "scientific" it degenerates into a very careful and systematic presentation and application of a conglomeration of assorted prejudices, caprices, dogmas, and question-begging assumptions.

Two examples of social problems and the kinds of knowledge involved. One of the most convincing ways of demonstrating that social science is neither pure natural science nor ethics, but presupposes both, is to begin with a typical problem in social science and analyze the nature of the reasoning involved, if such reasoning is pushed to the farthest limit. Let us first consider the problem raised by the question: Should capital punishment be eliminated? Certain propositions will be assumed to be true in order to illustrate the nature of the reasoning. On the assumption that there are conflicting views on the problem, let us see where the reasoning process leads us. Different types of problems will be encountered.

The first type of problem is that to be found on the level of a purely experimental science. The question is asked: In those places where capital punishment is legally practiced, does it in fact prevent murder? A study would be made and from it some kind of generalization would emerge, perhaps, to the effect that capital punishment does not prevent murder. In the process of arriving at the generalization historical propositions will of necessity have been obtained. The question is purely a matter of fact. Historical propositions and generalizations will be sufficient, as in any experimental science; and of course in arriving at the generalization the inductive technique peculiar to any natural science will be used.

We now have the answer to the question as to whether capital punishment does in fact prevent murder. The answer is, let us say for the purpose of discussion, that in general it does not. Does it then necessarily follow that capital punishment ought to be eliminated? From the facts alone such a conclusion certainly does not follow, for facts alone never prove or disprove any evaluation. The end for which capital punishment exists as a means is really an assumed end. If this end is agreed upon, then there is no further problem. But it may be that there is a disagreement as to ends to be obtained. It may be asserted that the purpose of capital punishment is not essentially that of eliminating murder; rather capital punishment is necessarily implied as the penalty for murder because of the nature of the concept of justice. A human being, just because he is human, has no right to be denied punishment in this manner. Of course, whether or not the concept of justice makes such a demand is not relevant to the point at issue here. The point is that in the case where there is a disagreement on the question of relative ends, there emerges another type of problem which is essentially an ethical one.

The problem now becomes the one having to do with the relation of instrumental ends to some ethical end or principle. The reasoning involved is essentially normative in contradistinction to instrumental reasoning. There is no appeal directly to generalizations or historical propositions. Different conceptions of what is ultimately good will of necessity lead to different appraisals of relative ends. If the ethical principle is taken to be the happiness (hedonistically conceived) of the greatest number of people, then it might be argued very plausibly (although Bentham did not do so) that the instrumental end, which is the prevention of murder, is the one to be obtained; and since capital punishment does not prevent that end, then capital punishment ought to be eliminated. However, if the ethical principle is not to be such a utilitarian principle, but some more "idealistic" principle is to be held, then a different answer might be obtained. It might be argued that it is the duty of anyone who has willfully committed murder, as a rational person, to demand capital punishment. If a person does not demand and accept capital punishment as a penalty for murder, then it is society's duty to carry out what he should have demanded were he acting rationally. If a common ethical end is agreed upon, then the problem is solved at this second level.

If no common absolute end is assumed, and if reason is to be pushed to the extreme, then one would encounter a different type of problem, the metaphysical. An appeal to the ultimate nature of things in the defense of an ethical end would be necessary. If there is disagreement on this level as to what the ethical end is, then from a rational standpoint, the problem can be pursued no further. If the disputants have pursued the problem all along with good will, then even though in the end there may still be disagreement, no accusation of arationality can be made.

Let us now consider another kind of problem—not the efficacy of a given means, but that of determining what the means shall be. For example: How shall the unemployment problem be solved? Let us assume that the time context is the fourth decade of the present century. What is the method of reasoning that is involved in the process of solving this social problem? In this problem there are three factors to be distinguished—the circumstances, the end or principles, and the proper means to the end. The circumstances are the set of events which give rise to the problem. It is these circumstances which are to be changed, for they are considered undesirable. If they are to be changed, then some end or goal is to be obtained. Considered very abstractly, the end might be said to be the elimination of unemployment. That simply means that a situation is to be arrived at in which men are working in industry and agriculture. Concretely, however, the matter is not so simple. When an end is considered so abstractly, it becomes vague relative to other ends; and no end is completely unrelated to any and every other end.

Without the clarification of the nature of the end to be obtained, it becomes almost impossible to adapt the means to the end. If all that is meant by the elimination of unemployment is that men are once again working at machines or in industry, then the means to obtain such an end might be inflation, some form of state violence, or imperialism of some form. The nature of the end requires clarification. The end cannot merely mean that men now unemployed once again work in industry and agriculture. It may mean at least this, but also there is the consideration that in so doing no other value of importance is eliminated by the means used to obtain that end. Clarification of the end requires a procedure which points in two directions. First there is a clarification of the end with respect to the possible means which may be used to obtain the end. Second, there is a clarification of the end with respect to other worthwhile ends. By the very nature of a means, in contradistinction to an ultimate end or principle, it must be related to both the end and the circumstances.

What is the reasoning by which a study of the set of events called circumstances is made? The method is essentially experimental, for the problem is to get the facts. Some kind of statistical analysis will be made, and generalizations formed. Before the actual means can be selected among the possible means, the nature of the end desired must be understood. This problem is essentially an ethical one. The relation of any end to other ends, and also the relation of that given end to some absolute end defines the nature of an ethical problem. How far the reasoning is to be pursued in any given case depends essentially upon the nature of the problem. Implicitly there is an ethical aspect to every social problem, but it may or may not have to be considered in a given case. With the facts about the circumstances acquired, and the nature of the ends to be obtained clarified, then the remaining part of the problem is concerned with the acquisition of means to obtain the end desired. The reasoning here is essentially on the experimental level, and it may be said to be somewhat as follows. If *X* circumstances are given, together with *Y* "means," then we may reasonably expect *Z* effects, which are the consequences desired in the light of ethical principles assumed. For the purpose of logical analyses, the emphasis we have put upon the distinction between circumstances, means, and ends is necessary.

How and why the ontological is constitutive as evidence in evaluations. An evaluational proposition in any moral science is singular or general, and is the product of the integration of kinds of knowledge from two contexts, the phenomenological and the ontological. If any argument were to be condensed, it would take the form of a syllogism. In this "practical syllogism" the major premise would consist of either a theological or metaphysical proposition; the minor of a historical proposition or generalization; the conclusion would be an evaluation. Whether or not the conclusion is singular or general depends upon the minor premise, whether it is a historical proposition or generalization.

In order to understand how and why the ontological is constitutive as evidence in evaluations, let us consider a particular example. A student is accused of getting help from his neighbor during an examination and is told that his act was wrong. What is presupposed is that cheating in examinations is wrong. If it is asked why it is wrong, the answer is that all cheating is wrong. If it is asked why all cheating is wrong, the answer is that it is dishonest. But why is honesty good? One might say that it is necessary for the harmonious development of the self, or, more specifically, to the development of all the potentialities that would make for the compossible actualization of the self. What is presupposed here is that such harmonious development is good. Again, why? One might say that the development of all the potentialities that would make for the compossible actualities of the self is conforming to the ultimate nature of things, or to *being*. The suppressed premise here is that whatever is conforming to being or the ultimate nature of things is good.

If one now asks why conforming to the ultimate nature of things is good, we have to stop. An answer would have no meaning for any problem of moral choice because there is no alternative. The most one can do is to explain why there is no alternative, and hence why this must be the case. We do not mean to say that a human being cannot go contrary in his behavior to the ultimate nature of things. Rather we are saying that if the human being is to lead a good life, then there is no alternative to that of conforming to the ultimate nature of things.

The reason why there is no alternative is that the denial would leave morals completely negative. There would be no morals at all, for the arbitrary will of man would be final. No standard assumed would be grounded in anything beyond man's subjectivity. However, this latter is identical with nihilism, which is simply man's rebellion against being. Furthermore, it would seem that every great ethical system has presupposed this general meaning of goodness, namely, that conforming to the ultimate nature of things is good. Some meaning of "natural law" is necessary for morality.

In the example we have given it was necessary for the purpose of illustration to give some definite answer to the problem as to the specific meaning of goodness. The specific answer given for the purpose of illustration may be rejected without invalidating the essential thesis as to the necessity of the ontological in evaluations. In any case the appeal is still to the ultimate nature of things. The good life is said to lie in conforming to that nature. Epicurus believed that the good life consisted in conforming to the ultimate nature of things, and so did Bentham when he pointed out that nature has placed man between two masters, pleasure and pain. The Christian also believes that the good life lies in conforming to the ultimate nature of things. Whether one be talking about a hedonist, a materialist, a Christian, or a Moslem, they all believe in conforming to the ultimate nature of things. The point of disagreement lies in what is believed to be the ultimate nature of things. Such differences of belief constitute the *basic* disagreement in ethical systems, and hence such interpretations are concerned with the metaphysical problem. Some ontological presuppositions are made by all ethical thinkers regardless of the degree of difference in their ethical conclusions.

Complete or absolute conformity is only to be found ontologically. If the ultimate nature of things is simply nature on a biological level as we find it outside of ourselves, then ontological goodness would be that very nature. Since the conformity of nature to itself is complete and not partial, then nature can be called good in an absolute sense. On the other hand, if the ultimate nature of things is not merely nature but the will and intellect of God, then ontological goodness would be completely identical with God's nature. If the nature of God conforms completely with itself, then God is absolutely good. We may notice that the propositions "God is good" and "Nature is good" are not evaluations. The subjects are not particulars that are being judged in terms of a standard. Nature or God, as the case may be, is the judge. Neither is that which is to be judged. Such propositions are ontological. The proposition "Nature is good" is metaphysical. The proposition "God is good" is theological, although it may also be interpreted as metaphysical. In saying that "God is good" one does not evaluate God. The description is not that of any *degree* of conformity, and hence the description is not that requiring a relation between the phenomenological and the ontological context.

This analysis rests upon the very real distinction between an ontological and a historical proposition or generalization. But no so-called Platonic doctrine of two worlds, one wholly finished or ready-made, is necessarily implied. To illustrate, we may point out that what is absolutely good must be completely actual and contain no potentiality. Whatever contains potentiality is only relatively good. When we say that God is good, we may mean that His nature is good. More exactly, God of necessity always wills the good. There is no potentiality for change in His will in this respect. Always willing the good, His will is always loving, and hence He is absolute love. Such an "absolute" need not imply that all good has been achieved and that it is useless for humans to try and achieve that which already is.

There are several questions that may arise as to the manner in which the ontological enters constitutively into the determination of evaluations.

(1) It may be pointed out that even if a singular evaluation is not a historical proposition, nevertheless general evaluations are still nothing but generalizations. Now undoubtedly, subjectively or psychologically, the way in which we learn about what is good (at least for the most of the race) is by making generalizations. We judge this to be good, and that to be good, and hence come to the conclusion that all *X*'s of a certain kind are good. For example, it may be held that it is good to treat each person as an end in himself and not merely as the means. One may generalize from a series of acts, each act being an instance of the generalization. Treating *this* person as an end rather than as a means merely, seems to work out satisfactorily and hence is good; treating *that* person as an end rather than as a means merely, seems to work out satisfactorily and hence is good. Therefore, we find that it is generally satisfactory and good to always treat people as ends in themselves.

Even if this be a correct account of how psychologically one or more people come to believe a principle, the distinction between a generalization and a general evaluation still remains. In the first place, some standard of goodness is presupposed in the judging of particular instances as good. In the second place, were there no conflict of values, and no problem of subordination of values—in other words, no problem of choice—then if X's *seemed* good they would *be* good. But something more than merely seeming to be good is necessary in the way of evidence to leap from "seem good" to "is good." In other words, there is a very real distinction between a psychological description of the way in which we may come to believe something, and on the other hand a rational justification or proof of the truth of the belief. The generalization is relevant to the former, the general evaluation to the latter.

Generalizations about values are still generalizations and not general evaluations. The anthropologist may study the values of, say, the Fijis, and he may report that they believe this is a value and that is a value and so on. He is telling us something about what the Fijis generally believe to be good, and perhaps he may tell us also the degree or extent to which they act on such beliefs. Such generalizations of the anthropologist are made from specific historical propositions which he has obtained in the course of his investigation of a primitive society. There is a further question, of course, as to whether the Fijis believe truly or not about the nature of goodness. But this question is an ethical one, and regardless of the answer that may be given an appraisal would have to be made of the Fiji society. Such an appraisal would be a specific evaluation, not a general evaluation. The evidence that is sufficient for determining the truth of the generalization of the anthropologist could not be sufficient as evidence to determine the truth of the singular evaluation. The content of such anthropological generalizations, each of which may be true, would vary from society to society and with time and place. The anthropologist deals with a history of codes of morals. Codes are always on the level of "means." If an appraisal is to be made of a code, then there must be some rational ground for choosing one code rather than another. No code can be its own ground. Such a ground would of necessity transcend any given code and hence the ontological would be implied, for such transcendence is not obtained through an infinite regress of codes.

(2) It may seem that the nature of man is not taken into consideration if universal evaluations have ontological propositions constitutive as evidence. However, the nature of man is considered indirectly in the major premise consisting of an ontological proposition. There is a metaphysics of man as well as of nature. The nature of man is also considered more directly in the minor premise which partly constitutes the syllogism establishing the universal evaluations. If, as we have pointed out, the evaluation is obtained through bringing the ontological and phenomenological contexts together, then the minor premise would be either a historical proposition or a generalization. These propositions through description take into account the nature of man, not ontologically, but specifically in relationship to the concrete circumstances in which man finds himself. Each premise, then, of the practical syllogism that establishes evaluations takes into account the nature of man, but each does so in its own way. The minor premise might be said to represent the horizontal; the major premise, which is ontological, represents the vertical relationship, and thus represents depth rather than breadth in man's moral consciousness.

(3) A critic may point out that the relation between the phenomenological and ontological context is nothing but that which has been called the particular-universal relation. The historical proposition "This is round" means that there is a universal "roundness" and that "this" participates in it, or the universal "roundness" is exemplified in a particular "thisness." So, there is a universal "goodness," and when we say "This is good" we mean that this "participates in the universal 'goodness,' " or that "goodness" is exemplified in a particular "thisness." In both cases there is a relation of "conformity," a relation which, if analyzed, would be found to be a case of cognitive identity. We are saying that "This conforms more or less to perfect roundness." In the other case we are saying "This conforms more or less to perfect goodness or absolute goodness."

The conclusion seems to be that there is no reason to make one a different type of proposition than the other.

Now "roundness" and "goodness" may both be universal, but that alone does not invalidate the distinction that we have made. From the standpoint of knowledge there are those concepts referring to restricted modes of being and those that are not so restricted—such as unity, existence, truth. Goodness belongs to the latter group, and these have been called transcendental concepts. Furthermore, the nature of the evidence necessary to demonstrate the truth of the propositions "This is round" and "This is good" is quite different. In demonstrating the truth of the proposition "This is round" an ontological premise is not necessary, although the universal "roundness" is implied and is purely a formal entity. However, "goodness" is not only an ontological "entity"; also an ontological premise is necessary as constitutive evidence to demonstrate that "This is good" is a true proposition. In the case of the one proposition, the formal and mathematical is appealed to; in the case of the other, the appeal is to the ontological, at least in part.

Unless there is some standard in terms of which evaluations of "good" or "satisfactoriness" are measured, how could one distinguish between true and false evaluations? What seems satisfactory would be satisfactory. The alternative is some objective test or standard. If so, then we are back to the ontological. This is true even though it be said that "man's needs" are the ultimate standard. Human nature and man's needs cannot be isolated or separated from nature and considered as if man existed in a vacuum. It is always a case of analyzing man's needs in relation to nature or in relation to God; or, if one wishes, in relation to some pantheistic absolute. One cannot escape the ontological. The most one can do is to avoid thinking about it.

It may be said that while it is true that man's needs are to be determined in relation to nature, our knowledge of nature is to be found wholly in the natural sciences and hence in generalizations. There is no esoteric so-called ontological knowledge to which appeal need be made. Now it may be true that a naturalist or a materialist uses only generalizations, chiefly of psychology and sociology, but the ground for such usage and limitation rests upon a metaphysical thesis to the effect that nature is all there is—the ultimate reality. This is the suppressed premise behind such antimetaphysical naturalism. If such a premise is not usually made explicit—and it is of the essence of a positivistic instrumentalism not to reason about such a premise, but merely to use it in reasoning instrumentally on the level of "means"—then a good question to ask is why it is not made explicit. In any case, the premise is "there."

Generalizations are obtained from data given by historical propositions. In the reasoning: All *X*'s expand when heated; this is an *X;* hence this expands when heated; the truth of the major premise depends upon the truth of the conclusion. The falsity of the conclusion can render false the major premise. This is simply to say that in natural science historical facts are coercive. If in the long run such facts are incompatible with a generalization that is a description of natural phenomena such as we find in a hypothesis, then it is a good procedure to modify or abolish the generalization. If the function of a generalization is to describe the behavior of natural objects, then such behavior is ultimately determining. It is perversion of the experimental method to fall in love with generalizations and to insist on holding to them when the evidence is to the contrary.

On the other hand, in practical reasoning which is moral the truth of the major premise which is ontological is independent of the truth of the conclusion. In the reasoning: Love is good; these acts are acts of love; these acts are good; even though the conclusion were false, the major premise could still be true. Only the minor premise would be proved to be false. The truth of the principle is not dependent upon historical facts in the same sense that generalizations are. In other words, such facts are not coercive for ethical principles. The principles may be misapplied, but that is not sufficient to invalidate them. In short, facts expressed either in terms of generalizations or historical propositions are to be judged; they are not themselves the judge. It is the general definition of ethical opportunism to make decisions according to facts alone and in the absence of principles, or to shift principles according to factual situations. What should be shifted under changing situations are "means," but "means" are expressed by generalizations and historical propositions. If theoretical ethical principles are to be changed at all, expressed as they are by ontological propositions, it is in the light of a more adequate ontological vision.

Further objection to the analysis made might be put in this manner. The form of derivation of general evaluational propositions we have said to be as follows: Whatever has a certain relation (degree of conformity) is good; all *X*'s have this relation; hence all *X*'s are good. The major premise is an ontological proposition and the minor is either a generalization or a historical proposition. Further, we have pointed out that the facts stated by the minor premise cannot be coercive. Now consider the following argument: Whatever has such and such properties is round; all of these ball bearings have such and such properties; hence, all of these ball bearings are round. Now in this reasoning facts are not coercive with respect to the major premise. Facts or material things do not determine the meaning of roundness. The truth of the conclusion, then, is partly determined by the nature of the relations constituting roundness. If this be the case, why select "good" to be a different category when the same analysis holds for other categories? Why should a proposition containing the category "good" belong to a different type than a proposition containing the category "round"? Furthermore, in the light of the future chapters it looks as if our analysis of generalizations is inadequate. We shall try to demonstrate that propositions of the formal domain of mathematics are related to generalizations instrumentally but not constitutively. However, it looks as if it may be otherwise. For in the example given is it not a generalization derived from a major premise that is formal and a minor that is a historical proposition?

Now it is true that facts are not coercive in the meaning of roundness, and it is also true that some formal relations are used in natural science to obtain generalizations. The formal does not determine what is evidence or truth, but it must be used in the process of such determination. When we say that all of these ball bearings are round, some system of reference is proposed, the system resting on a selection of some co-ordinates rather than others in the physical world. If the co-ordinate system were changed, the bearings might be elliptical. This is simply the principle of relativity. In changing a system of co-ordinates, the meaning of roundness is not changed. What is shown is that the major premise of the original syllogism is no longer applicable under the changed measurement. In the practical syllogism this cannot be the case, for there is no relativity because of measurement.

A more complete explanation would revolve around these considerations. "Good" is a transcendental which requires an interpretation in terms of analogy. "Roundness" is univocal. Also, it requires the notion of "intelligible matter" for its understanding, in a sense in which "good" does not. Finally, good is not a "property."

It is evident, then, that the reduction of general evaluations to generalizations is not only unwarranted but is equivalent not to explaining evaluations but to explaining them away. Moral knowledge is reduced to psychology or (positive) sociology. Goodness becomes relative merely to individuals or to group standards, which standards have no other ground than that they are in fact held at a certain time and place by the group. No one who is an ethical nihilist, no one who has ever denied the possibility of ethical truth, has ever meant much more than this.

It may be well to remark again that, regardless of the position taken as to the ethical or to evaluations, in general one does not escape from the ontological. The most that one can do is to escape from being rational about it. For practical purposes there are only a few "absolutes"; e.g., one's self, a group (nation, classes), nature, God. Even in the extreme case of absolute egoism, which is also nihilism in its strongest form, the individual ego is lifted from the realm of relativity into the ontological. The ego becomes identical with the ultimate nature of things.

Let us now consider formally the question as to what is described in evaluations. We may refer again to the theoretical and practical syllogisms.

Whatever conforms to the ultimate nature of things is good.

The will of God (or something else) conforms to the ultimate nature of things.

The will of God (or something else) is good.

This conforms (relatively) to the will of God (or something else).

This is (relatively) good.

In neither the premises nor the conclusion of the first syllogism is there an evaluation; they are all ontological propositions. In the second syllogism, by bringing together the ontological and phenomenological context, an evaluation is generated. An evaluation is just as descriptive as any other proposition. The difference is not that a generalization describes something that "is the case," while an evaluation does not describe anything at all, at the same time mysteriously presuming to say something. A historical proposition, a generalization, and an evaluation all state something that "is the case." They differ essentially in the matter of "what is the case." An evaluation brings a metaphysical category "down to earth." What is described is a degree of conformity, that is, relative conformity. Absolute conformity is ontological. When acts, natural and human, are described according to the degree of conformity, appraisals or evaluations are made. When human acts, mental and physical, are described in terms of degree of conformity, then those special evaluations that are called moral are made.

Problems of choice on a moral level can only be solved by judging *in terms of that which offers no alternative for choice.* If we are to be free, then we must conform to the ultimate nature of things; and while our freedom is expressed phenomenologically, the ground of freedom must be ontological. The formal categorical "ought" rests upon this necessity. "We ought so to conform." The meaning of metaphysical goodness is defined. The "material" categorical "ought" would state *what* one ought to conform to. It defines the ultimate standard or norm. The "hypothetical ought" on the level of necessary and contingent means is concerned with how the "material ought" may be relatively actualized under varying conditions. The two categorical "oughts" state the general and specific ground and possibility of our freedom. The "hypothetical ought" is concerned with the exercise of the freedom that is possible. The "formal" categorical "ought" allows no alternative, i.e., within the possibility of morality. There is of course always the alternative of rebelling against the ultimate nature of things, the repudiation of morality in any and every sense.

It is to be noted that the validity of this analysis, at least formally, is independent of what the ultimate nature of things is conceived to be. If nature has placed mankind between two masters—pleasure and pain—according to the hedonic interpretation, then ascetic practices would be evil as well as foolish, for they would imply rebellion against the ultimate nature of things—in this case, nature. On the other hand, if the will of God, as in the Jewish or Christian interpretation, is ontologically absolute, then to rebel against such a will would be both foolish and evil.

Some final remarks are now in order for the clarification of the moral. We have spoken of the theoretical and practical syllogisms. The theoretical ethical problem is concerned with the former, practical morality with the latter. Such subjects as political science, sociology, and economics are moral subjects or they are nothing at all.

The essential problem of practical ethics or morality is that of "means." The reasoning is essentially instrumental, and the methods of the experimental sciences are useful. The level of theoretical ethics is that of ultimate ends and principles; reasoning is essentially normative. Ethics is part of the metaphysics of man. As such it is partly constitutive of the moral sciences. The moral sciences are practical and synthetic, integrating as they do the ontological and the phenomenological.

The terms "theoretical and practical syllogisms" actually are shorthand references to a whole series of arguments. A religious person may believe that the United Nations program is good because it leads to some kind of internationalism, which in turn leads to positive peace, and that the latter is good because it conforms with the will of God. There is a series of means-ends relationships whereby spatio-temporal particularity is linked with the ontological. The concept of "conformity" may be expressed linguistically in other terms, and objectively it may be manifested in many ways. In the example just given conformity was expressed in the notion of "leads to."

Summary. Because the nature of the evidence is the same for both singular and general evaluations the value context has only one domain, and that is identical with the context itself. It differs from the phenomenological context in that the evidence for evaluations is partly constituted by ontological propositions. It differs from the ontological context in that evaluations are concerned with concrete particularity of spatio-temporal existence.

4

The Relation of Historical Propositions to Metaphysical (Cosmological) Propositions

Can historical propositions constitute evidence for metaphysical propositions? In appearance there would seem to be difficulties in either an affirmative or negative answer.

If the answer is affirmative, then metaphysical propositions are reduced to generalizations, even though they might be thought of as the broadest type of generalization. Historical propositions do constitute evidence for generalizations. If metaphysical propositions are of a different type, then that fact would not be recognized by saying that the evidence for a metaphysical proposition is the same as that for a generalization. On the other hand, if historical propositions are not constitutive as evidence for metaphysical propositions, then the latter would seem to have no evidence at all. Further, it would follow that the generalizations of natural science could not be constitutive as evidence for metaphysical propositions. Generalizations are constituted by historical propositions. If historical propositions cannot be evidence for metaphysical propositions, then neither can generalizations. It would seem that only theological propositions remain to which one may turn for evidence for metaphysics. But that is hardly possible. If the only evidence for metaphysical propositions are theological propositions, then metaphysics simply becomes a synonym for theology. For metaphysics to be even an instrument of theology, it must have some autonomy.

Are we faced with a dilemma? If historical propositions are evidence for metaphysical propositions, then the latter are reduced to generalizations, and hence metaphysics is reduced to experimental science. If historical propositions are not constitutive as evidence for metaphysical propositions, then metaphysics is reduced to theology. In neither case can there be metaphysics.

There is another problem. Either metaphysical knowledge is derived from sense experience, or it is not. If it is not, then we are faced with some doctrine of "innate ideas" or some doctrine of esoteric intuition. For many reasons the former is unsatisfactory. And even if some neo-Platonic doctrine of innate ideas were true, at best it would only tell us why we have certain metaphysical ideas and propositions. It would not tell us why they are true. The notion of "intuition" would seem no more satisfactory. It may be a name for a type of activity in which metaphysical propositions are pulled down from the ontological atmosphere, but it is not clear at all how it is relevant to the truth or falsity of propositions.

If the other alternative is taken, that metaphysical propositions are obtained from sense experience, then, if historical propositions are to be rejected as evidence, we are faced with a new kind of proposition for which allowance seems not to have been made, e.g., "This is a substance"; "This is something." Is there some kind of "induction" by which universal metaphysical propositions are obtained from "metaphysical singulars," just as generalizations are obtained from historical propositions? If historical propositions are "facts" for the natural sciences, are there some kind of special philosophical "facts" for metaphysics?

The sources of knowledge. There are only two sources of knowledge, sense and revelation from God. All knowledge other than the theological comes from sense experience. There are only three alternatives with respect to sense in relation to knowing: (1) The sense image "reveals"; (2) sense "veils"; (3) all we can know are the sense images themselves. The (3) is subjectivism. The (2) is a kind of skepticism; the real thing is forever hidden behind a veil of sense images. Only if sense "reveals" can knowledge be possible. How sense reveals is partly explained in the realistic doctrine of abstraction. We shall touch upon this only to the extent necessary for the problem at hand.

We sense or intuit the quality "yellow." "Yellowness" is also revealed to us through sense experience, but it can be obtained only by a process of abstraction. We do not literally sense yellowness. It takes some degree of intellectual sophistication to reach such an abstract concept. Hence we may say that yellow is a sense intuition, yellowness is an intellectual intuition. "Yellowness" is a metaphysical concept, "yellow" is a concept of the phenomenological context. The concept of yellow *qua* concept, as universal, is a being of reason and is therefore a purely logical entity. What the concept intends is this or that particular yellow existing at particular times and places. Any particular yellow is extended, and hence the concept of yellow is phenomenological. Yellowness, on the other hand, even as content, is not extended. It does not have any spatio-temporal boundaries, although it may be the transcendental foundation for the real quality of yellow, which is individuated and does have spatio-temporal boundaries.

Is the metaphysical concept of yellowness based upon sense experience? Yes, it is revealed through sense experience, although not immediately sensed as such. Sense reveals yellowness just as it does accidents of various kinds, and substances. It is only through an intellectual process of abstraction that we recognize these entities. In realism this distinction between what is sensed directly and what is sensed indirectly is expressed by the terms *sensible per se* and *sensible per accidens.* An accident, a substance, or yellowness would be classified under *sensible per accidens.* From the standpoint of the order of being we can sense yellow only because it has yellowness. From the standpoint of the order of knowledge we can know (intellectually) yellowness only because we can know (sense) yellow. But we know yellowness by a process of intellectual abstraction. When we describe the experience by means of a proposition we must say "This is yellow." This is a historical proposition. Is it the case, then, that if we say that "This is yellowness" we are uttering a metaphysical proposition? It is questionable whether such a proposition is literally meaningful. What we mean is "This has yellowness in it." While yellowness as a concept is the product of intellectual abstraction, the proposition "This has yellowness in it" is really a deduction from a metaphysical and a historical proposition. The minor premise would be a historical proposition: "This is yellow." The major premise would be a metaphysical proposition relating yellow and yellowness.

This answer, however, is somewhat forced. One feels a little uneasy about it. In a real deduction producing a proposition of the practical or synthetic context the matter is different. If "good" is an ontological concept, then we might say that "This is good" because it is an act of a certain kind, and all acts of that kind are good. This is a straightforward deduction. However, when we say that "This has yellowness in it" is derived from two premises, there is the suspicion of pseudo-deduction, of mere repetition. Therefore, let us rather say that after experiencing this yellow and that yellow, the mind by abstraction makes the judgment accordingly that whatever is yellow has yellowness. This is a metaphysical (cosmological) proposition, and is universal as it should be. The so-called "metaphysical singular" is not any new kind of knowledge, but is simply a weakened form of the universal proposition.

The same analysis would hold for such concepts as "substance" and "accident" when following the words "This is."

Let us consider another example, "This is something." This does not seem to be a historical proposition. One might reason as follows. "Something" is one of the transcendentals and as such is convertible with "being." Now, when we say that "This is something" we are stating a singular proposition and at the same time using a predicate that is not of the phenomenological context; nor is it one that can be reduced to it. Therefore, it appears to be the case that there are singular metaphysical propositions, and not merely universal metaphysical propositions or ones that are descriptive of universality.

An answer might be given by pointing out that "this" is equivocal. While this is true, it is hardly relevant. It would be better to question whether there is a proposition at all. Because of the absolute pervasiveness of the category what one is really saying is that "something is something."

A question might be asked at this point. Can all concepts be neatly arranged so that any given concept can be placed in a context and domain? Yes. No difficulty will be met if the order of being and the order of knowledge are not identified. The notions of "concept," "context," and "domain," are logical. These are not to be found in the extramental world with trees, dogs, and planets. Again, we must remember that some words or terms are notoriously equivocal. A word may stand for different concepts which do fall into different domains. If such a word is taken as univocal, then we will not know into which domain it falls. In any given case it may be difficult to place a proposition in a domain. But such a difficulty is irrelevant to the main thesis concerning the order of knowledge, which rests upon the fact that there are various domains. Without the truth of this fact there would be no problem of placing propositions.

Both the predicamental (substance and the various kinds of accidents) and the transcendental categories are metaphysical concepts. In the case of a transcendental relation the foundation and relation are the same. "Matter" is not one *thing,* "form" another, the two being related by some third entity. The predicamental relation and foundation are different. For example, similarity is a real relation between, say, two reds, but the foundation of the relation is the quality redness itself in the two objects.

Concepts such as "context" and "domain" are logical. Predicamental and transcendental concepts (but not *qua* concepts) are ontological in context, metaphysical in domain. However, the concepts that fall under the predicamental concepts belong to the phenomenological. In the order of being these contexts do not lie in juxtaposition to each other as beads on a string. In fact these contexts are not in the order of being at all. The cosmological and the phenomenological are distinctions of reason, but both are concerned with the realm of becoming.

The evidence for metaphysical propositions. The evidence for metaphysical propositions may be understood by recalling the levels of abstraction, and the definitions of metaphysics and cosmology. In the first order of abstraction the mind abstracts from the object all individual matter, leaving, however, sensible matter. For example, each dog has specific material conditions unique to it. When "total abstraction" occurs the concept of dog is obtained. Since dogs are composites of form and matter, the concept must take account of the sensible matter common to all such creatures. On the second level the mind abstracts from sensible matter, leaving only intelligible matter, that to which quantity is applicable. It is this level that defines the nature of mathematics. Finally, the mind can abstract from even intelligible matter and consider being *qua* being.

The realm of becoming, of motion, of material change is studied on the first level of abstraction. The ontological and the phenomenological are two logical aspects or contexts of one and the same being. On a nonrealistic view the two aspects either become two realms, with the former unknowable, or the one is reduced to the other. These alternatives correspond to Kantianism, idealism and materialism. In the order of being, both experimental science and cosmology are confined to the realm of nature, of becoming, to the first order of abstraction. We are using the term "metaphysics" broadly to include the inquiry into both being *qua* being and being *qua* becoming. The former is "general metaphysics"; the latter is a kind of "special metaphysics" called "cosmology." Since all natural knowledge has its source in the senses, and cosmology is directly concerned with sensible matter, from the standpoint of the order of knowledge cosmology is prior to general metaphysics. Without special metaphysics, i.e., cosmology, there could be no general metaphysics, or what is sometimes called "speculative metaphysics."

Now let us return to the question of evidence. We combine concepts and judgments and obtain historical propositions. With different concepts we do likewise to obtain certain cosmological propositions. Intuition, in some mode, is involved in both processes. Were it not so, an infinite regress would occur, leading to skepticism. But there is intellectual as well as sense intuition. With this in mind we may call attention to the fact that "substance" is revealed ("given") in experience just as is "red." "Substance" is given intelligibly, "red" sensuously. Even the "intelligible" is arrived at *through* sense experience. Sense experience is necessarily instrumental; without it we could not have such knowledge. Yet, though it be necessary, it is not sufficient. A substance is that which exists in itself and not in another, as does an accident. Through sense experience I can know that my Irish setter is a substance just as well as that he is red, although the former is grasped by an intellectual intuition and is not sensed *per se*.

When we combine concepts to get historical propositions, it is then through the inductive technique of experimental science that we arrive at generalizations. But when we combine metaphysical concepts, we do not first get metaphysical singulars and then by the same inductive techniques obtain universal metaphysical propositions. By the process of abstraction, and with reflection, universal metaphysical propositions are obtained directly. It is important to understand this difference. In the phenomenological context we are considering things according to their relations, qualities, or temporal and spatial situations. In the other case we are concerned with their metaphysical "parts," matter, form, potentiality, existence, and essence. The methods in the two cases are different because the "formal objects" are different, even though the existential object may be the same.

What, then, is the relation of historical propositions to metaphysical propositions? Historical propositions state "facts." Can the truth of metaphysical propositions be demonstrated through these historical propositions? To give an affirmative answer would be equivalent to reducing metaphysical propositions to generalizations. Moreover, there is no reason to believe that metaphysical thinking makes an appeal to such facts. To suppose so would be seriously to misunderstand metaphysics. And yet one might give innumerable examples apparently illustrating the opposite thesis, that metaphysics does appeal to scientific "facts." Also, one might well ask: If metaphysical thinking is to fly off into the upper intellectual atmosphere independent of such facts, then it would seem to have no foundation other than private intuitions, and intelligible communication and agreement is impossible. And so again we seem to be faced with an unpleasant dilemma. Either historical propositions are constitutive as evidence of metaphysical propositions, or they are not. In the one case metaphysics is reduced to natural science. In the other, it is rendered purely subjective and is reduced to a game of mental solitaire. In neither case is metaphysics possible as knowledge.

There is no answer to this dilemma if the only relation between kinds of knowledge is the constitutive relation. The argument really rests on this presupposition. The dilemma may be avoided by grabbing one of the horns. Historical propositions are not constitutive as evidence of, but are instrumental to, metaphysics. The world of facts is not irrelevant to the metaphysical quest. The problem is the nature of the relevance. One erroneous interpretation leads to positivism, the denial of metaphysics. On the other hand, there is a tradition stemming from Christian Wolff, and perhaps traceable to Plato himself, to the effect that cosmological truths can be known without the instrumentality of the senses, with the implication that the senses actually hinder rather than help in cognition. This way tends towards subjectivism, the consequences of which are avoided only by some notion such as "innate ideas."

Phenomenological concepts and facts are the means (but not the only means) by which one discovers metaphysical concepts and forms propositions. It is interesting to note that a "means" or an "instrument" itself limits, or "checks," the wildness of speculation. If historical propositions were not relevant in any sense to metaphysical propositions, then there would literally be nothing whatever to "check" metaphysical speculation. It would be limited only by formal consistency and extent of imagination. But historical propositions (or particular "facts") do not "check" in the sense of "determining the truth or falsity of," i.e., in the sense of constituting metaphysical propositions. Nor can they be "regulative of," descriptive as they are of that mode of being called "contingent." It would be nonsense to speak of historical propositions as regulative of metaphysical propositions, determining what is possibly true metaphysically. The converse is actually the case. *The "instrument" or "means" is a check in the sense that it is of the actual existent world of nature, of becoming, that we obtain cosmological truth, and not some hypothetical "nature" that is purely the product of man's creative imagination.*[1]

The dual role of "facts." An analysis of an actual bit of cosmological reasoning may aid in understanding the role of historical propositions as instrumental to metaphysical propositions. The following example is taken from C. N. Bittle, *Reality and the Mind,* a work dealing with that part of cosmology which is called "philosophical psychology":

> The mind is a mere instrument of my Ego, and this is clearly perceived by introspection: *I* think, *I* imagine, *I* remember, *I* judge, *I* reason. It is the Ego, then, and not the mind itself, which is the ultimate subject of intellectual knowledge. And the same is true of sensory knowledge: *I* feel, *I* see, *I* hear, *I* have a pain in my hand, *I* have a fever. Thus it is seen that the Ego is the real subject of both intellectual and sensory knowledge, that is, of *all* knowledge.[2]

There is a direct movement here from such historical propositions as "I imagine" and "I feel" to a universal cosmological proposition. The intellectual intuition is indicated by the words "thus it is seen." Let us compare the role of historical propositions in this example with the roles they play in history and natural science.

In chemistry one may be studying the degree of dissociation of an electrolyte. The degree of ionization is found by dividing the equivalent conductance of an electrolyte at a given dilution by its equivalent conductance at an infinite dilution. The equivalent conductance is the conductance of a solution containing a gram equivalent of the electrolyte. At the turn of the century Kohlrausch obtained the following values for the equivalent conductance of sodium chloride at various dilutions: 1, 74.4; 0.5, 80.9; 0.1, 92.5; 0.05, 95.9; . . . ; 0.0002, 109.2; 0.0001, 109.7. The first number of each pair is the concentration in gram equivalent per liter; the second number is the equivalent conductance.

Here we have a group of historical propositions representing the repetition of a type of fact under slightly different situations. Now let us suppose that one says that "thus it is seen" that conductance at infinite dilution is only a little above 109.7, that its value may be determined by extrapolation, and that therefore the equivalent conductance of other ionized electrolytes may be determined in the same way. Is the appeal here to historical propositions to establish a generalization the same as that in the cosmological example? No, there is a difference. Is the generalization "seen" by means of the "facts"? Only in the sense that "intuition" is required, in some manner or other, in all knowledge. At best all that is seen is something that is "probably" true. The point is that further experimentation might show that the generalization is false. *In fact* such experimentation has constantly confirmed the generalization. Of course, an infinite number of such experiments cannot, and need not, be made. A limited number establishes a high probability, and the generalization is said to hold, among other reasons, because there is no reason to believe that it does not. But because the historical propositions are *constitutive* of the generalization, there is always a theoretical possibility of disconfirmation.

If, as in the case of sodium chloride, the truth of the generalization might theoretically be undermined by additional historical propositions, the phrase "thus it is seen" must not be taken too literally. One may or may not "see" what one thinks he sees. Experimentation "checks" the "seeing." If the other generalization had been made, "that therefore the equivalent conductance of other ionized electrolytes may be determined in the same way," then experimentation could show that it was false, and that one did not *really* "see" this at all. It so happens that the determination of value by extrapolation does not hold for little-ionized substances such as acetic acid and ammonium hydroxide. One did not "see" correctly because he overlooked the condition "highly ionized" which is necessary in order that the generalization may hold. Correct "seeing" evidently depends upon first knowing everything that could be relevant. Since this is seldom, if ever, possible in dealing with phenomena, experimentation is necessary.

In the cosmological example the matter is different. When it is "seen" that "the Ego is the real subject . . . ," the appeal is to such historical propositions as "I feel," "I hear," "I have a pain." However, these propositions are only *instrumental* to the intellectual intuition, not of a generalization, but of a cosmological proposition. The relation is not that of "constitutive of." Let us recall that "type A knowledge is instrumental to type B" means that some true propositions of type B presuppose some true propositions of type A. In order to have metaphysical knowledge, some true historical propositions must be known. The "some" of type A is *indefinite,* whereas in the relations of "regulative of" and "constitutive of" reference is made to *specific* propositions. Now *some* historical propositions, such as those mentioned, are necessary in order to grasp the universal cosmological proposition. But it is an indefinite "some." A person who is stone-deaf, for whom the historical proposition "I hear this or that" is false, could still grasp the cosmological proposition by means of the other historical propositions. In short, and to put it crudely, if such historical propositions are merely *means,* then a part of the means can literally be destroyed, or be false, without causing the abolition or modification of the cosmological proposition for which the means exists. This would not be true at all if the historical propositions were "constitutive as evidence," as they always must be in the case of generalizations.

If a person could not feel, hear, have a pain, etc., if he could not have any sensory experience at all, then he could not "see" the truth of the cosmological proposition. But this merely confirms the point we have made, that without the instrumentality of sense metaphysical knowledge is impossible. All that is required is the indefinite "some." The truth of the cosmological proposition is "seen" *through,* but not proved by, the historical propositions.

There is another difference. There is no "probability" attached to the cosmological proposition, for there is a strong "either/or" involved. The proposition is in contrast to an idealistic position in which the self is identified with the mind merely, in opposition to the body. Man is not a disembodied spirit; a psychosomatic view is asserted. The truth or falsity of these positions is not the issue at present. What should be noted is: (1) that one either sees truly or one does not; (2) if one does see truly, then no additional historical proposition can abolish the cosmological proposition, as it can in the case of a generalization; (3) no experimentation is involved to increase probability constantly.

It must be granted that the argument as quoted is grossly simplified. One does not jump quite so easily from historical propositions to the cosmological proposition. A prior dialectic is involved that is not stated. But this is simply a requirement of economy in exposition. The case is analogous in mathematics. Equations will be laid down with great gaps omitted in the deduction. What is missing in the proof of a theorem is a prior linear deduction or demonstration rather than a dialectical analysis. Dialectical analysis is a kind of logical experimentation prior to the intellectual intuition of a metaphysical proposition, just as the experimental techniques are prior to the grasping of a generalization. The former kind of experimentation, because of the nature of the subject matter, requires no physical manipulation; the latter does.

The cosmological example may be contrasted with the role historical propositions play as constitutive of another historical proposition, as in historical knowledge. In the well-known kidnapping case it is believed that Bruno Richard Hauptmann was the kidnapper of the baby of Charles Lindbergh. What is the evidence to which appeal is made? (1) The writing on the ransom notes was identified by an expert as that of Hauptmann's. (2) A gasoline station attendant identified Hauptmann as the man who gave him one of the ransom bills. (3) Hidden in the garage by Hauptmann's home was a good part of the ransom loot. (4) The footprint left by "John," who got the ransom, closely resembled that of Hauptmann.

These and many other similar facts led to Hauptmann's arrest and prosecution. These are historical propositions "converging" as evidence on another historical proposition to the effect that he kidnapped the baby. Had certain historical propositions been different the probability of the truth of the conclusion would have been lessened. If one fact had been different, the case would have been dismissed, namely, if there was clear and unmistakable evidence that Hauptmann was a long distance away from

Lindbergh's home at the time of the kidnapping act. The reason for the decisiveness of such a fact, had it been discovered, is that it rests on a metaphysical presupposition having to do with the impossibility of a material body being at two widely separated places at the same time.

It should be observed that the cosmological or metaphysical principle is relevant only as "regulative." In itself it is not evidence as to which place Hauptmann was at a given time. On the other hand, the historical propositions are not regulative, but constitutive. How does this contrast with the cosmological example? In the quotation from Mr. Bittle historical propositions are instrumental to the grasping of the cosmological proposition. In the kidnapping case a cosmological proposition is regulative in the process of grasping a historical proposition which is a conclusion. Some one relevant historical proposition could, in the Hauptmann case, cause serious or unquestionable doubt about the conclusion. In the cosmological example it would be difficult to maintain that at some time or other some relevant historical proposition may turn up that would require relinquishing the cosmological proposition and accepting the contrary, which is a Cartesian view of the separation of mind and body.

Mr. Bittle either "sees" truly or he does not. But in any case historical propositions do not constitute evidence which determines the truth or the falsity of the cosmological proposition. Rather they function as a kind of means by which the intellectual intuition is obtained.

The problem here is both difficult and subtle. The contrast may be sharpened at the crucial point by putting the matter in the following way.

In the Hauptmann example:

(*a*) Some historical propositions can be true and the conclusion true.

(*b*) Some historical propositions can be true, and some be false, and the conclusion true.

(*c*) But if some historical propositions are true, and a certain specific one (or more than one) be false, then the conclusion is false. As we have seen, this alternative is determined not only by the constitutive relation of one proposition to another, but also mediately by the regulative function of a cosmological proposition. It is most interesting to note here that a specific historical proposition can be constitutive as evidence pro or con only because of the regulative function of the cosmological proposition (about the impossibility of a material thing being at widely separated places at the same time). Furthermore, it is always possible that such a specific historical proposition might be found.

In the cosmological example:

(*d*) Some historical propositions can be true and the cosmological proposition intuited be true.

(*e*) Some historical propositions can be true, some be false (e.g., "I hear"), and the cosmological proposition be true.

(*f*) But it is not the case that if some historical propositions are true, and a specific one be false, then the cosmological proposition is false.

The contrast is not between (*a*) and (*b*) as against (*d*) and (*e*). It is between (*c*) and (*f*). In the cosmological example there can be no cosmological proposition which, in its regulative function, could allow a specific historical proposition to be constitutive as evidence for or against the truth of the cosmological proposition in question.

The contrast may be pointed up in another way. In the one case I can say:

(*a*) I can know that "It is probable that Hauptmann is the kidnapper" is true because I know that the historical propositions are true.

But I cannot say:

(*b*) I can know without doubt that Hauptmann is the kidnapper because the historical propositions *are* true. It is theoretically possible for the given historical propositions to be true and at the same time Hauptmann not be the kidnapper.

In the other case I can say:

(*c*) I can know that the cosmological proposition is true because I know that the historical propositions are true.

However, "because" here does not have quite the same meaning that it has in (*a*).

But I can also say:

(*d*) I can know without doubt that the cosmological proposition is true because the historical propositions *are* true. It is not theoretically possible for the historical propositions to be true and also that the cosmological proposition be false.

The contrast between (*a*) and (*c*) is obscured by the fact that the two assertions are of apparently the same form, and the common word "because" is used. The difference is that in (*a*) the connective "because" must be interpreted in terms of the kind of inductive inference that is characteristic of the phenomenological context, whereas in (*c*) it must be interpreted in terms of abstraction and intellectual intuition.

The essential contrast is between (*b*) and (*d*). In (*b*) it is theoretically possible to have several hypotheses account for the historical proposition. The problem is: Which one is true? In (*d*) there is a sharp "either-or." The alternatives are truth or falsity.

After obtaining a cosmological proposition, it can be combined with another to arrive at still another, and in this manner that part of metaphysics called "cosmology" is constructed—not *a priori*, but from an experiential base. In order to illustrate how this is done we may quote a passage by the same author, one which follows after the previous quotation:

> Sense-perception is a vital act, certainly; but it is also an 'extended' act. The *subject* of sense-perception must, therefore, also be a *vital and extended reality*. And since the Ego is the real subject of sense-knowledge, it must be a reality which is both vital (perceptive) and extended. Only a body, however, is extended. Consequently, an extended body must form an integral part of the being of our Ego, in order to account for the *psycho-physical* character of our sense-perception as a vital yet extended act. We are thus forced to conclude that our Ego does not consist solely of our unextended mind, but is a *compound of mind and body*, united in such a way that our Ego is a unified living organism consisting of both.[3]

In the last two sentences we have a demonstrative argument. The former cosmological proposition is now a minor premise. The major, that whatever is extended is a body, is a cosmological proposition and so is the conclusion. This conclusion that the Ego or Self is a compound of mind and body is part of "philosophical psychology." From the standpoint of psychology as phenomenalistic, as purely experimental, the name "psychosomatic" is used. It is not surprising at all that the psychosomatic approach in psychology "works" so well in comparison with a neo-behavioristic viewpoint! In psychology, as an experimental science, do the generalizations confirm a cosmological proposition? Not in the sense that historical propositions and other generalizations confirm a generalization. To assert otherwise would be to reduce a cosmological proposition to a generalization. The generalizations "illustrate"; they are what we might expect!

The resolution of incompatible metaphysical positions. The reader may find difficulties in this explanation of metaphysical evidence. And this is understandable considering the history of philosophy. It may be pointed out that the author quoted is giving a realistic explanation of the mind-body problem, and the answer is chiefly in opposition to the view that stems from Descartes. Descartes conceived mind in terms of thought, and matter in terms of extension. The author conceives them in a different way. Starting with different presuppositions, different consequences are entailed. Descartes thought he was correct; the realist thinks he is correct. But how does one know which is *really* true?

Furthermore, have we not been begging the question all along? People appeal to the same "evidence" and get different metaphysical conclusions. As F. S. C. Northrop says, "That which is directly apprehended is roughly the same in any philosophical system, but how it is analyzed and correlated with other factors, whether immediately given or postulated, is different; it is precisely these differences which concern us in comparative philosophy." [4] There is no enlightenment in simply asserting that the one position is false and the other true. It is said that one either intuits truly, or one does not. Such a tautology is not helpful when the problem is to know which is true. Descartes "sees" the problem and answer in one way, someone else "sees" differently. Is it not dogmatism—which enters into philosophy whenever there is an absence of evidence—just to assert that the one "seeing" is true? Again, it has been pointed out a thousand times that intuition is "psychological." One may "see" that something is true, but it is not true because one "sees" it.

In answer we may say that the only way to know which is true is to discover which one has an experiential base. This is not the place to go into detail on the mind-body problem. It will be sufficient to indicate the difference in method between realism and Descartes.

How did Descartes arrive at the notion that mind and body were in juxtaposition, and did not constitute a compound? Through the use of experience as instrumental? No, not at all. The appeal to sense was used to doubt and to destroy. The positive part of Cartesianism was arrived at by *postulation.* Of course in his own mind it was a nonarbitrary type of postulation, in accordance with mathematical method as conceived at that time, and in contrast to the more arbitrary conception of postulation today. It was, nevertheless, the *a priori* approach. He did exactly what Whitehead later recommends as *the* metaphysical method, viz., take a limited category from the physical sciences, "generalize" it, and *make* it a metaphysical category. Whitehead merely objects to *what* Descartes generalized.

So Descartes took *a* (not *the*) conception of matter useful in physics at the time and made it a metaphysical substance. If "matter" is a substance, is extended, and "thought" is not, then the mind must be another substance. How, then, must "substance" be thought of? Not merely as that which exists in itself; it also exists *by* itself. Now what is the evidence? There is none whatsoever. To understand "why" Descartes did what he did one would have to understand him in terms of the history of philosophy (decadent scholasticism), sociological and psychological analysis—his rebellion, the repudiation of two thousand years of philosophy. Descartes never really explained why matter and form are not principles of being, and why the metaphysical category of matter must be a generalized notion from physics. Furthermore, what is intelligible through experience is the notion of substance as something existing in itself and not in another. Everyone recognizes the difference between "dog" and "red" as an accident existing in the dog.

Descartes' notion of substance (and Spinoza's too) was *posited a priori,* and was not derived through experience. Modern philosophy has often followed his method, even though rejecting the content of his thought. But once the postulation begins there is no end to it. It is just as easy to postulate that there is no such thing as substance, except as derivative from process. Whitehead and Alexander did so. Someone else can postulate that there is no nature except what is necessary to account for the "bumps" we get called "sensations." And so on to skepticism. It is then only natural to ask how we can know which postulated metaphysical notion is true. By this procedure the answer is: We can't know.

Which is true, Descartes' position or realism? Analyze sense and intellectual experience. Do you "see" the difference between substance and accident? If so, then one other question. Do you "see" that substances must exist *by* themselves? No, you will not find such "things"—not even *per accidens.* When we put it this way we can see that an answer can be given. If intuition functions in the proper manner through the instrumentality of experience, then if there is disagreement all one can do is wait for further enlightenment. In this sense, differences will always exist in metaphysics. They are healthy ones and the prerequisites of progress in intellectual depth. But if this metaphysical method is compared with the *a priori* postulational type, if the conclusions obtained by both procedures are examined, and then one asks: Which conclusion is true?—the only answer is that you can't get metaphysical truth, but only ideology, by the postulational procedure, and the widespread existence of skepticism and antimetaphysical positivism is the consequence of assuming that you can.

The contrast in the evidence for, and the reasoning to, generalizations and metaphysical propositions. Let us continue with the question of metaphysical evidence, for the matter is of utmost importance. The effort should be worth-while, since unfortunately in so many expositions there is too much generality and too little detail and actual demonstration.

Some time ago the question was raised as to whether there are cosmological (metaphysical) singular propositions. If so, are they in the ontological context analogous to the historical propositions in the phenomenological context? There are metaphysical singulars, descriptive of uniqueness, but they do not constitute a special type defining a domain. There is no kind of knowledge made up of metaphysical singulars corresponding to history as constituted by historical propositions. Secondly, the analogy inquired about does not hold. In the ontological context what is analogous to the historical proposition is the theological proposition. Both the historical and the theological proposition are descriptive of uniqueness; they differ essentially in context. The theological proposition differs from the metaphysical singular in that it can constitute a body of knowledge. The nature of metaphysical truth and evidence will better be understood by understanding the peculiar nature and function of these metaphysical singulars.

"Change" is something immediately experienced, although it is not a simple "idea." It constitutes the very essence of the realm of becoming, which is the subject matter of cosmology. We experience this change and that change. It might be a friend's dog we refer to, and which has grown from a puppy in our year's absence. Suppose we ask why it changes. The "why" here is ambiguous, and many answers could be given depending upon the listener's guess as to our purpose. But in the meaning-context at present relevant the answer is that it is "material." Implied is the proposition that all material things change. We then have the reasoning:

(1) All material things change. (generalization)
(2) This (and that, etc.) is material. (historical proposition)
(*A*) (3) This (and that, etc.) changes. (historical proposition)

The (3) is a historical proposition because we mean by "change" that the dog has increased so many pounds in weight, inches in height, and there is a slight color difference. The (2) is also a historical proposition because by "matter" we mean that which is extended, has weight, mass, etc.

Beginning with (3) one can go in two directions. By an ascending analysis one can go to the generalization which is the major premise in reasoning (*A*). But for other purposes, perhaps epistemological, one could start with the common sense "this changes" and trace back to a "this changes" in sensation. Of course, if we begin with sensation, the subjective, we can never get out. And we may remember that we do not experience our sensations, except in a reflexive sense. We experience things through, with, or by means of our sensations. The descending analysis is concerned with why I know this changes. The ascending analysis is concerned with why this changes.

Although reasoning (*A*) is set up in demonstrative form, does (1) give the "why"? No, there is a demonstration only in appearance. Actually, the conclusion helps to prove the major premise. From the experience of "this changes," "this is material," and many other similar propositions, we arrive by induction at the generalization. The historical propositions constitute the generalization. Because of this fact the form of the syllogism (in this case only) is only a pseudodemonstration, as Mill and other critics have been fond of pointing out. Historical propositions explain the "why" of the generalization.

There are other things to be noticed about reasoning (*A*). The (1) can be interpreted in terms of "material implication" if the experimental scientist so wishes: " 'That anything is material *and* that it does not change,' is false." Also, if he wishes he may, in interpreting (1), (2), and (3), use the notion of "function" instead of "cause." He can reduce "thing" to a set of "dispositional properties." We say he "can" because there are no rational grounds on which an objection could be based, even if one wished to do so. The experimental scientist has this freedom, and it is the mark of wisdom to recognize it.

But for any such freedom a price must be paid, for it is not absolute. His freedom must be responsible, and that means that it is restricted and limited. What he must not do is conclude a metaphysics from his operations and meanings. We say he "must not" because there are no rational grounds on which such conclusions could be based. If he does so, then it is an arbitrary act of will. This limitation does not restrict the freedom of the experimental scientist *qua* experimental scientist. *Rather it makes that very freedom possible.* It defines *responsible* experimental science, and prevents *irresponsible* metaphysics.

Where and how does metaphysics come into the picture? Is it not metaphysically true that all material things change? It may or may not be: that is the question. *In fact* it so happens that it is true. *But not because historical propositions are constitutive as evidence.* Moreover, while the words remain the same, the concepts are different. "Change" now means the actualization of that which is potential. "Material thing" now refers to a composite substance, of form and primary matter, and having potency. We have the reasoning:

(4) All material things change. (cosmological universal)
(5) This (and that, etc.) is material. (cosmological singular)
(*B*) (6) This (and that, etc.) changes. (cosmological singular)

In experience, (3) and (6) are usually confused, but they are different. In reasoning (*B*), are (5) and (6) constitutive of (4), the major premise? No, they are not. A "class" of cosmological singular propositions cannot be constitutive as evidence of a cosmological universal proposition, as a class of historical propositions can be constitutive of a generalization. Rather the relation is that of instrumentality. The (5) and (6) are instrumental to grasping of (4). It is to be understood, of course, that such intuition is not passive, that it comes after a great deal of dialectical or reflective analysis, and from wide experience of change. Our exposition and illustration is simple and condensed.

The point is that one can move from (5) and (6) to (4). But the conclusion (6) does not help to prove the major premise (4). By a long process of reflection one "sees" that composite entities must change. In reasoning (*B*), if there should be a case in which "this changes" is false, then it would be the minor premise that would be disproved, not the major. If "this changes" is false, then "this" simply isn't material. It still remains true that all material things change. In contrast, in reasoning *(A), and in absence of all cosmological considerations,* if "this changes" should be false, then the minor premise could still be true and the major would be disproved. This contrast illustrates the fact that historical propositions constitute generalizations, but that both historical propositions and cosmological singulars are only instrumental to seeing the truth of the universal cosmological proposition. In (*A*) the generalization is partly constituted by the conclusion. In (*B*) it is the major premise, the universal cosmological proposition, that is constitutive as evidence, not of the fact *that* "this changes," but of *why* it does so. "This" changes because it is material.[5]

It is to be noted that both historical propositions and cosmological singulars can be instrumental to universal cosmological propositions. It doesn't make much difference with which one begins. Actually, the two kinds of singulars are confused in the mind and are distinguished only by analysis. But while both may be instrumental to cosmological knowledge, historical propositions cannot constitute it. However, there can be a body of knowledge called history that is constituted in part by historical propositions. There is no corresponding body of knowledge composed of cosmological singulars.

But what shall we say to this problem: In reasoning (*B*) are we not talking about something quite different from that in reasoning (*A*)? For are not the concepts different, and only the words the same? Is it then identity of language that relates the phenomenological and the ontological context? If not, what is it?

These questions are innocent in appearance. Yet, to answer them is to understand and also to explain much of the chaos of modern thought. In our explanation thus far we have been stressing differences in predicates, sharply distinguishing phenomenological and ontological concepts. But the genius of realism is its existentialist nature, the fact that its aim is to understand the act of existence, while not ignoring the realm of essence. Now of course on the level of concept and of essence "matter" and "change" in (*A*) and (*B*) are different, though not wholly so. But the reason why one is talking about the same thing is that *there is an existential identity*. The "this" of (3) is the same identical "this" of (6). The *one* entity can be studied from two aspects. The two contexts are logical distinctions with a foundation in the entity. The real object is one; the formal objects are two. There is a real distinction between essence and existence, but they do not constitute different worlds.

The nonreductive nature of realism, and its capacity for total explanation, can better be understood by showing what happens when realism is repudiated. When epistemology becomes a substitute for metaphysics, instead of being subordinated to it, then the real tends to be reduced to the logical in order to avoid agnosticism and skepticism. Some kind of "essentialism" is the consequence. In this type of idealism the individual simply evaporates, becomes relatively "unreal." The only completely real individual "substance" is the absolute itself. But to say that there is only one individual is equivalent to saying there is none. Another way of saying it is that the individual is dissolved into a bundle of universals, the "this" becomes a concept. Existence is reduced to essence. But such idealism must still relate, first, the phenomenological and ontological concepts, and second, the "this" with such concepts. But how is this possible if there is no existential "this"? The logic here is inexorable. These concepts, which from the standpoint of realism are complementary, must be conceived to be in *opposition,* and it is this opposition which it is the task of the mind to overcome by the power of its own action. The dialectic ceases to be an instrumental means to intuitive discovery; *it becomes a method by which the world is created.* Since the order of knowing and the order of being are coalesced, logic is no longer a propaedeutic science but becomes ontologically descriptive. But as we have seen, when one kind of knowledge is reduced to another, both are destroyed. And so dialectical idealism is academic but inefficacious; dialectical materialism is not academic but is efficacious. If the "mind" cannot create the truth, the "will" always pretends to be more successful.

There is another alternative equally erroneous. But error has its own peculiar opposites, which are also other errors. The opposite of "essentialism" is "existentialism." In order to "correct" the error of essentialism, why not reduce essence to existence? This is the way of nominalism—or, more exactly, one mode of nominalism. We call attention again to an interesting characteristic of nominalism. Essentialism (idealism), at least in most of its forms, pretends to be rational. So much so that sometimes in its overemphasis of the rational it has been dubbed "intellectual*ism*." It must be criticized by showing that the "overemphasis" is really a misconceived function of reason. But its pretension is accepted at face value. On the other hand, nominalism is the metaphysical position which denies the possibility of rational metaphysics. But this means that nominalism allows, and is compatible with, many forms of pseudo-metaphysics as well as with skepticism. Whereas in essentialism existence is sacrificed to the conceptual, in the modes of nominalism the conceptual (essence) is sacrificed to existence. Only reasoning (*A*) is allowed.

Now what is to be done about metaphysics? There are only two alternatives, strict skepticism or some kind of *a priorism* The former becomes boresome, the latter more interesting. And so, instead of discovering ontological necessity modern man simply imposes it. The recipe for this is: *Select those generalizations that are most convenient and useful for control and manipulation purposes, and make them a priori. What truth man creates cannot be destroyed except by man; it can but lack utility.*

We have already explained the nature of metaphysical evidence, how one may arrive at a cosmological universal proposition such as (4). If all this is denied as impossible, as nominalistic existentialism does, then how may the proposition "All material things change" be more than merely a generalization? Simply stipulate or postulate it as something more. If anything appears to be material but does not change, then it simply is not material. Of course this is true. But why? *We find that it is not because of the nature of the being, but because of the will of the person.* One of the most amazing phenomena of modern times is man's attempt to escape skepticism through postulation. There is no doubt but that there is the immediate feeling of emancipation and freedom in playing the "postulational" game in metaphysics, for man is then responsible only to the rules he makes (individually or collectively). The truth is that man pretends to create truth only because he refuses to discover and know it. Postulation does not overcome metaphysical skepticism. One error cannot correct another error, especially the very one which is responsible for it. Man postulates and creates his own *a priori* because he first accepts skepticism, not because he wishes to escape from it.

By means of the distinction between "instrumental to" and "constitutive of" both skeptism and postulation may be avoided, and at the same time it can be understood how the metaphysical can be known. Facts (historical propositions) are as relevant to metaphysics as to experimental science, but not in the same way; for they are instrumental to the discovery of metaphysical truth, but are constitutive as evidence of the generalizations of experimental science.

Misconceptions often prevent understanding of sensory evidence for metaphysics. Sense-knowledge in itself has already been considered, and the distinction pointed out between what is known and that by which it is known. But sometimes a strange notion of intuition is assumed.

The general notion of intuition is not peculiar to realism. Any metaphysics or epistemology requires it in some sense or other. As used here the meaning of intuition is opposed to that of "naïve" realism, the doctrine that man intuits without taking thought, merely by "awareness," whole objects and whole complexes of objects. This doctrine is to be found in the behavioristic epistemology of the "new realists." In metaphysics it is found in the work of S. Alexander, in his notion of "enjoyment." [6] This notion is quite inadequate, as it requires the knower and the object known to be materially, not merely formally, identified. Moreover, it is both fantastic and false in fact that metaphysical knowledge is acquired through sense experience with the mind merely passive. The "intelligible" is given, is intuited, but not without a great deal of thought. Dialectical analysis is required. When dialectic becomes an end in itself, then at best there is the probable opinion, as Aristotle remarked. But when taken as a means, and as one factor in knowing, then it is a necessary instrument for the intellectual intuition that grasps true metaphysical propositions. The error would be only in making intuition a substitute for thought.

For one who is chiefly familiar with the phenomenological subjects there is a great difficulty in understanding metaphysical method and evidence. And yet in absence of such understanding he does not thoroughly understand his own field. There is a tendency for him to extend or generalize his own limited methods. He may set up experimental apparatus, make field trips, sail the oceans, and photograph the heavens. He selects, or manipulates and controls to acquire his evidence, and it is with lifted eyebrow that he may hear what he does not thoroughly understand about intelligible intuition.

But the truth that each subject has its own methods is as old as Aristotle. The historian pores over old manuscripts in the subbasement of a great library. And the pure mathematician is the prince of armchair sitters. But he knows that any fool or mechanical brain can deduce theorems. The trick is to find a proof for a potential theorem, and for that the mathematician has his own version of intuition, though he might fumble in explaining it. Pure mathematics is on the level of the second order of abstraction and, like metaphysics, it finds historical propositions and generalizations instrumental. Without some true propositions in the two domains of the phenomenological context mathematical knowledge would be impossible. Yet neither historical propositions nor generalizations constitute the truth of pure mathematics. In the light of this example the distinction between "instrumental to" and "constitutive of" should be more easily grasped.

5

The Relation of Experimental Science and Cosmology to General Metaphysics

Thus far we have considered historical propositions in relation to that part of metaphysics which is called "cosmology." We have chosen to use the term "metaphysics" as meaning something broader than its traditional use. The reason for this is that the broader meaning better conforms to modern usage. No harm can come from this change provided that no thought content is confused. Aristotle meant by "physics" what we would now call "cosmology." He was not acquainted with the experimental science of matter as we now know it. Hence, "beyond" physics would mean beyond cosmology, or beyond the realm of becoming. Metaphysics is, then, the science of being *qua* being. As we are using the term it means "beyond" physics as an experimental science. Hence, cosmology is a part of metaphysics, that part which studies the mobile *qua* being. General metaphysics is concerned with the formal object obtained by means of the third order of abstraction, that which is "beyond" both mobile being and quantity, viz., being *qua* being.

However sharp the distinction may be between being and becoming from the standpoint of the order of being, from the standpoint of the order of knowledge there is a continuity. Both special metaphysics (cosmology) and general metaphysics constitute one domain in the ontological context. This is not an arbitrary "positing." The reason is that propositions of both cosmology and special metaphysics are descriptive of universality, and the method and type of evidence is the same.

The primary notions, such as unity, being, truth, goodness,

are called "transcendental" concepts. They are called such because they are "transcendent" to those most pervasive categories applicable in a restricted manner to corporeal nature. This is not to be confused with the Kantian meaning of "transcendental" as an *a priori* cognition of objects. In cosmology we talk of matter, form, soul, body, number, quantity, space, motion, time, corporeal substance, transitive action, sensitive life. In general metaphysics we speak of potency, act, essence, existence, as well as of the other transcendental concepts mentioned. Since realism is first of all concerned with the act of existence, without neglect of essence, metaphysics is concerned with the various kinds of causes, and in particular, the "first cause," God. While the "God" of metaphysics and theology is existentially one and the same, from the standpoint of the order of knowledge there is a difference. In metaphysics or "natural theology" we consider what can be known of God through reason. The knowledge that is faith is that of "revealed theology." When we use the term "theology" without an adjective, revealed theology is meant. The distinction we have made is valid in itself independently of the answer that is given as to whether there is any actual revelation.

Our problem is that of the nature of the evidence for general metaphysics. (Henceforth the adjective will be dropped; the specific meaning of the term "metaphysics" should be grasped by meaning-context.) All metaphysical problems not bearing upon this problem we shall try to avoid. But not all can be avoided, for it is difficult to speak of evidence unless we are clear as to the nature of the "what" for which the evidence exists.

These questions may be asked. Why should there be any problem of being *qua* being? Why not call ultimate those categories with which we are familiar, such as space, time, quantity, quality, and let it go at that? Why not identify metaphysics with that part of itself called "cosmology"?

The object of metaphysics. In the first place, the transcendental categories are just as familiar in experience as are the others. In fact, more so. We are more familiar with "being" than with any other notion. And the child hardly gets out of the cradle before it hears of truth and goodness from its parents (e.g., "You should tell mother the truth"). As we proceed from these most general categories down to the most specific ones of the special sciences they become less and less familiar. One may study matter in experimental science for some time before coming across the concept of "electrical resistance." As we go deeper into the phenomenological context the concepts take on more and more the appearance of "constructs." In appearance, at least, what seems most real and least constructed and remote are the transcendentals. Even "substance" and "accident" are less immediate.

Second, if there are these most pervasive of all categories, they must be considered in relation to the others. And conversely, we can hardly leave the problem with the categories directly presupposed by the special sciences merely dangling in an intellectual vacuum. From the standpoint of physics there may be an interest in space and time; from that of mathematics, in quantity. But even these philosophical interests of the workers in special fields cannot be satisfied in abstraction from the systematic problem of metaphysics. If this is forgotten, as it has been in recent times, then instead of responsible philosophy we get innumerable conjectures reflecting the personal idiosyncrasies of experimental scientists who confuse wisdom and knowledge with subjective novelty in awareness of philosophical ideas. They do not understand that metaphysical "originality," while objectively very possible, is subjectively often directly proportional to one's ignorance of the history of philosophy!

Finally, to limit the metaphysical problem to that of cosmology is simply to settle the problem *a priori,* and reduce being to becoming. In which case we also have a contradiction, for the proposition to the effect that nature or becoming is "all there is" itself transcends the mere cosmological.

As with any other kind of knowledge metaphysics must have a formal object. What is it? In the words of Maritain:

> The being which is the subject matter of metaphysics, being as such, is neither the particularized being of the natural sciences, nor the being divested of reality of genuine logic, nor yet the pseudo-being of false logic . . . the intuition of being is also the intuition of its transcendental character and analogical value.[1]

Being is the most fundamental transcendental category, and like the others must be grasped analogically. For the problem of metaphysical evidence the meaning of "analogy of being" must be understood. Let us see why this is so.

Univocity and analogy. If our knowledge has a sensible origin, which means that it is directly connected even in meaning with material things, how can concepts of the immaterial have meaning? Note the following list of words [2]:

Consider	*sidera*	(to gaze at) the stars
Contemplate	*templum*	(to enter) the soothsayers' place of observation
Reflect	*reflectere*	to bend back
Ponder	*pondus*	(to use) a weight
Comprehend	*prehendere*	to take hold of
Deliberate	*librum*	(to balance on) a scales
Conceive	*capere*	to seize on
Discern	*circus*	(to mark off with) a circle or ringed area
Envisage	*visus*	(to use one's) power of vision
Cogitate	*agitare*	to shake up or turn over

These terms are all concerned with rational activity which is in itself immaterial. Yet the terms in their derivation reflect their origin, which is connected with physical activity. In "reflection" what is it that we "bend back"? Can a thought be bent?

There is also the phenomenon of the human use of words. Some terms are used univocally, e.g., dog, silver (in chemistry), cigarette. Other words are used equivocally. Such terms, those spelled and pronounced alike, have radically different meanings. For example, we speak of a "deck" of cards, and also of the "deck" of a ship. About the only thing in common in the two instances is the spelling. But there are also analogous terms, those which, though applied to different things, have a related or similar meaning. We speak of the "head" as applied to a part of the body of a human being and also to the chief executive of an organization. The application is different, but the meaning is not totally different. There is a similar-but-different signification.

Now an equivocal term is just that and nothing more, useful

either for puns or for sophistic confusion. Univocal terms are the ones scholars like to use; for in appearance the more univocal a term is the more clear and distinct it is. Unless some meaning can be given to analogy the alternatives would seem to be either univocity and clarity, or equivocation and confusion.

These alternatives seem to work out pretty well in dealing with phenomenological *detail* in the experimental sciences. They are satisfactory to some extent even in cosmology. But as we proceed from the less general to the more general we seem to be faced with the fact that strict univocity of terms is not only impossible but undesirable. No one would say that everything is "dog" or "cigarette." That would be equivocation. But is not this exactly what the metaphysician does when he says that everything is "being"?

Let us explore this matter further by beginning with things and events in nature. There are some who have pushed the demand for univocity to the extreme. If events or things are particulars and are made up of particular qualities and relations, then the ideal of perfect clarity would seem to demand that there be a separate word-symbol for everything. An ideal language for any discipline would be one in which there is a distinct symbol for every element in events, and also a distinct symbol representing each and every relation between events. There would be a perfect isomorphism between the symbols of language and the real world. Two systems are isomorphic if there is a one-to-one correlation between every distinct element and relation in the two systems. If there is an isomorphism between language and objects, then the former mirrors the latter. There would be no unclarity.

For this ideal it is not necessary that every symbol signify an object in the same manner. A symbol might be an "icon," which represents its object very directly through its similarity. A diagram would be an example of an icon.[3] Other symbols might be called "characterizing" because they point to their reference by *meaning* them rather than by picturing them.[4] At any rate, however the ideal may be obtained, the ideal itself is that upon which Wittgenstein once insisted—that every proposition should be a picture of a fact.

It has been recognized that this nominalistic ideal is impossible to attain. The complexity of nature being what it is, no dictionary or mind could encompass the innumerable symbols. Of course it might be maintained that though the ideal cannot be attained, we should attempt to approach it if we wish to be clear and not equivocal. However, it has also been pointed out that the ideal not only is impossible but also undesirable. If a map were as detailed as the events it wishes to portray, then the map would lose its value, for it is not detail *qua* detail that is always most important in knowing. We can only understand by abstraction from detail. What exists may be individual, but all science is general and universal. This is the ideal of science itself; however, it is not what science is because it falls short of the ideal of perfect isomorphism.

Whatever may be the difficulty with this view of terms in the phenomenological sciences, it is certain that it implies the impossibility of metaphysics. There can be no "map" of, say, form or primary matter even on a cosmological level. The notion would be even more meaningless on the higher level, the third order of abstraction.

One might attempt to hold to the strict univocity of terms in another way, avoiding extreme nominalism by a more conceptualistic approach, interpreting things and properties in terms of class-concepts. All concepts except the most elementary ones are generic with respect to the species (the differentiating factor) they encompass. As generic they can be subsumed under more general concepts, to which they stand as species. Individual things, substances and accidents, are "instances" of these concepts. Each concept is univocal. For example, a sheep is a mammal. "Mammal" is a concept subsumed under "sentient." "Sentient" in turn can be subsumed under "living." "Sentient" is a genus in relation to "mammal"; in relation to "living" it is a differentiating factor. Finally, we can go on to still more universal categories, "material" and "substance," ending up in the most universal of all, "being." Not everything we begin with will end up as "substance." But literally anything we begin with will finally fall under "being."

Now, if terms are considered only univocally, and if "intension" varies inversely with "extension," then the highest category of all, being, will be the emptiest. Everything is being; but what is everything is simply nothing. It is pure homogeneity, pure indetermination. But even that is not quite exact, for there is no "it." As Hegel says, being is nothing and nothing is being. As one descends from "nothing" (being) to less general categories, then one at least gets "something"; there is an increase in definiteness, in determination, as one decreases in generality and becomes more specific.

That such univocity has a function in the phenomenological sciences, or at least has some legitimate limit, may be granted. But if taken literally as the whole story, then the implication is definite that metaphysics is impossible. The science of being *qua* being is the science of nothing at all. Or, to put it in another way, if being is a genus, then metaphysics is impossible. Or again, if there is no analogy of being, but only pure univocity, then metaphysics *as knowledge* is impossible. Of course "postulational metaphysics" is still possible for "ideological" purposes.

The issue here is clear. One can assert the analogy of being, and assert the possibility of metaphysics, which will, of course, be realism of some kind. Or one can insist on univocity and deny the possibility. From a purely formal standpoint there is a logic to both alternatives, and the proponents of each position can be clear about their assertions and denials.

But such "logic" does not characterize modern philosophy since Descartes. Instead of having it either one way or the other modern man has insisted upon having it both ways. Let us deny the analogy of being and *yet* have metaphysics. But since this is impossible, how can it be accomplished? Impossible or not, men have attempted to do it, and it is only through understanding this fact that one can understand what is peculiar to modern thought.

Dialectic and postulation as alternatives to analogy. What can be done if one tries to have metaphysics and at the same time avoids the realistic analogy of being? There are only two things that can be done. (1) One can begin with being and then simply make it "something" by creating content. (2) Or one can take some category other than being, and hence a category that is of necessity limited, and make a metaphysical category out of it. Other than some form of metaphysical skepticism (Hume, Kant, some form of positivism), there are no alternatives other than these two. They are exhaustive. Of course there are various modes of accomplishing either alternative. If one thinks he has discovered a third alternative he will very likely find on closer examination that he has discovered only another mode of one or the other.

Our interest in these two alternatives is primarily that of the question of the evidence and only secondarily that of method, although the two cannot be separated. The metaphysics of Hegel and Spinoza would be examples of the first alternative. For illustrative purposes we may consider the former.

If being is considered a genus, a kind of abstract universal, then it must be "empty." And so Hegel says, "Being, as Being, is nothing fixed or ultimate: it yields to dialectic and sinks into its opposite, which, also taken immediately, is Nothing." [5] Hegel is consistent here. But in realism we have seen that what is determinate is form; pure indetermination is primary matter. We have not as yet considered the analogy of being, but it is already evident that being *qua* being would be perfect determinateness without matter. It would seem that Hegelianism is realism turned upside down. Is not being then practically identical with Aristotelian primary matter? Yes, for "we find Being identified with what persists amid all change, with *matter*, susceptible of innumerable determinations . . ." [6] In realism the concreteness of a corporeal substance is accounted for in terms of form, for the fundamental principle is the priority of act over potentiality. On the contrary, for Hegel "The truth of Being and of Nothing is accordingly the unity of the two: and this unity is *Becoming.*" [7] "Becoming is the first concrete thought, and therefore the first notion; whereas Being and Nought are empty abstractions." [8]

The Hegelian principle is, then, that of the priority of becoming over being, of potentiality over actuality. Being, the Absolute, *is* concrete, of course, because it *becomes* concrete. No longer can we say "out of nothing comes nothing; out of something comes something." Being acquires content, then, through generation. But from the standpoint of knowledge, "where" is the content to be obtained? What is the evidence? The evidence stems from the phenomenological sciences and the creative function of reason:

> . . . we may safely say that experience is the real author of *growth* and *advance* in philosophy. For, firstly, the empirical sciences do not stop short at the mere observation of the individual features of a phenomenon. By the aid of thought, they are able to meet philosophy with materials prepared for it, in the shape of general uniformities, i.e., laws, and classifications of the phenomena. When this is done, the particular facts which they contain are ready to be received into philosophy. This, secondly, implies a certain compulsion on thought itself to proceed to these concrete specific truths. The reception into philosophy of the scientific materials, now that thought has removed their immediacy and made them cease to be mere data, forms at the same time a development of thought out of itself. Philosophy, then, owes its development to the empirical sciences. In return it gives their contents what is so vital to them, the freedom of thought,—gives them, in short, an *a priori* character. These contents are now warranted necessary, and no longer depend on the evidence of facts merely, that were so found and so experienced.[9]

This thought development "incorporates the contents of science, in all their speciality of detail as submitted." [10]

Metaphysics, then, has no object, but does have a "purpose." But if it has no object the purpose of metaphysics cannot be that of *knowing* its object. Its purpose can only be something else—to *create* its object. For that purpose the raw material is obtained from the "detail" of the phenomenological sciences; ". . . in philosophy, to prove means to show how the subject by and from itself makes itself what it is." [11]

In our terminology the Hegelian answer is that historical propositions and generalizations are instrumental not to knowing but to creating. The Kantian revolution is completed. For Kant the mind as creative was at least limited to the phenomenological. There remained the thing-in-itself which was not created. Since knowing is creating, Kant was correct in saying that the thing-in-itself was unknowable. There is another alternative, that of refusing to admit that anything is intrinsically unknowable. If so, then the thing-in-itself must also be created if it is to be known. In this respect Hegel was also consistent.

The whole of this volume is a repudiation of the notion that knowing is creating. It is sufficient for the present merely to point out the nature of the alternative. Instead of the analogy of being there is creation by dialectic; instead of meta-physics there is meta-logic; instead of man's freedom being derived in part from knowing the truth, man's "spirit" is now conceived as thwarted unless he can create it. This, Hegel calls "freedom of thought." The issue here is not merely academic. It is not at all an accident that philosophy since Hegel has been relatively barren. Even Marx recognized it in his own way in speaking of the "poverty of philosophy." The twentieth century has reaped the "freedom" sowed by Kant and Hegel: "freedom" untouched and unsanctified by . . . Man's naked "spirit" has triumphed—and destroyed. Even Hegel could not today accept the child he fathered. There is reason to believe that Kant could.

The other alternative, if the analogy of being is to be rejected, is simply to take a limited category and make it equivalent to "being," even though the latter term is not used. When this alternative is taken there are always two problems: What method is to be used and what category or categories are to be elevated? Actually these are problems only for the critic looking on, not for the historical figure constructing his system.

This alternative is the one we have met with before, "postulational metaphysics." Abstractly speaking, there is nothing to prevent one from taking *any* category and absolutizing it. For example, one can say that everything is sound or is reducible to sound. The method of proof is "talking." All attempts to prove sound is absolute must be through talking. But talking will produce sounds and verify the thesis in the very act of positing it. Also, anyone who attempts to refute the fact that everything is sound must do so by talking and hence contradict himself by producing sounds. It may be pointed out that one can write and not talk; hence everything is not sound. That objection can be taken care of very easily. There are "liquid" and "frozen" sounds; in other words sounds in "process" and sounds "static."

All printing and writing are composed of "frozen" sounds. But there are colors and smells and tastes as well as sounds; hence, everything is not sound. No, it just appears that way. In reality "color is simply the way that eyes *hear*." Psychology has shown that colors can be correlated with sounds, and so on. But what about something like "thought"? "Proof" is thinking, not talking. No, that is a carry-over from the Dark Ages; and anyway it is prescientific. By scientific experimentation it has been shown that all thinking is really subvocal speech; in short, "talking."

If the reader thinks this is a little forced, he is correct. If he thinks such nonsense does not exist among the "learned," he is naïve. If he thinks it is funny, then he should also say that it is tragic.

It is tragic today, but it was not so in pre-Platonic times. It was one of the contributions of Plato and Aristotle (both realists, the one "extreme," the other "moderate") to show that such metaphysical procedure as had gone on before was sterile and fruitless because partial and arbitrary. If the judgment is correct, then it applies to modern philosophy also. To the degree that experience was appealed to there was a tendency to skepticism and a repudiation of metaphysics, e.g., Locke to Hume to Kant. To the degree that experience was not appealed to there was a tendency to rationalistic types of metaphysics which, to the individuals involved, were not meant to be arbitrary, e.g., Descartes, Spinoza, Leibnitz. However, the question at issue is one of fact. Either evidence relevant to metaphysics was appealed to or it was not.

The realist would point out that many *a priori,* rationalistic types of metaphysics can be understood only in terms of a faulty empiricism which they were intended to correct. If one begins with the assumption that sense experience is *what* we know, rather than *that by which* we know, then one is led into some kind of subjectivism. To escape this (in a non-Hegelian manner) one is forced to posit some ideas or propositions. At first this is not conceived to be arbitrary. The ideas may be thought of as innate, or as forms of the mind. Or propositions may be thought of as guaranteed by intuition—*not* in abstraction *from* sense experience, as in realism, but as *independent* of sense experience. Whereas in realism historical propositions are instrumental to, but not constitutive of, metaphysical propositions, in this kind of *a priori* rationalism historical propositions are neither instrumental to, nor constitutive of, metaphysical propositions. A good example of this would be Descartes' identification of the metaphysical category of "matter" with extension. This is to identify matter with a quantitative form. It is difficult to see how sense experience could even be instrumental to such identification. The reason must be sought for elsewhere; in this case in an unwarranted assumption that to be knowledge metaphysics must be mathematized. But this implies that the method of mathematics must also be carried over into metaphysics. From here on the logic is inexorable.

As is well known, after the first half of the nineteenth century, and partly because of the new approach to mathematics that developed from the generation of the non-Euclidean geometries, a postulational conception of mathematics came into being. The mathematician need no longer worry about whether or not the postulates of a system are materially true. They can be assumed, theorems generated and a system constructed. Formal validity, a relation between postulates and theorems, is sufficient for proof. Whether the system as a whole is "true" to anything in nature is irrelevant for the pure mathematician as such. Whether this is the whole story does not concern us at the moment. The point is that this change has taken place, and the truth of the fact itself is independent of the further questions of the philosophy of mathematics, such as the issues raised by the "intuitionalists" and the "formalists."

Now, what is the significance of mathematizing metaphysics? Fundamental metaphysical propositions become "postulates" having only a formal relation to their "implications." Of course this is quite unsatisfactory, for it is practically equivalent to skepticism. Again, the logic of the situation is inexorable, and one is forced into the "postulational" conception of metaphysics with which we have become familiar. For example, Whitehead objects that Descartes made the mistake of following the mathematics of his day and of attempting to begin metaphysics with clear and distinct ideas that were true. And so he did. But Whitehead's objection should have been that he "followed" at all. Unfortunately that is not Whitehead's objection. The consequence is that the objection simply comes down to the fact that Descartes did not have the advantage of living in the twentieth century and of knowing contemporary mathematical and physical methods. While it is true that in a sense every philosopher is a victim of the limitations of his age, Whitehead's postulational conception of metaphysics reduces it to an ideological reflection of the "learning" of a culture. Presumably if mathematics and physics change radically in some respect a century hence, metaphysics must necessarily reflect it, and to the degree that it does "progress" will be made.

The realist rests his case on the fact that the evidence for metaphysical propositions ultimately is the "intelligible" obtained intuitively through sense experience. That there are difficulties attending this notion is not to be denied. It shares that in common with any metaphysics. But there is no gain in shifting to the arbitrariness of postulation. For where is the ground for either method or evidence? If one insists on univocity and denies the analogy of being, then one is faced with either one of two alternatives. The first is that there must be a science for every univocal concept. Needless to say, this alternative is both impossible and undesirable and hence is never taken. The other is, as we have seen, to choose some univocal categories and "generalize" them. This alternative, though undesirable, is possible, and hence is taken. To exaggerate we demonstrated a moment ago with "sound." That category is too restricted; usually more general ones are chosen. One can choose "mind" and "matter," the one from experimental psychology, the other from physics. Or the one might be taken and the other reduced to it. Or, in the case of Alexander, why not choose the two "accidents" space and time, put a hyphen between them just as the latest physical theory does, and then proceed to reduce everything to points and instants? If there is no reason why one should not, then metaphysics becomes a formalistic game of worth only to the solitary soul.

The answer that is given to this criticism is that the right of postulation carries with it the duty to "check" it with experience. It must pass the pragmatic test; it must "work," be "successful," and "explain." And so it must. The question is: What does this mean in terms of "postulation"? And what is the "experience" that tests? For example, Whitehead was confronted with the experience of a methodological procedure of physicists in which a thing is considered to be what it does, and he was also confronted with the experience of three thousand years of theism. He "generalized" the former notion into a metaphysical principle, and then very consistently pronounced the whole development of theism to be a tragic error. Now what experience "checks" what; and which is "checked"?

The question can be put in this way: Exactly how does recent physics prove something metaphysical? Either it does or it doesn't. If it does, it should be shown. But neither Whitehead nor others give a demonstration as to how historical propositions or generalizations enter constitutively into metaphysical knowledge as they do in history or the natural sciences. The priority of physics is simply posited. Instead of being interpreted in terms of metaphysics, physics becomes the interpreter. But isn't it the case that physics is "empirical," and theism is not? No, not unless the question is begged, or a doctrine of experience is posited in terms of which theism is impossible. This solves nothing. In fact such positing is what a person does when he has no solution. Further, that a methodological principle of physics can justifiably be elevated to a metaphysical principle is or is not "experiential" in just about the same sense as is theism; it certainly is no more justifiable as to truth, and probably less.

Let us suppose that a theologian "postulated" something theistically and then argued that the contemporary principles of physics are false. This would be the inverse of the aforementioned error. Both the theologian and the postulational metaphysician assume the physical principles to be metaphysical, which they are not. The difference is that the one assumes them to be metaphysically true, the other to be metaphysically false. It is from such confusion that strife is born.

It may be objected that it is only from a psychological standpoint that generalizing a limited category to metaphysical status seems to be arbitrary. But there is always the "check" of experience on such generalization. When particular categories are so generalized and postulated, then the pragmatic test through experience may reject them. What more can be asked? It may even be granted that there is always an appeal to intuition in some sense. What one experiences, that he experiences. And so intuition enters into the verificatory experience by means of which the successfulness of metaphysical postulates is explored. Now, Whitehead sees it the way he sees it. It is his experience, and a metaphysical system always comes from the experience of someone. One may or may not agree with the system. If one does not agree, that does not make it false; nor does it mean that his method cannot be fruitful. The realist is stuck with his own thesis. Let there be intuition; Whitehead admits it. But if so, then if two or more people do not intuit alike, and hence arrive at different conclusions, one cannot appeal to intuition to say that one is true and that the other is false. If one attempts to do so, then the person is simply being dogmatic through begging the question; for he is saying, *without evidence,* that he intuits correctly, and that whoever disagrees intuits incorrectly.

This kind of argument seems to be most potent and conclusive. But it "proves" too much. Such an argument is not *for* a given postulational metaphysics and *against* realism. It is an argument for skepticism, and *against* all metaphysics as knowledge. It makes Whitehead's metaphysical pursuit quite as worthless as that of the realist. The skeptic's argument still has to be met, but it is irrelevant in the present context. Of course, if metaphysics is impossible, then there is no question of evidence. But the present problem is that of evidence.

At this point it may be helpful to recall again the distinction between sense intuition and intelligible intuition. The former is relevant to historical propositions, the latter to metaphysical propositions. An example of the first is: This tastes bitter. An example of the second is: Whatever reality a being has, it must have it either of and by itself or from and by another being. There is a good deal of thought in connection with the second. Of course, ultimately, as with any other proposition in any kind of knowledge, one does or does not see it to be true. But there is a great deal of difference between beginning with being as immediately experienced, then through reflection arriving at the metaphysical principle of sufficient reason, and on the other hand beginning by elevating a phenomenological principle through postulation to metaphysical status, then discovering what is and what is not compatible with it. In the latter case what we can "see" is already limited by what one postulates, for as Whitehead has pointed out, theory "dictates" the relevance of evidence.

The notion of a pragmatic test of postulated metaphysical propositions is based upon a faulty analogy with the method of the physico-mathematical sciences. In the latter some meaning can be given to postulational technique. The reason is that historical propositions are constitutive of generalizations. *Postulational technique would have the same meaning in metaphysics if likewise historical propositions were constitutive of it.* But historical propositions are not so constitutive. To maintain that they are is equivalent to the reduction of metaphysics to experimental science.

Postulational metaphysics is, then, either formalistic and arbitrary and not knowledge at all, or else through reduction to experimental science it ceases to be metaphysics. It is the alternative to some kind of Hegelianism when metaphysics is denied a formal object of its own, namely, being. Metaphysics comes to be conceived as a kind of a logical, epiphenomenal reflex of the experimental science of an age. One then reads this false conception back into history.[12] Aristotle's natural science is then said to be the evidence for his metaphysics. Since much of Aristotle's natural science is no longer held (and correctly so), it is then inferred that the "adequate" metaphysics of the moment must be demonstrated by the very latest natural science (usually mathematical physics). A perfectly logical deduction, but from a false premise—false historically and theoretically.

In the first place it is false to interpret Aristotle's metaphysics as postulational or the notion of being as a "generalization" from the science of his day. This is independent of the question as to whether his metaphysics is essentially true or false. Realism is in relation to Aristotle and Plato through a continuous development, not through slavish imitation. Some of his metaphysical notions were clear and true, some clear and false (e.g., we have quite correctly "naturalized" the stars), and some were not clear at all. It makes some sense to say that his notion of "substance" is false, and likewise the proposition that what a thing *does* is partly determined by what a thing *is*—if one takes the proper responsibility. But it is to confuse kinds of knowledge to say, as does Mr. Northrop, that while such principles were "scientifically verified" at the time, they are "now outmoded" because of recent science; or with Whitehead, that it must now be metaphysically true that anything is what it does because that is the reigning notion in present physics. A metaphysical principle is true or false at all times, and is more or less understood at different particular times. If something in Aristotle was true then, it is true now; if false now, it was also false then.

What was not proved by natural science to begin with cannot later be disproved by it. Whatever in metaphysics is later "disproved" by natural science was not really proved in the beginning by earlier natural science. Recent science does not overthrow Aristotle's notion of substance or primary matter. *If it overthrows anything it is the many systems of postulational metaphysics constructed at various times through generalizing the latest fad in natural science.* For example, what recent physics overthrows is the "substance" of Descartes, not that of Aristotle. Descartes' notion was "generalized" from the science of his century, and it is overthrown by the science of another century. These "postulational" systems of the past are accepted by no one as essentially true. Nor will they ever be. Rather they function even historically as a museum of errors. What is lasting is Descartes' contribution to mathematics, not his philosophy. On the other hand, what is lasting in Aristotle is his philosophical contribution, not his natural science. Had Aristotle's metaphysics been postulational, merely derived from the science of his day, it would have died long ago. On the contrary it has provided the base for the continuous development of a realism now over two thousand years old.

There are signs that scientists themselves are recognizing more and more the error of lifting their notions to metaphysical status.

In discussing the relation of philosophy and natural science the British physicist and astronomer Martin Johnson devotes a chapter of his book to "Misleading Transfers of Argument from Physics to Metaphysics." In the final sentence of the chapter he says, "As elucidator of the logical status of physics, Eddington led well his generation: as metaphysical speculator, he seems unlikely to do more than exemplify with the materialist and with Alexander the danger of transferring into theorems about the nature of existence the devices which are legitimate technique for physics." [13]

We have been considering the two alternatives to the "analogy of being." The one is to make being a genus. The other is to choose a limited category and make it equivalent to being, or at least metaphysically ultimate, by postulation. Both are "reductionist" in tendency. The first makes metaphysics a "metalogic." On the second metaphysics either becomes formalistic and arbitrary, or it is reduced to experimental science.

Realism has long recognized the problem which seems to demand some kind of inference from limited categories. For example, from knowledge about limited "essences" is there not reasoning leading to statements about God's essence? And is it not admitted that God's essence is not the same as any other essence? If so, then in realism is there not a "generalizing" of a limited notion, a kind of "postulating"? No, it is rather reasoning by analogy; and it is something more than that meaning of analogy which is usually given a few paragraphs in the back of a logic text. The problem of analogy is most difficult, and a thorough discussion of it is not necessary for our purpose. It will be sufficient to indicate the nature of analogy insofar as it bears upon the problem of the nature of metaphysical evidence and reasoning.

The analogy of being. Realistic metaphysics is based upon a fundamental proposition to the effect that being cannot be a genus. Logically a "species" is the consequence of the union of a "genus" with a "specific difference." For example, "metal" is a genus in relation to "silver" as a species. The specific difference which partly makes silver what it is, is extraneous to the genus. What makes metal metal is something other than what makes silver silver. What makes silver the kind of metal it is also adds something positive to the notion of "metal." It follows also that if a specific difference does not add something positive, if it is not extraneous to the genus, then the genus cannot really be a genus at all.

This is the case with being in relation to substance and accident. Substance is that kind of being which exists in itself and not in another. But being is not a genus. "Existence" is something positive, but it is not something extraneous to being. Rather it is in itself a modal form of being. There is nothing other than being which can positively differentiate. The only "thing" that is outside of, or extraneous to, being is "nothing." "Nothing" cannot be combined with "being" in order to get the determinateness that a specific difference usually gives to an abstract and relatively indeterminate genus. To assume that this is possible is, of course, to follow Hegel. Being is nothing and nothing is being, but by the dialectic a synthesis occurs which is "becoming." The dialectic becomes a power and a substitute for analogy. Dialectic is a *power* whereby incompatibles and contraries are *forced* together. Analogy is a way of *knowing* how the "same" and the "other" are transcendentally related. Dialectic is a power by which something presumably comes from nothing, by which the determinate arises from the indeterminate. Analogy is a way of knowing how determinateness and concreteness of being permeates its kinds. In realism the "dialectic" is a valuable logical instrument, but it is not a "power."

If being is not a genus, is not "nothing," then it must be interpreted analogously. A univocal term designates many different things, but all in the same sense. An analogous term is applicable to different things because there is a likeness in some respect and an unlikeness in another respect, a sameness and otherness. Being is such a term. Everything is being in some sense or other. Nothing is nonbeing. There is nothing extrinsic to being which, as a differentia, could divide it into species. Being permeates and cuts across the categories, and hence its univocity must be denied. On the other hand, it is not merely equivocal. "Being" is not said of (say) substances and accidents as "blade" is said of a bit of grass and also of the edge of a knife.

There is another way in which the contrast between univocity and analogy may be understood. There is a creature in my house that delights in chasing skunks. This creature is an animal. I can apply the term "animal" to both this creature and the skunk in a univocal manner; that is, the thought-content of the term is present in the creature and in the skunk in the same sense, in the same uniform manner. Now this creature happens to be a certain kind of animal, a Gordon setter. What distinguishes a dog from a skunk is not contained within the concept of animal. It is added from without. In other words, "animal" applies to that nature in which they both agree, but not to that nature in which they disagree.

The case is different with "being." Being is in substances and in accidents just as (but not quite as) animal is found in dogs and skunks. But there is a difference. The way in which substance and accident are unlike is "being" just as much as the way in which they are alike. "Being" is not only that in which they agree; it is also that in which they disagree. It is for this reason that we say that being is not in a substance and in an accident in the same way, in the same uniform manner, and hence being must be considered analogously and not univocally. The same identical meaning of "being" is not applicable to substance and accident, or to quality, or to quantity, etc., for "being" is applicable to the way in which these differ as well as to the ways in which they agree:

> To be is to be in a certain way, and the way is the very heart of the being. So the whole order of beings, of *entia,* from the triune deity down to the speck of dust and the electron, consists of nothing more and nothing less than analogical instances of being: self-existent being and dependent being, actual being and possible being, substantial being and accidental being, real being and notional being, not in any pantheistic or monistic sense, as if being were some kind of cosmic material, a metaphysical modeling-clay appearing now in this shape and now in that, but in the far more profound sense that every being must *be,* and must be in some determinate way, and—the theist will add—in the sense that the way in which it has being depends in the last resort upon its relation to self-existent being which is the prime analogate of all.[14]

The notion of "prime analogate" must be explained. But before proceeding further we must give a hint as to how this notion of analogy bears upon the question of metaphysical evidence in reasoning. Since all knowledge can be traced back to sense experience, there is the problem of how to get from such experience to universal metaphysical principles, and especially how to talk about God as first cause. Are we just to "generalize" some limited category, or "posit" the nature of some finite existent as "God" and call Him infinite? We experience finite essences, existents, beings. Are we merely to take some one of these and "blow it up" conceptually and call it "God," call it infinite? Hardly, if we wish to escape a crude anthropomorphism and also care about evidence and rationality. If we do it, then all we have done is to take something that is univocal and relatively clear and make it equivocal. This would not be knowledge, but confusion. But if analogy is a mean between univocity and equivocation, then the matter would be different. Let us see.

There are two fundamental kinds of analogy, analogy of attribution and analogy of proportionality. To use an example that realists are fond of, we say that a human being is healthy and also that a certain food is healthy, or that his complexion is healthy. Now the way in which human beings and foods are healthy is not the same. Health is formally in a person, and only derivatively in a food or a complexion. A given complexion is a sign, or an effect, or health in a person. A food conduces or causes health in a person. Food, person, and complexion are called "analogates." The thing to which health strictly applies, that which has it formally, is called the "prime analogate." The property in question (health) which is referred to the objects is called the "analogue."

Now, when we say that both human beings and God are good we must interpret "good" analogously. Just as food is healthy because it causes health in us, so God is good because He causes good in us. Yet God's goodness is not the same as our goodness. However, this kind of analogy, that of *attribution,* is only a part of the story, not the whole of it. For we are faced with the finiteness of man's knowledge. Health is formally and strictly in man, and only virtually in the food. That is to say, while health is actually in a person, only the foundation of health is in the food. And so we are saying likewise that goodness is formally (but in a finite manner) in a human being, but that all that we can attribute to God is the cause or the foundation of goodness. It may occur to someone that if this is the case there is no reason to use the word "God." All that has been shown is that "something" is the cause of goodness in us. The "something," for all that the analogy of attribution can tell us, might just as well be "Nature" as "God." This is true. And there the matter would rest were it not for the other kind of analogy, that of proportionality.[15]

Let us suppose that we are thinking of "life" in connection with both man and dog. Both are living things, and yet the life of a man is not quite the same as the life of a dog. The reason for this is that that which makes a man a man is not identical with what makes a dog a dog. But when we speak of the "what" we are speaking of the "essence." How anything is alive is determined in part by what the thing is. The way in which the essence "dog" determines the life of a dog is the same, and yet not quite the same, as the way in which the essence "man" determines the life of a man. This can be expressed as a kind of "proportion": the life of dog is to the essence of dog as the life of man is to the essence of man. This is the *analogy of proportionality.* "Life" is proportionate to the "natures" that have it.

Whereas in the analogy of attribution the analogue (property) was formally in one analogate and only virtually in the other, in the analogy of proportionality the analogue (in this case, "life") is formally in both analogates and also is determined by both. Through this kind of analogy, based upon sameness and difference, we can know something of the life of a dog through knowing the life of man. What is the "same" is the fact that in both cases essence determines life. What is "different" is the way in which such determination occurs.

On levels of being below that of man this kind of knowing by analogy is not so important. Before the development of the biological sciences it was the only way man had of conceiving of lower forms of life. At the present time it is not only supplemented, but far surpassed in worth, by the biological sciences which have given us a great deal of detailed knowledge about "life." The value of analogy is on the metaphysical level itself, and especially when considering natural theology—what can be known of God, not only through revelation, but through reason.

Essence, existence, potency, act, and such transcendentals as good and truth must be interpreted by analogy. Otherwise such propositions as "God is Truth," "God is Good," if taken univocally (literally), can be made to seem silly. The goodness of both man and God is proportionate to their respective natures. It is through such analogy of proportionality that metaphysical propositions can be known, and also some knowledge of God may be had, however little. Of course, it is understood that here the argument to God's nature is merely indicated, that it is used for illustrative purposes, and that independent evidence for the existence of God is assumed.

The bearing of analogy upon the question of metaphysical evidence and reasoning may better be understood by considering the implications of its denial. We are faced with the question as to how we may reasonably speak of infinite and necessary being when our terms are taken from knowledge of finite and contingent being. How, for example, from the notion of cause as applicable to nature, and as treated in cosmology, can we speak of God as first cause? From our knowledge of man's goodness how can we speak of the goodness of a perfect being? If such terms were merely univocal, then the answer would have to be that we cannot so speak. But of course man does so speak. The mystical silence of skepticism is but a convenient fiction.

Let us assume that "good" can only be univocal, and we say that man is good. Then if we say also that God is good we must mean the same identical thing by "good" in both cases. This is a sort of "pellet" conception of a character or property. The nature of "good" would be completely independent of the "nature" to which it is applicable. One could pursue this line of thought and show to where it leads on purely epistemological grounds. But most important to note is that of necessity it tends toward a crude anthropomorphism, the reduction of God to a "thing." If "good" and other terms are to be applied to God univocally, and if at the same time there is a knowledge-claim, then consistently God must have a sufficiently finite nature to be compatible with the univocal concept applied. God can't be infinitely perfect and at the same time be "good" in the same sense as a human is good. It is not an accident at all that in modern times, with the tendencies toward positivism and away from realism, there have been attempts to conceive of God as finite. And so God both lacks and strives for the good just as human beings do. He even "rolls up his sleeves" and helps us fight evil. God is no longer the creator. Rather He is partly a victim of the world, created by it in the very process of introducing order into the world He did not create!

This way of answering the question is simply to get rid of the question. There is no movement in knowledge from finite and contingent to infinite and necessary being. The demand of univocity eliminates the latter, and terms are applied in the same sense to different finite beings. This requires the denial of at least one kind of knowledge-claim, that of revealed theology. "Natural theology" may remain in name, but *what remains in fact is a form of naturalism with the borrowed language of theism.*

There is a countertendency which represents the swinging from one extreme to the other, from the univocal to the equivocal. The notion of an infinite God is asserted, but all hope is given up of discovering any reasonable link between terms descriptive of Him and terms descriptive of nature or man. A term like "good" now becomes purely equivocal, meaning one thing in application to man, but something quite different when applied to God. The content of the "good" of God's nature is furnished by revelation. The discontinuity between reason and faith becomes absolute, as it has in certain forms of the neo-orthodox movement in Protestantism. Metaphysics either becomes useless or is a potential danger to faith.

Either one of the two extremes of pure univocity or equivocation bodes ill for general metaphysics as knowledge in addition to the purely cosmological, for there is no way of "getting" from the latter to the former. But it must also be observed that it is only in terms of some kind of realistic cosmology that analogy can have meaning. Analogy implies, and is implied by, such notions as those of "potentiality," "act," and "primary matter." They would seem to stand or fall together. There are some principles which have ontological and not merely logical status, and which may be said to be grasped intuitively, although not without the instrumentality of sense experience. Examples would be the principle of contradiction and the principle of sufficient reason. The principle of contradiction is presupposed in proof, and cannot itself be proved without begging the question. But most of the propositions of general metaphysics are obtained by demonstration from evidence supplied from cosmology (special metaphysics). The analogy of being makes this possible. In the example we have been using the argument has been from nature to God. From the standpoint of the order of being the dependency is of the former on the latter. From the standpoint of the order of knowledge the converse is the case. Apart from special revelation we know God (however little) by first knowing nature. But affairs of nature can be evidence for propositions about God only if the concepts used are interpreted analogously.

An example of metaphysical evidence and reasoning. There is almost an insuperable difficulty in understanding the nature of metaphysical evidence for one who has never subjected himself to the discipline of metaphysical thinking. Of course the same holds true in discussing the nature of evidence for any kind of knowledge. It is to be doubted whether the full understanding of the nature of scientific evidence can be had by anyone who has not had any scientific training. Nor does it follow that if a person has been disciplined only in the experimental sciences, he automatically understands fully the nature of science and what is and what is not the range and limit of its evidence. However, for most people the difficulty is greater in the case of metaphysics for the reason that no disciplined thinking in, or even acquaintance with, metaphysics can be assumed. It may be helpful, therefore, to relieve the abstractness of this analysis by examining a bit of metaphysical reasoning. We shall choose an example from the writings of St. Thomas.

Consider, for example, the notions of "essence" and "existence." How can we reason from the essences and existential acts we know in the world of nature to some statement about God's essence and existence? In the following quotation the term "suppositum" means a substance self-contained and autonomous in its operations:

> God is the same as His essence or nature. To understand this, it must be noted that in things composed of matter and form, the nature or essence must differ from the *suppositum,* for the essence or nature includes only what falls within the definition of the species; as humanity includes all that falls within the definition of man, for it is by this that man is man, and it is this that humanity signifies, that, namely, whereby man is man. Now individual matter, with all the individuating accidents, does not fall within the definition of species. For this particular flesh, these bones, this blackness or whiteness, etc., do not fall within the definition of a man. Therefore this flesh, these bones, and the accidental qualities designating this particular matter, are not included in humanity; and yet they are included in the reality which is a man. Hence, the reality which is a man has something in it that humanity does not have. Consequently, humanity and a man are not wholly identical, but humanity is taken to mean the formal part of a man, because the principles whereby a thing is defined function as the formal constituent in relation to individuating matter. The situation is different in things not composed of matter and form, in which individuation is not due to individual matter—that is to say, to *this* matter, but the forms themselves are individuated of themselves. Hence it is necessary that the forms themselves should be subsisting *supposita.* Therefore *suppositum* and nature in them are identified. Since, then, God is not composed of matter and form, He must be His own Godhead, His own Life, and whatever else is so predicated of Him.[16]

The conclusion is a proposition of general metaphysics, and the evidence to which appeal is made is from nature; but it is nature as ontologically conceived, which is special metaphysics or cosmology, and not nature as phenomenological. This may be more easily seen if we set up the argument in strict demonstrative form:

> Any suppositum that is individuated by matter is that which is different from its essence.

(*A*) Any substance composed of matter and form is a suppositum that is individuated by matter.
Any substance composed of matter and form is that which is different from its essence.
Any substance composed of matter and form is that which is different from its essence. (also convertible)

(*B*) Nothing that is individuated in itself is a substance composed of matter and form.
Nothing that is individuated in itself is that which is different from its essence.

(*C*) Whatever is individuated in itself is the same as its essence. (by obversion)
God is that which is individuated in Himself.
God is the same as His essence.

In the major premise of (*A*) "essence" refers to finite being. In the conclusion of (*B*) the reference is to infinite being. The whole point of the argument is to demonstrate that God's existence is His essence, and that such cannot be said of anything else. Evidently the meaning of essence is not identical in (*A*) and (*C*). Now if analogy were to be abolished in favor of univocity, then regardless of the apparent strictness of the demonstration, at the most we would have but an exercise in equivocation; for "essence" cannot be predicated of (say) dog and God in the same sense and in the same way in which we predicate "animal" of dog and cat. But the matter is different in terms of the analogy of proportionality. The essence of a finite being is to its existential act as the essence of God is to His existential act. If on some other grounds there is some notion as to what existence of God might mean, then by means of analogy together with the demonstration some knowledge (however meager) may be had of God's essence. In the case at hand the knowledge is that His essence is His existence.

If the cosmological knowledge is correct, if the doctrine of analogy is correct, and if the logic of the demonstration is valid, then we have (general) metaphysical knowledge. The particular exposition of analogy that has been given is not universally accepted by all realists, and for the purpose of indicating the nature of metaphysical evidence it has been greatly simplified.[17] What is important, however, is the recognition of some doctrine of analogy.

Abstraction, intuition, dialectic, analogy, and demonstration, all have their place in metaphysical knowing. Metaphysics as science begins to break down when one or more of these are neglected. Abstraction without intuition leads to some kind of "essentialism," idealistic or materialistic. Existence is known through intuition, not abstraction. If only intuition and logical demonstration are recognized some kind of *a priorism* is the consequence. Without analogy dialectical analysis, if ontologically conceived, becomes a power, a kind of mental violence; if only conceived logically it can at best produce probable opinion, and instead of analogical knowledge we have merely reasoning by resemblances, by examples. Without demonstration we are left with a few metaphysical first principles, all else remaining potential.

How reductionism and skepticism are generated. The key to general metaphysics as a science lies in the fundamental nature of special metaphysics, cosmology, and especially in the realistic notions of "form" and "matter." If this is not recognized, confusion occurs and the end is skepticism. Let us see how this comes about in a step by step process.

If one begins with propositions of the phenomenological context, historical propositions and generalizations, and then asks for some trick whereby through generalizing some particular relation in experience metaphysical knowledge can be obtained, the answer would seem to be that there is none. It is this that Dorothy Emmet did not see in her critique of the analogy of being. In contrast to many who reject analogy, she does make a valiant effort to understand it. However, she insists that it comes to this: ". . . the appropriateness of . . . analogy depends on the reality of the relation which it exemplifies. The existence of the relation cannot be established by analogical argument; but if there are independent grounds for asserting it, it can be described analogically." [18] In other words, there can be no analogical *knowledge,* but if something can be known on other grounds, then it can be *illustrated* analogically. It will be of interest to see why she insists on this, for her difficulty is also that of many others.

Miss Emmet informs us that "metaphysical theories can only be 'compositions,' products of the mind's form-creating power, and born in particular types of selective experience." [19] This is the conception of metaphysics as "postulation-through-selection." Miss Emmet admits that her view here is that of Whitehead. On this view some limited experience is "selected," generalized, and postulated metaphysically. Furthermore, the so-called "pragmatic test" really means that one's theory is selected by a value-judgment. Miss Emmet is quite consistent in following Whitehead when she says that metaphysical judgments "are judgments of importance and significance which govern the development of a theory. If you ask from whence are these basic judgments derived, I should suggest that they are derived predominantly from some particular type of experience, e.g., intellectual, aesthetic or moral, which has seemed to provide a clue in terms of which a *Weltanschauung* or philosophical attitude could be developed." [20]

From here it is only one step to saying: "What the metaphysician does, therefore, is to construct a theoretic model drawn from analogy from some form of intellectual or spiritual relationship which he judges to be especially significant or important." [21] As we have seen, everyone can get into this game of metaphysical solitaire. At any rate, the point that we wish to make is that if one assumes such a subjective and arbitrary approach to even cosmology, then it will follow that analogy can only be illustrative and not itself knowledge. Granted this, the question now is whether metaphysics as a science is possible at all. In this respect Miss Emmet follows Whitehead to the bitter end when she says that these "alternative" metaphysical theories may be "co-ordinated." A nice question arises here as to whether the person who "co-ordinates" what others postulate, himself postulates also!

It would seem that realism is an appropriate name for systematic metaphysics as knowledge. Of course, its denial is "metaphysics" too. But it is not at all clear in what sense postulational metaphysics can be called knowledge. It is perhaps safe to say the assumption that it is stems from the belief that in some manner or other historical propositions and generalizations are constitutive of metaphysical propositions, and hence arbitrariness is avoided. It has been our purpose (1) to show that this cannot be true even theoretically; (2) that in fact it has never been shown; (3) that the attempt to do it does not avoid, but *is,* arbitrariness. It is because realism (in the broadest sense of the term) has never "played that game" that it has had a continuous development of over two thousand years, and that it cannot be identified with the temperament or personal convictions of any one man.

There are difficult and unsolved problems in realism. And perhaps no one is more aware of the vagueness of the best attempts at explanation of metaphysical evidence than the realist himself. But what is the alternative? Here we must be tough-minded instead of tender-minded. Is not Mr. C. D. Broad tender-minded when he says of "Speculative Philosophy" that:

> Its object is to take over the results of the various sciences, to add to them the results of the religious and ethical experiences of mankind, and then to reflect upon the whole. The hope is that, by this means, we may be able to reach some general conclusions as to the nature of the universe, and as to our position and prospects in it.[22]

It is not clear at all how this differs from saying that speculative philosophy is but a series of happy guesses. Exactly how does it differ from the metaphysical speculation that has nothing to do with knowledge at all? The answer to this question is never given.

The arbitrariness remains, however. A rule may be laid down for which it would be difficult to find an exception: Examine any nonrealistic metaphysics and it will be found that some knowledge-claim is not satisfied. Another rule, more specific, is: Examine any system of postulational metaphysics and it will very likely be found to be an *a priori* kind of naturalism in which one or more knowledge-claims are eliminated; in particular, revealed theology. This applies to Mr. Broad's statement. There is no "science" in connection with religion. Knowledge lies elsewhere, in the "various sciences" to which something called "religious experience" is added. In a footnote we are told: "Theology, whether 'natural' or 'revealed,' is a form of speculative philosophy, in our sense of the word." [23] Now it is impossible to have revealed theology, which transcends reason, and at the same time have *only* speculative philosophy, which is based on reason. To throw natural and revealed theology together as speculative philosophy is simply to get rid of revelation. No better example of the elimination of a knowledge-claim by "initial predication" could be given. After having got rid of three thousand years of theistic interpretation of religious experience as found in Judaism, Christianity, and Mohammedanism, by means of a definition in a footnote, Mr. Broad asks us now to "reflect on the whole" with the "hope" of finding some answer as to our "position and prospects" in the universe.

What is there to reflect upon? The answer has been given—a naturalism or materialism. What is the evidence? What is the method? Is this seriously offered as a way of obtaining metaphysical knowledge? Or is it really a procedure, a method of happy guesses, that one indulges in because metaphysics cannot be knowledge? Even this is not quite exact, for the elimination of the knowledge-claim of theology is dogmatic.

What Mr. Broad asks us to reflect upon is man's place in nature after a naturalism has been dogmatically posited. The possibility of reflecting on whether naturalism is itself true is eliminated wholly and completely—in other words, that on which we need to be most "empirical" is prevented a priori.

We are now in a position to understand the nature of postulational metaphysics (together with the idea that historical propositions and generalizations of the special sciences enter constitutively into metaphysics) in a sense in which it was impossible before the treatment of analogy. *In the analogy of proper proportionality the analogue must be formally present in both analogates, although the mode in which it is present is determined by the nature of the analogate.* In a spurious form of this kind of analogy, called "metaphor," the analogue (characteristic) is formally present only in one analogate. *What is present in the other analogate is something imposed or selected by the human mind for the purpose for which the metaphor is made.* Metaphor has literary value, but is ontologically worthless. To compare it with mathematical proportion would be like a case in which two of the four elements were "unknowns." The equation could not be solved. And so with metaphor; it does not produce knowledge. At best it can but illustrate something known on other grounds. We say that the lion is king of the beasts because he has a relation similar to that which a king has to his subjects. But, of course, "kingship" is not formally present in the lion.

Postulational metaphysics is based upon *improper* analogy. And it cannot be otherwise, for in its essence it is a denial of realistic cosmology, of hylomorphism. The meanings of "formally" and "virtually," which are necessary in order to understand the analogy of being, have no place in nonrealism. Hence, an improper analogy is the only alternative. Some limited category is "generalized" to metaphysical status. It is extended by metaphor and "tested" by seeing how it "works." One improper analogy leads to another. The notions of "working" and "success," so far from being a test, themselves need a criterion. In fact the criterion is some personal value judgment, a "judgment of importance." Instead of its truth being ontologically grounded, it determines the satisfactoriness of the postulates. If the personal value judgment is the "urgent" need to secularize society, as Whitehead says, then, as we have already pointed out, metaphysics becomes an ideological weapon against traditional religion.

The personal value judgments can vary. Sometimes there is a sincere hope to arrive at truth for truth's sake by postulational procedure. Analogy can never be abolished completely. What can be abolished is proper analogy, with all it implies, in favor of improper analogy or metaphor. Since the range of similarities in any case is indefinitely indeterminate, the possibilities are many. Mathematics "looks like" metaphysics in many respects, and since we seem to "get somewhere" in the former, why not mathematize metaphysics? If realism is to be rejected, why not? There is no answer. One can reject today the "systems" of Descartes and Spinoza because they do not "work";

and anyway mathematics has changed. But otherwise there can be no objection. If "mechanism" happens to be the reigning concept of the natural science of the age, why not interpret the world as a machine and God as the perfect mechanic? If "relativity" happens to be the reigning concept of another age . . . ? Why not? Why not take the notion of "evolution" from the field of biology, where alone it has validity, blow it up to ontological status, deduce that thinking must be a form of biological activity (when organisms become "socialized"), and that the denial of this reflects a "class bias," a lack of appreciation of "natural science," an attitude that is fascistic, authoritarian, totalitarian, dogmatic, and antidemocratic?

Why not? It is false to say that such ideas do not "work." For example, the latter ideas are those of John Dewey, and they have "worked" unusually well in the last half century. One of the chief aims of Dewey and his followers was to secularize the public schools and shift faith from "religion" to the "scientific method." Who will deny that this philosophy has been a relative success? But is it true? To the degree that it is successful, yes. Any other answer is irrelevant from the standpoint of "postulation."

Why not? It is difficult to see how an answer can be given once it is assumed that one can argue from experimental science to metaphysics. What can be done is what we have tried to do, to show that there is no evidence for such an assumption, and that an improper conception of analogy is necessary to give it the illusion of success.

6

The Formal Context of Mathematics

A full treatment of the nature of mathematics is not necessary in order to understand its relation to other disciplines, and hence we shall be concerned only with the minimum requirement sufficient for the purpose. The problem before us is the nature of pure, not applied, mathematics, and its relation to experimental science, metaphysics, and logic. The problem of mathematics as a kind of knowledge is not itself a mathematical problem.

Mathematics has been defined in many ways. It has been said to be the science (*a*) of quantity; (*b*) of magnitudes; (*c*) of numbers; the science which (*d*) has for its object the indirect measurement of magnitude; (*e*) deals with the universal laws (forms) according to which things must behave as existents; (*f*) deals with the investigation of concepts which express the relations of any objects to each other. It has also been defined (*g*) in terms of ordered classes and relations. Professor C. I. Lewis gives this definition (*h*): "A mathematical system is any set of strings of recognizable marks in which some of the strings are taken initially and the remainder derived from these by operations performed according to rules which are independent of any meaning assigned to the marks." According to A. N. Whitehead (*i*) "Mathematics in its widest significance is the development of all types of formal, necessary, deductive reasoning." [1]

In the light of these, and many other definitions, how can one say what the real nature of mathematics is? There seem to be only three alternatives, all of them unsatisfactory. (1) If one of the definitions is chosen for convenience, then it is arbitrary. (2) If one is chosen and asserted to be the real definition, then that will appear to be dogmatic. (3) The final alternative is skepticism; the nature of mathematics cannot be known. Actually there are not three alternatives, but only one—skepticism. The first two alternatives are really modes of the third when some sort of decision must be made and acted upon.

If an answer is to be given it must not be arbitrary. If it is not to be arbitrary, then it must be metaphysically grounded, for the definition of mathematics is not itself a mathematical problem. As must any other fundamental discipline, so must mathematics have a formal object. It will also have a method, but a method must be understood in terms of the subject matter, the object studied. It may be suggested that the nature of mathematics might be discovered by means of a phenomenological description of what the mathematician is doing when he is functioning as a mathematician. It has already been pointed out that such an approach is not satisfactory for two reasons. The description would pose the problem, not solve it. It would disclose the various answers from (*a*) through (*i*) that were listed. Second, the question is begged, for without a prior knowledge of what mathematics is it is impossible to know whether a person is functioning as a mathematician, or as a natural scientist, or as a philosopher.

The Problem of the Object of Mathematics

In abstraction from the metaphysical problem there is no answer as to the nature of mathematics or any other kind of knowledge. An equivalent manner of saying this is that there are as many "answers" as can be "thought" of, and one is as good as another. It will be observed that answers (*a*) through (*d*) define mathematics in terms of an object of some kind. Definitions (*b*), (*c*), and (*d*) are narrower forms of (*a*). Definitions (*e*) and (*f*) in effect make a metaphysics out of mathematics. For (*h*) mathematics appears to be without content, and in (*i*) mathematics is identified with a method.

To define mathematics so that it is indistinguishable from logic is to distort both disciplines. It is likewise arbitrary to make a metaphysics or a methodology out of mathematics. In abstraction from any formal object why should mathematics be identified with the method of formal deduction? Why not identify it with the method of induction and make mathematics an experimental science? But, again, why not identify it with "dialectical method"? This answer, too, can be found historically. And so on. These modes of defining a discipline do not solve the problem; rather they create the chaos that makes a solution urgent.

In considering the three orders of abstraction we have already seen that mathematics is the product of the second order. In the first order, that of total abstraction, the individual matter is mentally discarded. The piece of copper tubing that I see is cylindrical, about twelve inches long, and has a definite weight. Copper is subject to scientific knowledge, but *this* piece of copper is not. Experimental science can deal with copper as a thing having "common matter," but not as having "individual matter." By formal abstraction I can go further and think of the copper as something which has a certain length, is cylindrical, and so on. I am not thinking of the thing in terms of sensible matter at all. Common sensible matter has been mentally discarded; only intelligible matter as quantitative being remains. I can think of solidity, cylindrical shape, and length without any intrinsic reference to physical matter. Matter considered "intelligibly" is considered quantitatively. Mathematics is the name given to such consideration. Quantity, which is an accident and not a substance, is the metaphysical category expressing the kind of reality or mode of being which is the foundation of mathematics. As we shall see presently, mathematics as a positive science has quantity as its formal object. The object of the philosophy of mathematics is quantitative being.

In the brief definitions of mathematics that were given it is to be noted that those that considered the content of mathematics, in contrast to those stressing method or confusing mathematics with metaphysics or logic, emphasize quantity or some species of it. This is not surprising. Even a phenomenological description should approximate the same conclusion. The working mathematician deals with points, lines, planes, projections, numbers, functions, groups, and matrices. He is not dealing with metabolism, cancer, God, or a number of other objects. Geometry is concerned with points, lines, and planes. Topology or *analysis situs* is the study of properties of spaces or their configurations invariant under continuous transformations. "Configuration," "transformation" are quantitative categories. *Mengenlehre* deals with multiplicities conceived as unities. "Multiplicity" and "unity" here are quantitative. "Unity" is a predicamental category in *Mengenlehre,* and is not the transcendental concept of "one."

The meaning of the foundational category of "quantity"—which is a metaphysical concept, but makes mathematics possible—is taken in the realist sense. If it is not so taken, then there may be a confusion between quantity and other categories such that the foundation of mathematics is not clear. It is sometimes said that mathematics is concerned with the qualitative as well as the quantitative. For example, H. Poincaré says:

> . . . magnitudes need not always be measurable; there is, for instance, one branch of geometry independent of the measure of magnitudes, in which we are only concerned with knowing, for example, if, on a curve ABC, the point B is between the points A and C, and in which it is immaterial whether the arc AB is equal to or twice the arc BC. This branch is called *Analysis Situs.* It contains quite a large body of doctrine which has attracted the attention of the greatest geometers and from which are derived, one from another, a whole series of remarkable theorems. What distinguishes these theorems from those of ordinary geometry is that they are purely qualitative.[2]

Contrary to appearance, what Poincaré says is not incompatible with the identification of mathematics with the quantitative. The difficulty lies in the rather strange use Poincaré makes of the category of "quality." He is contrasting "quality," not with "quantity," but with "metric." Magnitudes that are not measurable he identifies with the "qualitative." This is questionable metaphysics, to say the least. At any rate, the issue is a metaphysical one, not mathematical. The realist would point out that a magnitude, whether measurable or not, presupposes quantity. We can know quantity by means of measurement, and only quantity can be measured. It does not necessarily follow that only the measurable is quantity, and that the nonmetrical must be qualitative. Otherwise one would be identifying *that by which* quantity is known with *that which* is known. We have already seen, in analyzing our knowledge of nature, that this is the error that produces subjectivism. And subjectivism is nihilism regardless of the kind of knowledge to which reference is made.

Although we believe that this sufficiently answers Poincaré's statement, nevertheless there is more of a problem posed than at first meets the eye. The problem is essentially one in the integrative science, the philosophy of mathematics, and is not primarily one of the order of knowledge itself. And yet, because some believe that mathematics is not confined merely to the quantitative, we may pause long enough to at least give a few hints in the way of a solution. In advance we may say that the protest against limiting mathematics to the quantitative, insofar as it is something more than merely questionable and unthought-out metaphysics, is perhaps really against a restricted view of the quantitative.

The subject matter of *analysis situs,* to which Poincaré makes reference, overlaps with that of the theory of sets and topology. Topology is concerned with geometrical structures which remain constant under continuous transformations, and finds important such concepts as dimensionality, connectivity, continuity, neighborhoods, and ordered sets. There is the study, apart from what are usually considered to be metrical relations, of properties of closed, open, and interlacing curves; the connectivity of surfaces, and so on. The point seems to be that in contrast with the old-fashioned notion of mathematics as limited to quantity the new conception of mathematics is that it is a "science of order" or of "relations." By identifying quantity and metric it is then possible to show that there must be the nonquantitative because there is the nonmetrical. The nonquantitative must be the qualitative, and hence mathematics is concerned also with the qualitative.

The conception of mathematics as the science of order or relations has been furthered by the recent attempts to reduce, if not identify, mathematics and logic. This has been made possible by conceiving logic as nonintentional, and shifting the emphasis from "concepts" to "classes," and "propositional functions." "Class logic" becomes the same as "class algebra." In the new algebras we have such laws as "aa = a" and "a + a = a," which, according to Mr. C. I. Lewis, "result in the elimination of all notion of number or quantity from the algebra." Now over and above the questionable view of logic as nonintentional that is implied, it may be pointed out that the notion of "class" presupposes that of "multiplicity," which in turn presupposes "quantity." In comment on this statement of Professor Lewis, Mr. Henry Veatch gives a quite sufficient reply:

> Now while it is true that laws of this sort serve to differentiate the class algebra from arithmetic, it would hardly seem that they would make the algebra non-quantitative. On the contrary, the fact that classes are compared with one another in respect to 'more and less,' 'equal to,' 'inclusive of,' 'exclusive of,' 'coextensive with,' etc., would certainly indicate that such classes had quantitative aspects and that it was in virtue of these aspects that the classes were susceptible of algebraic treatment.[3]

There is another reason why mathematics has been thought to be concerned with something more than the quantitative. Consider a pure deductive system dealing with points, lines, and planes. All the theorems would be formally valid if these are replaced by *X*'s, *Y*'s, and *Z*'s. Now why not conceive the terms as variables such that literally anything could be substituted? The system then becomes a purely formal framework of relations. These difficulties occur: (1) When conceived of in this way mathematics becomes a science of relations without anything in particular being related. (2) This means that either mathematics has no object of its own, and is set off uniquely as "knowledge" by this fact, or it is so conceived that it overlaps or becomes a substitute for metaphysics and/or logic. This would either be false or an unfortunate use of a word.

Another reason why mathematics is thought to deal with the qualitative, and not merely the quantitative, is that there is a confusion between pure and applied mathematics. Applied mathematics is always some kind of physical or natural science, and hence is never limited merely to the quantitative. Quantity is but an aspect of the physical world of motion, of change, and of course there is always the qualitative. Mathematics is concerned with (say) abstract topology, and it is that of which we have spoken. A physical science (physics) is concerned with physical topology, and hence with sensible and not merely intelligible matter. Furthermore, physical topology will be concerned with the relation between events. In abstract topology, which is strictly mathematical, there are no "events." Now events require a time co-ordinate and the relations of before and after. If "metric" is defined so as not to include such relations, then the "temporal order" may be identified with the nonmetrical, which is in turn identified with the qualitative.

When we turn to find out what the working scientist means, this is apparently what is meant. According to L. L. Whyte, ". . . the temporal order (succession) of two events is a descriptive or qualitative relation which can never be given pure metrical expression since it involves a criterion or definition of the non-metrical relation of before and after." [4] The meaning of "qualitative" is here to be understood in terms of physical theory. And this is as it should be, for physical theory, however much one may wish it could be otherwise, can never be reduced to the metrical or the quantitative. If the distinction between abstract and physical topology is kept in mind, the qualitative will be seen to fall outside of the former. If confused, then abstract topology, and hence that much of mathematics, will be thought of as considering the qualitative, which really is an affair of physical topology.

Another misunderstanding may occur, not by identifying metric and quantity, but by identifying metric with a restricted notion of quantity. Quantity and metric may be thought of in connection with the ordinary numbers dealt with in elementary and higher algebra. If so, then some matrices must express the nonmetrical, namely, those which do not obey the commutative law of "ordinary" mathematics. If a and b are matrices, then ab may not equal ba. Furthermore, $ab - ba$ is no longer zero. Now, is a matrix a number or a quantity, or isn't it? If it isn't, then it must be some kind of "form" for which even "quantity" is a variable. It is, to speak the language of a "school," a language constructed syntactically, its "strings" having no denotation. Mathematics becomes a game played with meaningless marks according to prescribed rules. Mr. C. I. Lewis has described this kind of game as follows:

> Mathematics so developed, achieves the utmost economy of assertion. *Nothing* is asserted. There are no primitive ideas. Since no meanings are given to the characters, the strings are neither true nor false. Nothing is assumed to be true, and nothing is asserted as 'proved.' [5]

This is a rather indirect way of saying that mathematics is simply "nothing." Mathematics has no "being"; it is relegated to nonbeing, for it has no object. If a type of knowledge has no object, then it can have no being as knowledge.

To interpret matrices in a completely nonquantitative manner implies, then, the impossibility of mathematics. The issue is clear thus far: either there is or is not mathematics. And there the matter would rest were it not for a contemporary procedure with which we have become familiar, namely, the attempt to have it both ways even though it is impossible. From a rational standpoint the outright denial of anything must be made in the name of something else. The procedure we refer to may be stated as a principle: Deny a thing in the name of the thing. The tendency today is to deny Christianity in the name of Christianity, to deny logic in the name of logic, to deny the nature of man in the name of man, to deny democracy in the name of democracy, to deny love in the name of love. And so with mathematics. It seems that the *name* must be used even after its *being* has been denied. After following out the implications of extreme formalism Mr. Lewis, although not necessarily subscribing to the view, says:

> For when mathematics is no longer viewed as the science of number and quantity, but as it is viewed by Mr. Russell or by anyone who accepts the alternative definition offered in this chapter, then the logistic treatment of *any* subject *becomes* mathematics. Mathematics itself ceases to have any peculiar subject matter, and becomes simply a method.[6]

There is an "art" and a "logic" aspect to any kind of knowledge. The art aspect consists of those peculiar techniques of discovery that are in part a function of the formal object defining the kind of knowledge. For example, there is the art of experimental discovery in the natural sciences. When these techniques are absolutized, then the "logic" of a discipline is reduced to its "art." But art is concerned not with discovery, but with reaction. So the name of a discipline becomes identified with its art, with its method, which now is an instrument of creation *ex nihilo*. Any subject becomes mathematics if treated mathematically! One could play around with this for some time and exhaust its absurdity were it not for the restraint imposed by a sense of humor.

Even to call such a view "mathematicism" would not do it justice, but it is the best descriptive term we have. As found in recent literature an "ism" occurs whenever a metaphysics is made out of a kind of knowledge or whenever its method is absolutized. The latter alternative is found most frequently in recent times. And of course others can play the game. When history is identified with its method we have "historicism." When natural science is identified with the "scientific method" we have "scientism." And likewise when mathematics is identified with its method we have "mathematicism."

The absurdity of making mathematics contentless is not merely a deduction from realism. Even the nonrealist may take his stand on this matter in no uncertain terms. Paul Rosenbloom, himself a "mathematical logician," has this to say:

> . . . we emphasize that a language must have an interpretation in order for it to serve as a language, namely as a tool for communication, and that those who neglect this, and those who dogmatically insist that the study of a language independently of its meaning is the only rigorous procedure, are wrong. This statement is itself somewhat dogmatic; it is difficult not to be dogmatic when one feels strongly about something.[7]

We suggest, then, that the alternative of interpreting matrices as irrelevant to quantity had best be rejected. From the standpoint of the working scientist it would seem to be understood that the interpretation of a matrix is relevant to quantity. He may call matrices "non-ordinary numbers." One physical scientist says that "A matrix can itself be treated as if it were a number . . ." [8]

Another speaks of a matrix as a "higher number" which expresses nonmetrical properties, while an "ordinary number" expresses metrical properties.[9] Mathematics may be said to deal with order and relations provided a proper restricting adjective is used.

Quantity as the Object of Mathematics

The insistence that the foundation of mathematics is the category of quantity is a thesis of realism. However, it is worth noting that one may be forced to this conclusion who is not in that tradition. For example, L. O. Kattsoff takes a dialectical and idealistic approach to mathematics. He says that it is understandable "why some have defined mathematics merely as the structure itself without recognizing the nature of the mathematical object." [10] But mathematics must study something, some objects or properties—and "these properties have been called the *quantitative* properties of objects." [11] He adds that "the word 'quantitative' has lost a great deal of its original clarity."

Most contemporary statements of what mathematics is go into some detail describing method and technique. Thus far we have said nothing of these matters, and have seemingly overstressed one particular notion, that of quantity. But it will now be better understood why we have done so. In the definition of a kind of knowledge subject matter is prior to method. The denial of this has produced the chaos which it is the purpose of the order of knowledge to eliminate.

Quantity is an accident, not a substance. As an accident it is real being and not merely a being of reason. This is not to say that mere beings of reason are not to be found in mathematics. They are to be found there just as they are to be found in any other kind of knowledge, e.g., absolute zero in physical science. It is not the function of the working mathematician as such to be concerned with the ontological status of his concepts. That is a problem of the integrative discipline, the philosophy of mathematics.

As an accident quantity does not determine the essence of any composite thing. It determines *how much,* but not the *what* of anything. Quantity may be continuous or discrete, and hence geometries, arithmetics and algebras are possible. Being the kind of accident it is, quantity is limited to a species of formal cause. Hence, pure mathematics cannot deal with material, efficient, or final causation. Although the object of mathematics is intelligible matter, matter insofar as it is quantitative, the emphasis must be on the accident and not on "matter," which is one of the two constitutive principles of a composite substance. But if the "matter" is forgotten, then, it becomes very easy, as with Descartes, to identify matter and quantity (or a species of it, extension). Quantity is not all there is to matter, but it is that about matter which is the peculiar object of mathematics.

Quantity, as a metaphysical category which is the foundation of mathematics, presupposes the hylomorphic notions of form and matter. Mathematics deals with a specific kind of form which matter can take. But it is intelligible, not sensible matter to which reference is made. Its function is to discover the various quantitative forms and relations which matter can take. Hence mathematics is a formal science and may be distinguished from experimental science by the fact that it does not describe actual, sensible matter. As formal its method is essentially that of deduction. Since it is concerned with certain forms that matter can possibly take, whether they actually do so or not, it has an *a priori* character that is unbecoming to experimental science.

It is considerations such as these that enable one to understand the method of the working mathematician. In that function he is not concerned with the philosophy of mathematics, or what is often called "meta-mathematics." He is dealing with mathematics in its *positive* sense as relatively autonomous, and he wishes to get results. For this purpose he has a method, or methods. He will construct the symbols necessary for system generation—term-symbols, operation-symbols, relation-symbols. Nominal, formal, or "created definitions" may be used. Postulates or axioms will be laid down. A distinction will be made between those which relate entities in the system, and those which prescribe the rules whereby theorems are drawn from the former. Proof will consist in showing that a theorem follows from the descriptive axioms in accordance with the prescriptive axioms. The evidence for a theorem lies in the postulates or axioms, or in other theorems which have been deduced from the postulates.

From the standpoint of positive mathematics the axioms need be self-evident only with respect to the system. But they will be tested for independency, consistency, and categoricity or completeness. An axiom that can be deduced from the other axioms should be a theorem and not an axiom at all. If there is not consistency, the system is not a system. The problem of categoricity is that of determining the axioms that are both necessary and sufficient for the system.

These are problems which concern matters internal to mathematics, and hence are strictly mathematical. The mathematician may use other kinds of knowledge, but he does not have to reflect on what he is using. It is here that the pure mathematician *qua* mathematician is relatively absolute and autonomous. Philosophy is just as much a distracting factor as it is for the experimental scientist *qua* experimental scientist. But the problems of mathematics in its positive sense must be distinguished (1) from those of the philosophy of mathematics and (2) from those of the order of knowledge.

Is mathematical infinity actual or potential? If actual, is it so as a "thing" or as a "rule"? In mathematics what entities are (1) purely fictions? (2) beings of reason, but not fictions? (3) real beings or relations? Questions such as these belong to the integrative discipline of the philosophy of mathematics because neither mathematics *qua* mathematics nor metaphysics *qua* metaphysics can answer them. Both are necessary. The order of knowledge is concerned with the nature (essence) of mathematics and its relation to other fundamental kinds of knowledge. This is the problem at hand, and to that we may now turn.

The relation of experimental science to mathematics. What is the relation of historical propositions and generalizations to mathematical propositions so far as evidence is concerned? With respect to the theorems of mathematics they have no relation, for the evidence for the proof of theorems lies wholly within the postulates. It is this fact which explains the relative rigorousness of the reasoning in a mathematical system. No summation of historical propositions or generalizations proves theorems. The theorem that in a Euclidean triangle the sum of the angles equals 180° is not proved by examining triangles. Field trips are not necessary because the theorem makes no pretense to describe material things. Neither does an axiom, and hence the same fact is relevant for it. Mathematical propositions should be true to intelligible matter as quantitative, but they need not be true to sensible matter as actually existing. The latter problem is experimental, and is concerned with the application of mathematical propositions.

Historical propositions and generalizations are not constitutive as evidence of mathematical propositions for the reason that the actual physical world, metaphysically speaking, is contingent and not necessary. What exists is a selection among possibilities. Likewise historical propositions and generalizations cannot be regulative of mathematical propositions. The contingently actual cannot delimit the possible any more than it can be constitutive of it on the level of knowledge. The so-called empirical approach to mathematics, e.g., that of Mill, was falsely conceived because an antimetaphysical bias led to the relative absolutizing of a method. It was also to overlook the whole process of abstraction which allows the very possibility of mathematics.

The relation of historical propositions and generalizations to mathematical propositions is that of instrumentality. They are instrumental to, but not regulative or constitutive of, mathematical propositions. Without sense experience, which can be expressed in simple and relatively primitive historical propositions, there would not be the intuition of the intelligible. Socrates taught the slave boy about the nature of a square by drawing a figure in the sand. What the boy saw in the sand can be expressed in terms of historical propositions. These were *instrumental* to the "seeing" of forms. The truth of this is, of course, independent of any explanation of it, e.g., the theory of reminiscence. Intuition is as important for mathematics as for metaphysics. For both, forms are obtained by abstraction; and for both, sense experience is merely, though necessarily, instrumental. The denial of the instrumentality of sense experience would mean that quantity is considered without matter. This leads to the notion of mathematics as dealing with pure, contentless symbols—fictions wholly created by the mind. In this case mathematics is denied by denying it an object. On the other hand, if historical propositions and generalizations were constitutive of mathematics, then the latter would be denied by reducing it to an experimental science.

The evidence for mathematical propositions other than theorems is essentially through intuition. This statement needs some qualification. For as we shall see when we come to define the nature of the philosophy of mathematics, intuition in mathematics cannot be considered in abstraction from the metaphysical. When intuition is spoken of it is not always clear whether mathematics as a positive science, or the philosophy of mathematics, is referred to. "Intuitionism" is strictly a philosophical position *about* mathematics. From the standpoint of mathematics as a positive science a postulational technique may be used which is quite nonintuitive.

In contrast with mathematics experimental science is the least intuitive. The evidence for generalizations rests upon historical propositions, which in turn rest upon intuition. For mathematics the evidence is more directly through intuition. But whereas in primitive historical propositions intuition is limited to the actual sensible matter, in mathematics intuition is not so limited. It is limited only by the imagination. The imagination is rooted in, but not limited to, actual sense experience, and hence mathematics can consider forms and systems for which there may be no known exemplification. Historical propositions give rise to the simpler mathematical forms, while generalizations may be instrumental to the more complex. The generalizations of pre-Newtonian science were instrumental to the development of the mathematical theory of "fluxions" by Newton. On the other hand, because imagination transcends the sensible, because intelligible matter is "wider" than common sensible matter, it is possible to develop systems for which only the future may discover applications.

We may say then that mathematics is the name for that discipline which has as its purpose the seeking of propositions descriptive of universality, the context being that of form; and by form is here meant that which is obtained by abstraction, the forms of intelligible matter. We say that the context is "formal" because, of the four causes, only the formal is relevant in pure mathematics. The rules of mathematics represent formal causes. There is no efficient or material causation in mathematics, for all actual matter has been abstracted. Only intelligible matter remains. Mathematics is an "ideal" discipline for this reason, although the term "ideal" requires careful interpretation. What things exhibit what mathematical forms is irrelevant to mathematics *qua* mathematics. That there are no final causes is obvious. Mathematical forms do not have natures that strive for perfection, for there is no motion or change. Forms are just what they are. Even in the integral calculus the forms of change are not themselves changing forms. Triangles are perfect triangles; only in the realm of nature, of motion, do triangles fall short of perfection. In summary, as one author has put it:

> Mathematics . . . is a science in which effects are deduced from their causes and vice versa. The rule here represents the formal cause . . . It is universal because pure extension prescinds from individual differences among the mobile objects; the rule is immutable because pure extension prescinds from motion (mutation); it is necessary because the matter to which it applies, being pure and undifferentiated, cannot impede it and thus produce exceptions to the rule; the rule is negatively eternal because pure extension makes no reference to time.[12]

The proper definition and explication of the nature of mathematics preserves its uniqueness and relative autonomy. If the aforementioned considerations are confused, mathematics is reduced either to a metaphysics or experimental science. The latter occurs when material or efficient causes are introduced. When final causes are introduced the former occurs. This is found most frequently. There is a reason for this. Mathematics is the discipline most useful for *dominating* and *controlling* the material world, though not necessarily for *understanding* it. The very freedom that the pure mathematician has, e.g., through postulational techniques, and the fact that imagination is not limited to physical fact—all of which in itself is legitimate—this very freedom, when not understood in terms of the formal object, becomes absolute. Mathematics becomes an instrument of man's "spirit," and a kind of idealism results which allows man almost to assume the attributes of deity, contrary to the warning of the Greeks that man should not "play Zeus." Mathematics acquires final causation and becomes a metaphysics.

The relation of metaphysics to mathematics. What is the relation of mathematics to metaphysics as a relatively autonomous, positive discipline? It is that of being "regulative." But since mathematics is essentially a formal discipline, in the sense already defined, metaphysics exerts a minimum of regulation. Through logic, which rests upon metaphysics, the latter is regulative of mathematics essentially through such principles as those of "contradiction" and "identity." There is a reason for this. The pure mathematician *qua* mathematician deals with only one of the four causes, the formal. The material, efficient, and final causes are irrelevant. Hence, metaphysics is regulative only in its most formal aspect.

This explains why the mathematician enjoys a relatively high degree of freedom from metaphysics that is greater than that of the experimental scientist. Even the experimental scientist must be concerned about "material consistency," the problem of verification. The mathematician apparently needs to worry only about "formal consistency." This also explains why it is "easier" to make a metaphysics out of mathematics than with any other subject. This error can be accomplished by reducing identity to equality, and also by making the principle of contradiction mathematical rather than logical and metaphysical.

Metaphysics is regulative of any discipline, for one of its functions is to define what is and what is not possible, what is being and what is not-being. The necessity for metaphysics to be regulative of mathematics may also be understood by following out the implications of its denial. There are two alternatives. If metaphysics is not regulative of mathematics, then mathematics is self-regulative. In this case mathematics becomes absolute, and metaphysics is reduced to mathematics; in which case its (mathematics') uniqueness, and hence its nature, is destroyed. On the other hand, if metaphysics is not regulative of mathematics, then the other alternative is that it is constitutive of it. In this case mathematics is reduced to metaphysics, and of course the former is destroyed. For the being of mathematics, whether it be reduced to metaphysics, or metaphysics is reduced to it, there is no difference. The uniqueness and relative autonomy of mathematics demands that metaphysics be only regulative. This seems to be the only answer that can be given of the relation of metaphysics to mathematics. Any other answer eliminates one term of the relation, and hence the question itself.

It might be objected that this is a very old-fashioned answer, the kind that might have been given before the work of Cantor, Brouwer, and Gödel, before the era of the discovery of transfinite numbers and the construction of three-valued logics. How can a principle such as "a whole is always greater than any of its parts" be regulative when the mathematician pays no attention to it and takes infinity to be a kind of collection, aggregate, or set in which any subset is equal to the whole? In a three-valued logic it may be the case that "if a proposition is not true, then it is either false or undecidable." How can metaphysics, through logic, be regulative, when what is supposedly impossible is in fact actualized, namely, a system that is constructed which rejects the law of the excluded middle (for the nonfinite)? Either the recent advances in mathematics are valid and justified, or they are not. If they are, then metaphysics is not regulative. If they are not, then they would have to be ruled out on metaphysical grounds. But in that case metaphysics would be constitutive of mathematics, and we have already shown that this is impossible. Hence, the thesis that metaphysics is regulative of mathematics is shown to be without any foundation.

The rigorousness of this objection is in appearance only, for it rests upon a confusion of mathematics with the philosophy of mathematics. To understand this we must consider the nature of the philosophy of mathematics.

7

The Philosophy of Mathematics

A distinction must be made between a science in its relative autonomy, and the same science as integrated and concrete. Of course the latter is not quite the "same" science. Hence, the words "philosophy of" must be put before the name of the science. There is mathematics and the philosophy of mathematics. There is experimental science, which is concerned with nature, and there is the philosophy of nature, which is the same as "natural science" when properly conceived. This distinction is of great importance, and it is the failure to recognize it that has been responsible for a large amount of intellectual confusion in modern times.

The meaning of "positive" science. What is the ground of the distinction? The various formal objects that partly define the fundamental kinds of knowledge—for each kind of knowledge must be *of* something—are modes of being. Each formal object is an "aspect" of being, not the whole of it. One can study mobile being, or changing being, and that is called the "philosophy of nature." From a linguistic standpoint when we say "mobile being" we have before us an adjective and a noun. We can study them in three ways, each separately and both together. When we study being *qua* being it is called "metaphysics." When we study motion or change without considering being at all, it is called "experimental science." When we study them both together it is called the "philosophy of nature."

These distinctions are beings of reason (*ens rationis*), but they are not fictions. They have a foundation *in* things. Such distinctions are familiar. We distinguish a thing and a property which a thing has. We can consider each separately, admitting all the while that in reality the two are together, and that only for the purpose of analysis do we separate them in our minds. So when we say that we can study "motion" without considering "being" we do not mean that motion can really exist without being. Even the attempt to express the thought results in a contradiction. But we can consider the nature of motion, and in its endless details, without considering being *qua* being at the same time. It is this fact that both defines and makes experimental science possible. In more familiar terms this means that the experimental scientist can consider his subject without having continually to bother about metaphysical considerations, i.e., without having to do so while he is functioning strictly as an experimental scientist.

Even "mobile being" is an abstraction, as we have seen. But here we have a further abstraction, and one of a peculiar kind, for it is an abstraction from being itself. No longer is one studying a mode of being, but rather a mode *qua* mode. Of course what is real is the mode of being; the mode *qua* mode is a distinction of reason. Does this mean that when one is studying a mode *qua* mode one is not studying something real, but only something logical? No. But it is true that the science which is defined in terms of abstracting "mode" from "being" cannot itself determine which among its concepts are those that represent real as opposed to logical being. In other words, for the real to be determined the science which studies the mode *qua* mode must be brought together with the science which studies being *qua* being. When this is done we have an integrative or synthetic discipline, in this case the philosophy of nature, a metaphysical interpretation of experimental science.

Now, whenever a science is considered from the standpoint of the mode studied, and not from the standpoint of the being that the mode is of, then that science is considered in its *positive* sense. A positive science is one which is defined in abstraction from the metaphysical because it is concerned with a mode *qua* mode and not with a mode of being. Experimental science is positive in this sense. This does not mean that it is antimetaphysical; it is simply nonmetaphysical. What is antimetaphysical is positivism, which is the position that knowledge is limited to a "mode," and that there can be no knowledge of a "mode of being" because there is no science of being *qua* being. Experimental science is positive science, but it is not the same as positivism. Positivism is a doctrine *about* it, and hence is not *of* it. A proposition about experimental science is not necessarily a proposition of it.

Mathematics as a positive science. And so with mathematics. The foundational category for mathematics is quantity. We have sometimes spoken inexactly, referring to the object of mathematics indiscriminately as quantity or as quantitative being. Instead of using the term "mathematics" in a slightly equivocal manner we can now give the name to the study of quantity. The philosophy of mathematics studies quantitative being. From the standpoint of the order of being what is common to both the philosophy of nature and the philosophy of mathematics is "being." From the standpoint of the order of knowledge what is common to both is the "philosophy of," which means that metaphysics enters constitutively into each. What distinguishes mobile being from quantitative being is not the noun but the adjective. It is understandable, then, that when a noun is given as the name of a discipline it is the adjective of the formal object that is referred to. This also defines a discipline in its positive, nonmetaphysical sense, and distinguishes it from another positive discipline.

In mathematics as a positive science the emphasis is on what is unique to it, not on what it has in common with some other type of knowledge. Thus its relative autonomy and independence is established. And rightly so. For if knowledge could not be obtained by this type of abstraction *away* from being there would be nothing to integrate. In the order of knowledge there cannot be a science of the philosophy of mathematics unless there is first a science of mathematics *qua* mathematics. There cannot be integration if there is nothing to integrate. There is first the understanding through separation (mental only) of factors in order to obtain a more thorough understanding through integration. For in reality quantity and being are together, and only for the purpose of analysis are they separated.

The worker in a positive science is free from metaphysics as constitutive, but not as regulative. As regulative metaphysics will be determining as regards what can possibly be true in the science, but it will not be determining as to what is actually true. Metaphysics is not constitutive as evidence of any positive science. But it is constitutive of the "philosophy of" that science. Therefore, a careful distinction must be made between the problems that are strictly of a positive science and those that are of the philosophy of that science. Problems of a positive science are solvable, if they are at all, within the science; the problems of the philosophy of that science are not. To put it another way, it is one thing to deal with a mode of being in abstraction from being; it is something else to consider the mode in relation to being. The kind of evidence cannot be identical in the two cases. If this fact is not recognized, then one may wrongly assume that the evidence sufficient for a positive science is also sufficient for the philosophy of that science.

One problem of the philosophy of a positive science is to determine, among the entities to which concepts refer, which are real and which are not. Or, more exactly, since all entities have being in some sense, the problem is to determine the kind of reality they have. Positive science, in abstraction from consideration of being, cannot do this. What it can do implies a limitation. The discipline which investigates a mode in abstraction from being cannot of itself relate being to the mode. It cannot determine or relate the content of its own concepts to that from which the abstraction was made. On the other hand, the metaphysical has its limitations. It is what it is partly because it is not something else. Like any kind of knowledge its virtue lies in its limitations. The nature of a mode cannot be known merely by knowing being. In other words, the details of a positive science cannot be deduced from metaphysics. Does this mean that metaphysics is about being and the positive sciences are about nonbeing? No, this would be a serious misunderstanding. Both are concerned with being. Nonbeing is nothing, and any kind of knowledge must be of something. Furthermore, being is not a genus. It cuts across the categories. Hence, a mode of being is also being. Experimental science and mathematics, as positive, are concerned with the real, but the sense in which they are so concerned cannot be determined by them since their very nature is defined by the fact that they are confined to a mode *qua* mode. For example some concepts of experimental science may have a foundation in nature, and some may not. Fictions are logical entities which may serve a purpose. But what is real and what is fiction in a positive science cannot be determined by it. This question can only be determined by bringing the mode together with being, reuniting what was separated, interpreting the positive science metaphysically.

How metaphysics constitutes evidence for the philosophy of mathematics. Some examples may illustrate how metaphysics is constitutive as evidence for the philosophy of mathematics, although merely regulative for mathematics as a positive science.

Are there just as many points on a long line as on a short one? Yes and no. From the standpoint of mathematics as positive one may construct a system such that in terms of the axioms and definitions it must be the case that the number of points are equivalent. On the other hand, someone else may construct a system with different axioms and definitions such that it would follow that the number of points are not equivalent. But which is *really* the case? Which system is true? The answer is that each conclusion is "true" within the system in which it is found. Each is formally valid, and that is all truth can mean in mathematics as positive. As to what is really the case, that has no answer because it has no meaning within the positive science. Mathematics as positive is not concerned with such a notion. If one insists on using the term, then there are as many "reals" as there are different systems.

It all depends upon what is meant by "point." If in one system it has a given meaning, then certain conclusions follow in terms of the axioms. It may mean something else in another system. But what is the *real* meaning of "point"? Now the working mathematician may be somewhat irritated by such a question, forcing, as it does, the metaphysical on one whose work apparently does not require it. Furthermore, does it not show the naïveté of the questioner and his lack of understanding of "recent developments," viz., "axiomatics" and "postulational technique"? The meaning of "point" is that which is given by the system. As Mr. Northrop puts it, ". . . the meaning which such a concept has is that which it gains by virtue of the properties or relations assigned to it by the postulate or set of postulates within which it is a member term. It means what the postulates prescribe it to mean." [1]

What is one to say to all of this? The proper thing to say is that the mathematician is quite correct. If the mathematician is working with quantity in abstraction from being, then it is obviously impossible for him to answer questions about quantitative *being,* i.e., quantity in relation to being. To insist that he do so is to insist that he, *as a man,* should come to grips with the problems of the philosophy of mathematics, a synthetic and integrative discipline. This demand is legitimate. The only error would be to demand that mathematics as positive must give answers that require a metaphysical premise, and of course this is impossible.

And there the matter would rest were it not for another fact, namely, that if means are not to be mistaken for the end, it is necessary to proceed to the philosophical question of what is real. The question still remains, and it is a good one. All that has been demonstrated thus far is that mathematics alone cannot answer the question. If the purpose is to understand "intelligible matter" or "quantitative being," then the principles of being are quite as necessary as the principles of quantity. Now in terms of such metaphysical principles as act and potency let us consider two alternatives for the purpose of illustration. The "infinity" of points on the two lines is (1) actually logical and potentially real, or (2) actually logical and real. The second is really a condensation of two other alternatives. All that is required for illustrative purpose is an alternative that blurs over act and potency and the two modes of being. In terms of these two incompatible metaphysical premises let us answer the question originally raised.

In terms of the second alternative mathematical infinity is actual, and since there are an infinity of points on both a short and a long line, the number of points is the same. In this case points are conceived to be unextended, and numbers are correlated with them. The metaphysics constitutive here may be some kind of idealism, neo-Parmenidean or Leibnitzian.

The first alternative is realism, and in terms of it a critique can be made. From the standpoint of quantitative being, and not just quantity, numbers should be correlated with segments, not unextended points. A line is to a point as act is to potency. A point is indeterminate until determined by a line drawn through the linear continuum. No summation of unextended points can produce extension. One cannot get something from nothing. Therefore, the actual infinity of the points on a line is logical (mental) only. Really, and objectively, the infinity is one only of potency. It is false to say that actually there are as many points on a short line as on a long line. The two are not comparable because the points on each are indeterminate.

What we have tried to demonstrate is that the two incompatible answers as to whether there are really the same number of points on a short and a long line are the consequences of two different and incompatible metaphysical premises. If one metaphysical premise is applied to two different axiomatic systems, then two different answers are obtained. Or one can apply the two metaphysical premises to one axiomatic system and get two different answers. It doesn't make any difference. It might seem that what is responsible for the different answers is purely a mathematical consideration. But this is not the case. Two axiomatic systems do not give different answers about the same thing. It is the "things" that are different. Given the meaning of "point," "line," etc., each system is "correct" because the terms are defined differently. And this is perfectly legitimate because mathematics as positive, as axiomatic, does not have the function of determining which is being, this being the function of the philosophy of mathematics.

In the structure of an argument in mathematics the two premises and the conclusion can be mathematical propositions. But in the philosophy of mathematics, when the argument is condensed, the major will be a metaphysical proposition, the minor a mathematical one, and the conclusion a proposition of the integrative discipline, the philosophy of mathematics.

In this way metaphysics is constitutive of the philosophy of mathematics, although it is only regulative of mathematics as a positive science.

It may be objected that two different axiomatic systems are not about different "things" when they deal with points and lines, but rather are different systems about the same "things," namely, points and lines. It is not an accident at all that "point" is used as a term in both, and not "planet" or "cat." If this is so, then we simply have two mathematical systems about the same things. There are only two alternatives. Either the one is true and the other is not, or the question of truth cannot be determined, and the choice of system is left to convenience in use. On the latter alternative metaphysical truth would be impossible. On the first alternative the issue must be determined on mathematical grounds, and hence metaphysics is irrelevant. Hence, metaphysics is either impossible or irrelevant, and therefore cannot enter constitutively into something called the "philosophy of mathematics."

This dilemma may be met by grabbing a horn. Let us assume that the two systems are not about different, but about the same, "things." And let us grant that one is true and the other is false. It does not at all follow that mathematics as positive can tell which is which. Actually, so far from being able to solve the problem, mathematics as positive creates it. Of course, if by "true" all that is meant is formal consistency, then there is no problem. Both are "true" in this sense. But the only reason for asking the original question is that something more than mere "validity" is meant by "true." In other words, the issue is not one concerning mere quantity *qua* quantity, a mode *qua* mode, but one that concerns quantitative *being,* matter as intelligible and not sensible.

Properly speaking, then, quantitative being is the formal object of the philosophy of mathematics, a discipline made possible by the second order of abstraction. Quantity is the formal object of mathematics as positive, and is made possible by abstraction from being itself. Mobile being is the formal object of the philosophy of nature, a discipline made possible by the first order of abstraction. Motion is the formal object of the phenomenological discipline of experimental science, and is made possible by abstracting motion from being.

It may be pointed out that to abstract from being is to get nonbeing, and that a positive science is for this reason about nonbeing, nothing. This would be a misunderstanding. The details of a mode of being cannot be furnished by metaphysics. The details of a mode are just what they are, and must be investigated and discovered. In doing so one forgets about "being." In fact one may not even know about it. Such abstraction is not only possible but is an accomplished fact. The world is full of mathematicians and experimental scientists who know nothing whatsoever of metaphysics, yet work satisfactorily within the limitations of their positive sciences. This is both possible and actual, although perhaps not desirable. A positive science is a necessary means to an end, the *philosophy* of the science. A science of quantity is necessary in order to know what *quantitative* being is. But it is neither sufficient nor an end in itself.

Nonbeing (and nihilism) enters the picture when the means becomes an end in itself, being is identified with a mode, when a positive science is taken as sufficient. But even this is not an affair of the positive science itself. It is wholly innocent. The doctrine to the effect that positive science is the only kind of knowledge possible, that it is sufficient, is a proposition *about,* not *of,* positive science. The doctrine is that kind of "ism" called "positivism." But the nonbeing which is positivism is not the consequence of abstracting from being for a limited purpose. *It is rather the consequence of denying that from which one has abstracted.*

There is a great deal of difference between "giving rise to a problem" and "being able to solve a problem." Mathematics may give rise to problems that it cannot solve without metaphysics. The structure of mathematics seems to rest upon the natural numbers, whether or not God created them and left it to the mathematician to create the others. Now, let us suppose that the mathematician defines number in terms of "class" or "aggregate." Having done so, over a period of time he discovers that the concept of "aggregate" leads to difficulties, to what are called the mathematical "paradoxes" or "antinomies," usually in connection with the notion of "infinity." For example, consider the sum of all the cardinal numbers in aggregate K, when K is itself the aggregate of all cardinal numbers. The sum must be a cardinal number, and therefore in K. Yet it is greater than any in K. Now clearly something seems to be "wrong." This and many other paradoxes can be developed, e.g., that a whole may not be greater than one of its parts.

Now what is the relation of metaphysics to all of this? It has no relevance, except as "regulative" through the principle of contradiction. It is not "constitutive." What the philosopher dares not say is that the mathematician cannot, or should not, do what he does. Of course he "can" do it, for he has done it. Further, it is not the business of the metaphysician to tell the mathematician what he ought or ought not to do *qua* mathematician. As regulative metaphysics does not tell him what to do, but rather holds him responsible for what he does, i.e., he must accept the consequences of his axioms and definitions. But if metaphysics pretends to do any more than this, then we would have a kind of *a priorism* in the worst sense of the word.

But the paradoxes remain. What the mathematician does not do is identify the difficulties that arise from considering quantity *qua* quantity with the nature of quantitative being. The "evidence" that produced the paradoxes does not at all produce this conclusion. Well, then, what can be done? Why not solve mathematical problems mathematically? The answer is that such ought to be done for the simple reason that there is no other way. But since our purpose is to show the nature of the "philosophy of mathematics" we have chosen examples that can only be handled by that discipline. But we are getting ahead of ourselves. Let us first see what can be done mathematically with the paradoxes.

The mathematician may try to eliminate a paradox by adding an axiom or changing a definition. The criticism here must not be on the grounds that this would be an *ad hoc* procedure. It is doubtful whether "ad hoc" can have any meaning at all in mathematics. The validity of such criticism would seem to be confined to experimental science. However, a legitimate criticism of such an attempt would be that it does not really eliminate the paradox, but merely avoids it.[2] Another attempt might be made by way of a "theory of types." In this theory no class can contain itself as a member and no propositional function can take itself as an argument. Any proposition about an aggregate must be of a "higher type" than the proposition defining the aggregate. Thus we are prevented from constructing paradoxical aggregates, i.e., no aggregate can have itself as an element. However, the trouble with this is that it gives rise to its own kind of difficulties. The problem of infinity in connection with number is shifted to that of an infinity of "types" or even "logics." Of the two attempts the first avoids, and the second but shifts, the problem of mathematical infinity.

Of course, there is another alternative. One can cut at the very root of some of the paradoxes by simply denying the existence of the infinite aggregates which "cause" them. This is the procedure of the intuitionists. But if so, then the denial is made on metaphysical, not mathematical grounds. For when one asserts or denies "existence," the formal object, whether one realizes it or not, is not merely quantity, but quantitative being. And this is the formal object of the philosophy of mathematics, in which integrative discipline, in a condensed argument, the major premise is metaphysical.

What is important to recognize is this, that a distinction must be made between what is positive in mathematics, and what are positions taken *about* mathematics. Intuitionism is not a *positive* mathematical doctrine, but a doctrine of the philosophy of mathematics. And so is formalism, to which intuitionism is opposed. This fact is often obscured rather than recognized by the use of such terms as "meta-mathematics" or "meta-logic." Such use is not accidental. It reflects a twentieth century trend to reverse the proper relationship between positive science and metaphysics. To continue with the example of mathematical infinity, instead of solving the problem by applying metaphysics to mathematical developments, bringing together what for the sake of a division of labor was separated, namely, quantity and being, the procedure has been to try to prove something metaphysical by using the mathematical as evidence. But in following this procedure the "philosophy of mathematics" becomes nothing more than a reflective image of the positive science. Different mathematical approaches generate different philosophies of mathematics, the latter reflecting and being determined by the very difficulties they are supposed to solve.

Another way of saying the same thing is to say that a metaphysical premise is chosen, postulated, to fit a given mathematical procedure. The difference is verbal. For whether the metaphysical premise is thought to have been produced directly by the mathematical, or to have been chosen as most compatible with it, the error is still the same, namely, that of supposing that a positive science can determine the metaphysical. To make this clearer let us begin with realism and then show how (say) formalism is generated.

How formalism is obtained. We have already suggested the realist answer as to what mathematical infinity really is, as opposed to the nominal meanings which it may have in postulational systems. As actual, mathematical infinity is logical; as potential it is real (nonmental). What is actual in mathematical infinity is a rule. A rule is about something, (say) numbers; but a rule is not a number. These distinctions have a foundation in the formal object "quantitative being," which can also be spoken of as "intelligible matter." The being that quantity is *of* is matter. Matter as such is pure potentiality, the indeterminate. The determinate is form, which is quantity.

Now the first fatal step is taken when "form" and "matter" are identified, when being and mode are coalesced. This is what occurred when Descartes identified "matter" and "extension." When we consider the offspring of this error it is understandable why he is called the "father" of modern philosophy. From having begun mathematization of being, other developments were inevitable. Logic as the science of intentional forms is no longer possible. But since it still remains formal it is conceived to be a science of real relations of a kind. The question then arises as to what is the difference between logic and mathematics. The difference is little, if any; logic is perhaps more general. What seems to be left of it are such principles as those of contradiction and excluded middle, which seem to be prescriptive in the construction of mathematical systems. But if matter and form have been identified, and quantity is form, and logic is concerned with forms also, some of which seem to be non-quantitative, and there isn't much if any difference between mathematics and logic, then why not identify mathematics with the science of forms and not merely with the science of quantity?

After taking the first step there are now many alternative second steps. Since form and matter, being and a mode are identified, mathematical forms can no longer be conceived to be obtained by abstraction. If the forms are not in things, or in a Platonic heaven, then they must be in our minds. If so, they are either within or beyond our control. If the latter, then we have Kantianism. Forms are not abstracted, but *imposed*—not on matter, but now on something called "experience." If the forms are within our control, then we have some kind of conceptual pragmatism or idealism—experience is again the raw material from which the world is fashioned in the *act* of knowing it, but there are alternative ways of "acting." By this time logic and mathematics have become so completely identified that it follows that there are alternative "logics." It is easy to take the next step and question whether there are "forms" at all. Perhaps there are only "names." Mathematics and logic now become languages. But of course languages are made up of "marks," and therefore . . .

Where is the check point to stop all of this? There is none if the first step is taken. However, let us return to the end of the first step and consider one of the alternatives.

Having identified mathematics with the analysis and construction of formal systems, an important problem becomes that of proving formal consistency within the system. As is well known, this was Hilbert's problem, and there were difficulties. It was Gödel's function to show that for a formal logic L, satisfying certain conditions, there are undecidable propositions in L, i.e., propositions F such that neither F nor not-F is provable. Further, for a suitable L, the consistency of L cannot be proved in L. In other words, within a formal system consistency cannot be demonstrated, although it might be in a "meta-system." The implications of this may seem rather startling when we realize that the difficulty is but transferred from a system to a metasystem, and also when we remember that from such a formalistic standpoint a mathematical entity, if constructed, exists if its nonexistence is inconsistent. Whether or not they are startling depends upon what we mean when we ask about the significance of Gödel's theorem.

What should be meant when we ask about the significance of the results of a positive science? This is a question, not *of,* but *about,* the science. For the question at hand the science is *given,* which means that its results will constitute minor premises in arguments in which the major premises are metaphysical. The conclusions will be propositions of the philosophy of the science, and they will state the "significance." How else can the significance be obtained that is not merely guesswork and conjecture? In asking, finally, about significance one is seeking the end for which the positive science is a means. The question is about quantitative being, not just about quantity or about being. We shouldn't expect the means to give the final answer. We do not expect investigations about quantity alone to give us answers about quantitative being. But if we have knowledge about being *qua* being and about quantity *qua* quantity, then it is reasonable to expect that some knowledge may be had about quantitative being.

Since our problem is one in the order of knowledge, and not one in the philosophy of mathematics, it is not our purpose (nor do we have the knowledge) to appraise Gödel's work thoroughly. Rather we are using it as an illustration in order to demonstrate what is involved in a correct procedure of appraisal. In the first place, it is not the function of the philosophy of mathematics to change or modify the results of mathematics. Gödel's theorems are what they are. If there has been an error in the method of proof, and they are not really theorems, then one makes his discovery and criticism as a mathematician and not primarily as a philosopher of mathematics. However, one must accept the theorems as true and not merely valid, or reject them, on metaphysical grounds, for being as well as quantity is determining.

A realistic analysis would then point out as regards the value of Gödel's work, that if one begins with a mode of being, but in abstraction from being, an infinite regress of systems is necessary; for at any given stage the system of rules, of mathematics or "logic," is incomplete. Now if any infinite series of steps must invalidate the series as both real and actual, then it follows that Formalism in mathematics is limited and in logic is impossible. The mathematician has demonstrated its limitation in detail. The metaphysician would suspect the same on other grounds, for he knows that predicamental categories and relations are limited, and that naturally one would encounter difficulties if they were made transcendentals and absolutes. So far as logic is concerned the significance of Gödel's work is that the conception of logic implied is wrong because of the conclusions obtained. It is important to note here that from the standpoint of mathematics as a positive science all one can say is that the conclusions follow. But it cannot tell one whether the premises (axioms and definitions) should be accepted and the conclusions accepted, or the conclusions rejected and hence the premises rejected. The positive science presents the problem but does not solve it. In this case the latter alternative is the correct one because logic is concerned with intentional forms and relations and not with real relations.

Such is the procedure. Fundamental to it is the necessity that the metaphysics which is constitutive of the philosophy of mathematics must be obtained by appealing to evidence independent of mathematics. The reasons for this need not be repeated. Also it is to be noted that the truth of this principle is independent of the truth or falsity of the metaphysics that is constitutive. In order to demonstrate the relation of metaphysics to mathematics and the philosophy of mathematics we have used realistic principles. But the metaphysical premises might be, and often are in fact, nominalistic. Nominalism may be a false metaphysics, and we believe it is. But it is metaphysics nevertheless. The thesis we are demonstrating is that metaphysics, whether true or false, is constitutive of the philosophy of mathematics, but only regulative of mathematics. No more than is any other kind of proposition, a metaphysical proposition as a type is not defined by its truth. Its type must first be known in order that the kind of evidence relevant to its truth or falsity may be known.

It is perfectly legitimate, therefore, so far as the relation of metaphysical and mathematical propositions is concerned with respect to evidence, to consider mathematics as positive in the light of nominalism, the very antithesis of realism. Provided of course that the evidence in terms of which nominalism is upheld is independent of the positive science, in this case mathematics. Otherwise, to put it mildly, there would be a begging of the question in drawing conclusions about the philosophy of mathematics. Actually, what would occur is an arbitrary positing of a metaphysics on no other ground than that it is necessary in order to assert the conclusion one wants to assert. And, of course, this is identical with absolutizing a positive science, making a metaphysics out of it, or supposing that it proves something metaphysical.

Mathematics does not "prove" what is metaphysically presupposed. The practical importance of the principles thus far developed are twofold. Their recognition would prevent much useless waste of energy and scholarship on the part of those who suppose the problems of the "foundations of mathematics" or the "philosophy of mathematics" can be solved by some new development in mathematics, some new set of definitions or axioms, or alternatively by constant conjectures about the philosophy of mathematics, the conjectures being merely reflective of the mathematics the philosophy is supposed to be about. Such conjectures are tagged and identified by name, and constitute at best but a museum of half-truths. "Scholarship" may then consist of further commentaries on the commentaries, further conjectures on the conjectures.

The principles are of even greater practical importance in establishing the possibility of intelligent communication in case of disagreements. For this it is necessary to know the type of proposition in question, i.e., what kind of knowledge it represents, and what kind of evidence is relevant to it. In absence of this, disagreement becomes either quarreling or confusion with good will. We may illustrate with the Gödel example. With nominalistic premises one may come to a conclusion in the philosophy of mathematics quite contrary to that which would stem from realistic premises. For the sake of illustration, and not of argument, in terms of nominalism one might conclude that no one system of formal logic can embrace all forms of reasoning that are correct. From realistic premises certainly a contrary conclusion would be drawn.

Now we have here a disagreement in the integrative discipline, the philosophy of mathematics. Abstractly speaking, where could the locus of the disagreement lie? In either one or both of two places, the minor or major premises; in the mathematics or in the metaphysics or in both. In the particular case in question where is the source of the disagreement? It is not in Gödel's mathematics as such. Both parties accept the theorems as relative to the system. The source of the difficulty is, then, in the metaphysical differences of the two parties. The issue now shifts to that of metaphysics, with each party recognizing as he must that the evidence to which appeal is made, in order to settle the issue of nominalism versus realism, *must not include Gödel's theorems.* The reasons why this must be so have already been sufficiently explained. It would be foolish as well as fruitless to use the mathematics on which both parties agree to settle a metaphysical issue on which they disagree.

An example or two will be helpful in illustrating the confusion in the order of knowledge of which we have spoken. In expressing sympathy with Intuitionism and Brouwer's criticism of Formalism, Mr. Kattsoff says:

> It has been shown (by Gödel) that mathematics can never be completely formalized; that in every arithmetical system it will be possible to construct propositions which cannot be decided in that system, i.e., propositions such that it is impossible to decide whether they are true or false. This does not mean a temporary lack of proof but a permanent one so far as the given system is concerned. This itself it seems to me leads to the necessity of a three-valued logic.[3]

Now Mr. Kattsoff's conclusion not only does not in fact follow—it is impossible for it to follow. For he is saying that Gödel's work in positive mathematics demands necessarily a three-valued logic. What makes the demand, however, is a metaphysical premise, in this case suppressed. Unless a collection of numbers can be denumerated, or yield a law of denumeration, it cannot be taken as *A* or not-*A,* but must be considered as indeterminate. Do we then have a limitation on the law of the excluded middle? Let us see.

If a metaphysics is assumed which has no room for potency as well as act, an affirmative answer may follow. A pure form is act. As we have seen, it is just what it is. Something is a triangle, or it isn't. Something is either *A* or not-*A,* and there is no middle ground. Now let us suppose that mathematics, in the positive sense dealing with quantity *qua* quantity—in itself legitimate as a means only—is absolutized. Not intelligible matter but just the intelligible; not quantitative being, but just quantity. What should be mentally abstracted for the purpose of understanding becomes metaphysically real, *reified.* If, now, difficulties arise in mathematics of the kind given, then it would seem as if a three-valued logic is implied. A proposition is true, false, or indeterminate (undecidable). We are assuming, of course, that the "undecidable" is real, and not merely a psychological matter. Otherwise there is no problem, and one does not have a three-valued logic.

Something like a three-valued logic is implied only if a metaphysical premise is assumed which takes account of being and nonbeing but has no room for potency. The indeterminate would have to be that which is both being and nonbeing, or neither. Just what kind of metaphysics this would be is not clear. If it is nominalism, then the indeterminate would have to be psychological, and we have already assumed that this is not the case. More likely the metaphysical would be some kind of dialectical idealism. There is evidence that it is this which Mr. Kattsoff is assuming.[4]

However, if an Aristotelian realism is the metaphysics assumed, then no three-valued logic is necessary at all. There is no third position between *A* and not-*A* as act. The indeterminate is real, but as potency. The realist would point out that the intuitionist's critique of formalism is essentially correct. In its own way it is rediscovering potency after it has been eliminated.

And now for the main point to be made. A three-valued logic is not necessitated by Gödel's work. What demands it is a certain kind of metaphysics used in interpreting his work. If another metaphysics is used, there is no such demand. Realism can admit Gödel's work as positive mathematics, and of course the logic of realism is two-valued. Mr. Kattsoff's error is not essentially one in the philosophy of mathematics, but one stemming from a false conception of the order of knowledge. He assumes that a positive science can prove something metaphysically. This is impossible, and hence any discussion that proceeds on this assumption makes communication difficult. What appears to be communication turns out to be a mutual commentary on each other's conjectures. Unfortunately many books and journals today are filled with such conjectures, attempts to do the impossible. Since what Mr. Kattsoff does is typical of much of those writings, rather than multiply examples, in which there is no virtue, let us continue with the example at hand in order to understand even more clearly the nature of the error involved. According to Mr. Kattsoff Gödel's work necessitates far more than a three-valued logic:

> If, as is agreed, the formal systems can be used to systematize fields of knowledge, and if the Gödel theorem applies to such applications, it would mean that no field of knowledge so systematized can ever be complete. At any stage there will always be questions formulable in the system that need a wider system for their solution. Since it is the contention of the author of this book that logic and mathematics do tell us something about reality, the Gödel theorem tells us that there can never be a complete and final theory of reality, i.e., metaphysics. This does not lead to mysticism, but to an evolutionary scheme of reality.[5]

There is no doubt but that mathematics is a most wonderful science, and that Mr. Kattsoff believes it to be the "queen" of them all. But by such statements Mr. Kattsoff turns it into the court jester. It would be an understatement to say that Gödel's theorem proves no such thing. Not having any metaphysics Mr. Kattsoff cannot be clear about the nature and delimitations of a "field of knowledge," "formal," and "logic." But let us confine ourselves to one consideration. The reasoning is that metaphysics can't be complete because Gödel's theorems tell us it can't. It is true but not sufficient to say that the theorem tells us no such thing. We must ask: On what grounds does Mr. Kattsoff think it does? Is it merely because mathematics tells us something about reality? Hardly. This happens to be true, but even so the conclusion would be a *non sequitur*. Any kind of knowledge is about reality in some sense. The whole point is that the "sense" in which a positive science is about reality cannot be determined by the science itself. The denial of this is the recipe for intellectual chaos—scientists and mathematicians constantly "postulating" and "generalizing" the notions and results of their limited disciplines, supposing that in this manner metaphysical knowledge may be obtained. What is obtained has as little relation to metaphysics as astrology to astronomy. One may suspect that it is not an accident at all that "philosophy" has about the same standing in higher education today as astrology.

What Mr. Kattsoff pretends to do is to discuss the "philosophy of mathematics." What he actually does is arbitrarily make a metaphysics out of mathematics. Specifically, what he does is commit the first fatal error on the way to intellectual nihilism that was mentioned some pages back, namely, identify "matter" with "form." He says:

> We wish merely to indicate the possibility of a metaphysics based on the applicability of mathematics to reality. Such a metaphysics would clearly be a return to a rationalism of the Cartesian type. This tendency is indicated in Eddington and reflected by Korzybski . . .[6]

If this is true, then, it is not very surprising to learn that mathematics is "queen," and that "the purpose of the philosopher is to understand and to establish firmly this 'queen of the sciences.' "[7] At this point a sense of humor is perhaps helpful. But it is tragic comedy. All semblance of the order of knowledge has vanished, and in its place we have a kind of academic imperialism. In the absence of law and order of knowledge, philosophy is reduced to a "name," a name of a kind of weapon that is used for power purposes by the various claimants to the throne. For in the absence of any objective criterion many want to become queen. It may be physics, or biology, or some more youthful claimant such as grammar or language. What we have is war waged by a positive science under the name of the "philosophy" of that science.

Let us now briefly relate the example used to illustrate the principles in terms of which it must be understood. Intelligible matter is quantitative being, the object of the philosophy of mathematics, made possible by the second order of abstraction. For investigative purposes quantity can be separated from being, thus defining mathematics as positive. Now let the Cartesian error enter. Formalize mathematics and identify a mode of being with being itself. The object now is not "intelligible matter," but "intelligible being"—*and this is exactly what metaphysics is.* The title of Mr. Kattsoff's book is *A Philosophy of Mathematics.* But if mathematics is metaphysics, what can the philosophy of mathematics possibly be? Nothing at all. It becomes a "name" for the reduction of metaphysics to mathematics. This is not knowledge, or a kind of knowledge. It is a kind of intellectual nihilism.

Before continuing further let us summarize with a statement of ten principles:

(1) Metaphysics is regulative, but not constitutive, of mathematics.

(2) Metaphysics is constitutive, together with mathematics, of the philosophy of mathematics.

(3) The formal object of the philosophy of mathematics is quantitative being or intelligible matter.

(4) The foundation of mathematics as positive is quantity, which can be considered in abstraction from being.

(5) The nature of the reality of mathematical entities cannot be determined by mathematics itself because these entities have been considered in abstraction from being.

(6) Therefore, to determine the kind of reality mathematical entities have—e.g., what is logical but with a foundation in reality, what is logical but mere fiction—requires knowledge of being itself. Hence, metaphysics must be determining.

(7) In order that metaphysics may so determine, it must be applied to the results of mathematics. The conclusions obtained constitute propositions in the integrative discipline called "phi-

losophy of mathematics," the two parts of the name referring to the two kinds of knowledge that are constitutive.

(8) Although neither mathematics nor metaphysics constitutes evidence for the other, each is necessary, and both together are sufficient, as evidence for the philosophy of mathematics.

(9) A proposition of mathematics alone cannot determine any proposition in metaphysics or the philosophy of mathematics. A proposition of metaphysics alone cannot determine any proposition in mathematics or the philosophy of mathematics.

(10) Propositions of the philosophy of mathematics cannot constitute evidence for either metaphysics or mathematics.

Communication and the relevance of kinds of evidence. Since these principles are violated in much of the contemporary literature on the relation of mathematics and philosophy, it is necessary to explain why this is so. We have already done this to some extent in a very general way. But it is necessary to do so more specifically, with a further explication of the conditions demanded by intelligent communication. A correct understanding of the relation of mathematics and metaphysics to each other as kinds of knowledge is a precondition to a correct solution of problems involving each of those kinds of knowledge as evidence. Confusion in communication on the latter level often has its source in not only a false but an impossible notion of the nature of the kinds of knowledge involved. In other words, confusion in discussing the problems of the philosophy of mathematics often has its source in a prior confusion as to the order of the kinds of knowledge.

What is involved in asking the "meaning" of mathematics, or the "meaning" of some theorems? What does it mean to speak of "interpreting" mathematics? Or to say that something in mathematics "presupposes" something "philosophical"? Such terms as "interpreting," "presupposes," and "implies" often obscure rather than clarify. For example, we turn to an article by Mr. John Myhill called "Philosophical Implications of Mathematical Logic." [8] Overlooking for the moment the non-intentional use of the term "logic," we might ask what the phrase means? It means that mathematics implies something "philosophical." Now we have tried to demonstrate that this is impossible, if by "philosophical" is meant "metaphysical," and this is presumably what he means when he speaks of Platonism and the "conventionalism" of nominalism. The question arises, then, as to what Mr. Myhill can possibly be doing. The answer to this we shall postpone for the moment, and continue with other questions.

Mr. Myhill raises the question of Gödel's theorem "presupposing Platonism," meaning "Platonism as a precondition of its meaningfulness." [9] After discussing the reasons for believing this is not necessarily the case, he concludes: "We merely observe that we have not seen any *compelling* reason to infer Platonism from Gödel; . . ." [10] Now it may be asked: What thesis is it that is being discussed? Is it that Platonism implies Gödel, or that Gödel implies Platonism? When we say that *A* presupposes *B* we mean that *B* implies *A*. Further, we have already seen that there are several senses in which this is true. The way in which a theorem presupposes axioms in mathematics is not the same as the way in which (say) experimental science presupposes the "uniformity of nature," or "limited independent variety," or some equivalent. In the first case there is a constitutive relation; in the latter a regulative. These are not distinguished by Mr. Myhill in saying that Platonism implies Gödel. In the conclusion we are led to believe that a quite different question was being discussed. Disregarding the psychological connotation of "infer," the phrase "to infer Platonism from Gödel" means "Gödel implies Platonism."

Not only is there confusion about the two meanings of "implies" (constitutive and regulative), but Mr. Myhill is not even clear as to the question he is discussing, as to what implies what. And yet there is reason to believe that he thinks that Gödel *proves* something philosophical, for at the end of the article he gives "hints" as to how mathematics may "make more precise and fruitful the future sciences of ethics and aesthetics." [11] Now we should like to point out that this is both impossible and unintelligible, and it is only confusion in the order of knowledge that would allow one to think otherwise. Furthermore, even the phrase "philosophical implications of mathematical logic," the title of the article, represents something quite as impossible as "bitter tasting parabolas." The more awkward phrase, "the mathematical implications of philosophy," would be more correct. Yet neither phrase brings out exactly what is involved in the "philosophy of mathematics," that which is or can be knowledge rather than conjecture and commentary.

If this is true, then it is important. That philosophers and graduate students should know more mathematics than they do is to be granted. But it would be a very un-divine kind of comedy to have them furiously study mathematics in the hope that somehow or other—and it is all very unclear—ethical and philosophical wisdom may be obtained. This is tragedy, of the kind that characterizes so much of modern "thought."

What, then, can it mean to "interpret" Gödel? Or mathematics? What are the possible sources of disagreement?

(1) One may be asking whether certain propositions "follow." Are they really theorems? This is a mathematical question, just as much as is the problem of solving fifth degree equations, and is to be handled accordingly.

(2) What do the theorems mean in terms of the system, the axioms and definitions? For example, a novice might dismiss Gödel on the ground that he says nothing new, that there have always been undecided problems in number theory. It would then be pointed out that his theorems mean that there are undecidable, not merely undecided, problems. Or one might think that he shows that some instances of a law concerning numbers are not provable. It may then be pointed out that, on the contrary, his theorems mean that in a system in which there is a normal formulation of number theory there exists a law concerning numbers such that every instance of the law is provable, but the law itself is not. These problems, too, are problems within mathematics. Metaphysical considerations are not relevant at this stage.

(3) A quite different kind of question may be asked. What does a system, axioms and definitions as well as the theorems, mean in reference to the formal object, quantitative being? The problem here is the relation of mathematical and metaphysical notions, and hence is a problem of the philosophy of mathematics. In being an integrative discipline a conclusion in the

philosophy of mathematics is a terminal product, an end product. It is itself not evidence for anything else, either for mathematics or for metaphysics. Rather, mathematics and metaphysics constitute evidence for *it*. Where, then, can there be disagreement and to what kind of evidence is appeal to be made?

(*a*) If the disagreement is about the metaphysical, the appeal is to metaphysical evidence.

(*b*) If the disagreement is about the mathematical, the appeal is to mathematical evidence.

(*c*) If the disagreement is about the conclusions of the philosophy of mathematics, then there is no peculiar type of evidence to which appeal can be made. One must return to (*a*) or (*b*).

However, if we can assume the "logic" of an argument to be correct, and the mathematical problem settled, then disagreement about conclusions in the philosophy of mathematics is really disagreement about metaphysics. At any rate, to debate the matter on the level of (*c*), in abstraction from (*a*), is fruitless. *A problem of the philosophy of mathematics is always a problem of the relation between metaphysics and mathematics, not on the level of second intentions, which would be a problem of the order of knowledge, but on the level of first intentions.* Furthermore, in the application of metaphysics to mathematics neither can be evidence for the other, neither can force a change in the other.

Is this not to make both equally absolute and autonomous? In which case we would seem to have the impossible situation of either having two "metaphysics," or else mathematics itself becomes a metaphysics. No, let us remember that we are working from the standpoint of the order of knowledge and not the order of being. From the latter standpoint quantity and being are already together—true quantity and true being, making true quantitative being. There is no "application" of being to quantity. They simply are—together. But for cognitive purposes there is a separation, and a synthesis (again mental) demands the relating of one to the other. In addition there is the fact that since we are not omniscient beings there can be and are different metaphysical and mathematical positions. Hence, while a disagreement in metaphysics or mathematics as such is one within the discipline, a disagreement in the philosophy of mathematics cannot in the same sense be within that discipline but must be within either metaphysics or mathematics, and can be within both. For an omniscient being there are no disagreements. But neither can there be a question of the relevance of evidence and the order of knowledge, for the latter and the order of being are the same. But since we are human beings and there is disagreement, it becomes of utmost importance to understand the relations of kinds of knowledge to each other, and especially the nature of the evidence that is relevant in order intelligently to communicate on matters.

If the mathematical cannot be evidence for the metaphysical, why should anyone think otherwise? We have explained why the fact must be so, but we have not as yet clarified the nature of the error which would lead one to the contrary. After all, there are people who do believe that, for example, Gödel's mathematics implies something philosophical, and in the sense of "proving." Let us see how they "reason." For a working example we choose the question of the mathematical infinite, one that we have used before. We shall now attempt to "demonstrate" the impossible, how mathematics alone can prove something philosophical.

Explanation of the error of assuming the mathematical to be evidence for the metaphysical. Let us suppose that a person is discussing the philosophy of mathematics and he says: "If mathematical infinity is a quantitative form, then it is a transcendental real." He continues and says that there is evidence that mathematical infinity is a quantitative form. Therefore, he concludes that it is a transcendental real. The conclusion is called "Platonism," and the evidence to which appeal is made is mathematical. The form of the reasoning is: If p, then q; p; therefore, q. This is admitted by everyone to be valid. In order to draw the conclusion p must be asserted. If p remains hypothetical we merely have a repetition of "If p, then q." What allows us to assert p is mathematical evidence. Therefore, it is also the reason why the conclusion can be drawn, and the conclusion is a proposition of the philosophy of mathematics.

In the major premise of this hypothetical syllogism neither the antecedent nor the consequent is asserted or denied. Since q is neither asserted nor denied in the major premise no philosophical position is asserted. A philosophical position *is* asserted in the conclusion. But the reason or ground for the assertion is the mathematical evidence which allows the assertion of the antecedent or minor premise.

This argument would seem to demonstrate rather conclusively that metaphysics is not constitutive of the philosophy of mathematics. Rather, what implies or proves something philosophically is mathematical evidence. In practice this means that if we wish to understand the "philosophical implications of mathematics," then we should study the mathematics that does the implying. This kind of reasoning seems eminently sensible and crystal-clear. So much so that when it is expounded in contemporary academic groups it is honored as ultimate wisdom. Yet the "logic" of it is based on a questionable view of logic itself. What is the error?

In a hypothetical proposition it is said that neither the antecedent nor the consequent is asserted. This is true. But in the argument we are examining it is not made clear what is asserted. A proposition must assert something; otherwise it is not a proposition. Nothing *merely* psychological is meant by the term "assert." Hence, the difference between "inference" and "implication" is not relevant. By "assert" is meant "intend." Now the proposition is an implicative compound, and what is asserted is a relation between two propositions, the relation mediated by a middle term. In other words, the hypothetical proposition is an enthymeme stating a minor premise and a conclusion, the former being hypothetical. What is presupposed is a premise not stated, namely, "whatever is a quantitative form is transcendentally real." Of course, if mathematical infinity is a quantitative form, then it is transcendentally real. What is conditional is the minor premise. What is unconditionally asserted is the major premise, which is metaphysical and not mathematical. If, because of mathematical evidence, the conditionality is eliminated, then we may say "*since* mathematical infinity is a quantitative form, *therefore* it is transcendentally real." But in either case the metaphysical premise (major) is asserted unconditionally.[12]

What we have, then, in the argument under examination is actually a syllogism expressed in enthymeme form with a metaphysical premise presupposed. When sufficient mathematical evidence allows one to assert that mathematical infinity is a quantitative form, then we have a categorical syllogism. What is removed is the conditionality of the hypothetical proposition which is really an enthymeme. If one wishes to speak of a conditional and a categorical syllogism, the difference is this, that in the former the minor premise is asserted conditionally and in the latter categorically. But in both instances the major is categorical. Were it otherwise we would be faced with an infinite regress such that nothing could be asserted. If reasoning is to *intend* anything, and hence be more than a "manipulation of marks," then for something to be hypothetical something else must be categorical.

What is *intended?* The kind of implicative compound which a conditional proposition is, asserts a connection between an antecedent and a consequent. If it did not, it would remain the barest of forms. In being an enthymeme it is able to intend the connection, a *cause,* by means of the middle term. There is nothing mysterious about the notion of "cause" here, if we remember that there are four species of cause, and that reference is to the formal. If an enthymeme or syllogism is considered as a "pure" structure without content, then no conclusion can be drawn. The structure merely allows the conclusion to be asserted as true if one already knows that it can be so asserted. The reason why the conclusion "mathematical infinity is transcendentally real" is believed falsely to follow from mathematical evidence, that "mathematical infinity is a quantitative form," is that it appears that only the latter is asserted. This appearance is taken to be true when logic is thought of as nonintentional. Especially is this true if, instead of recognizing the conditional proposition as an enthymeme it is reduced to a categorical proposition. However, in this case, though we do have an assertion, we do not have an argument.

We see, then, that so far from mathematics proving something metaphysical, or even being sufficient as evidence for a proposition in the philosophy of mathematics, metaphysics is constitutive of the latter—standing as a major premise to the latter, which is a conclusion. The philosophy of mathematics *presupposes* metaphysics. We may recall that if type *B* knowledge presupposes type *A* knowledge, then *A* constitutes *B* if by this is meant that some specific proposition of *A* must be asserted as true if some specific proposition of *B* is asserted as true. In the light of the analysis given, if *B* is "mathematical infinity is transcendentally real," and *A* is "whatever is a quantitative form is transcendentally real," then it is seen that the metaphysical premise satisfies the defining criterion of "constitutive."

Let the major, minor, and conclusion of the argument we have been examining be designated respectively as Mp_1 (metaphysical), Ma_1 (mathematical), and Pm_1 (philosophy of mathematics). The "Platonism" stems from Mp_1, and it is only derivatively in Pm_1. (Whether or not this is questionable Platonism will not concern us.) Now an Aristotelian might argue that (Pm_2) mathematical infinity is merely logical because (Ma_2) it is a rule. What is presupposed is that (Mp_2) whatever is a rule is logical. Which conclusion is the correct one, and to what kind of evidence is appeal to be made? On what level is the disagreement?

We have seen that it cannot be on the level of the "conclusion." This is true for any synthetic or integrative discipline. Such a discipline is a sterile hybrid; it is produced, but it cannot produce. This fact, however, does not reflect at all on its importance. Therefore the difference would seem to stem from Ma_1, Ma_2 or from Mp_1, Mp_2. Since metaphysics and mathematics are both constitutive of a proposition of the philosophy of mathematics there are three possibilities. (1) Agreement metaphysically, disagreement on the mathematical. (2) Agreement on the mathematical and disagreement on the metaphysical. (3) Disagreement on both. We can then say that mathematics implies a proposition of the philosophy of mathematics by means of a metaphysical premise. Also, metaphysics implies a proposition of the philosophy of mathematics by means of a mathematical premise. But neither implies directly and unaided, although both are constitutive. Hence, in any given case the problem is to find the locus of disagreement in one of the three possibilities and proceed accordingly.

Having come this far we might do well to let the matter rest. Unfortunately, although containing some truth, it is all too simple as stated. Some questions will bring forth this fact. What is meant by disagreement in mathematics? Is just any kind relevant? Do metaphysics and mathematics equally constitute the philosophy of mathematics? In what sense does each contribute? Is there any significance in the name "philosophy of mathematics"? Why not call it "mathematical philosophy" or the "mathematics of philosophy"? Are all three possibilities of disagreement equally likely? Or is one always basic and essential?

We must proceed cautiously here, and also with some difficulty and risk of misunderstanding. The difficulty is that the distinctions that have been made are confused so often that unless they are very consciously kept in mind it is almost impossible to avoid misunderstanding. We shall show that disagreements in the philosophy of mathematics are essentially metaphysical disagreements, and only mathematical in appearance. There are metaphysical disagreements that arise from coming to grips directly with metaphysical problems. Then there are those metaphysical disagreements that are occasioned by asking certain questions about the content of nonmetaphysical disciplines. This does not mean that there are not genuine disagreements in mathematics. But insofar as they are purely mathematical they are not relevant to the philosophy of mathematics. Therein lies the negative freedom (free *from* metaphysics) of the positive scientist. Such problems as whether a theorem "follows" from the axioms, the test for the independence of axioms in a postulate system, are mathematical. They are not directly involved in the philosophy of mathematics. This is sometimes obscured by the fact that the term "foundations of mathematics" is applied both to the problems of the philosophy of mathematics and to fundamental mathematical problems.

Also to be remembered is the fact of the great amount of

agreement to be found in any positive science. It is this that comprises most of the material in textbooks, however advanced. For example, the student of calculus learns Rolle's Theorem, Taylor's Theorem, and many others. There are no disagreements and no philosophical problems. Furthermore, when he begins his study he does not encounter such terms as "marks" or "strings." He learns that mathematics is concerned with quantity; that a quantity which changes is called a "variable"; that a quantity that has a fixed value is called a "constant." He is introduced to "function," "limits," "derivatives." He learns that when the difference between a variable x and a constant a becomes and remains less, in absolute value, than any preassigned positive quantity, however small, then a is the limit of the variable x; also, that $a-x$ is an "infinitesimal." He then learns the theorems about the properties of limits. He has been studying mathematics as a positive science. It has all been quite clear, and this is made apparent by its continual usefulness in engineering.

Let us suppose now that the student loses his original innocence through asking questions. What is a limit? What is the "meaning" of mathematical infinity? He turns to books on "the philosophy of mathematics" and finds that mathematicians and/or philosophers disagree. Now he is introduced to such terms as "intuitionism" and "formalism," "logistic," as well as "class," "aggregate," and other terms. In one system there are transfinite aggregates, and in another "infinity" is something like a law of construction. Thus, he comes to the two positions we used as examples.

Is the problem still mathematical? That depends upon what the problem is. What is mathematical infinity? The answer is that it has one meaning if certain axioms and definitions are used and it means something else in terms of different axioms and definitions. That is the answer from the standpoint of mathematics as a positive science. But what about the *existence* of mathematical entities? The answer is that in one system an entity exists only if it can be constructed; in another if it can be constructed and its nonexistence is inconsistent.

But which answer is *true?* Which is the real meaning of

mathematical infinity? Of existence? And not just relative to a system. What the question is about now is the truth of the axioms themselves. Mathematics must be true to something. The problem here is a philosophical one; and metaphysics is determining when such predicates as "truth," "existence," and "real" are used. The responsibility cannot be avoided by any verbal trick. What is asked for is not some meta-language that may prove useful for certain purposes.

Are there, then, two different meanings of such terms as "infinity" and "existence," the one mathematical and the other metaphysical? If so, then we have the possibility of conflict. It will be said that metaphysics won the "battle" in the past, but mathematics is winning today. Of course, this is nonsense. If there is conflict and war it is within the soul of the scholar or, unfortunately, between men whose motives are questionable. The positive scientist has a certain freedom in experimenting with "working hypotheses." If the experimental physicist wishes to define "thing" as a "set of dispositional properties," in the belief that it will prove "useful," then he is free to do so. It was a grave error and a tragedy for scholarship when certain people thought that it was the function of metaphysics to protest this freedom, a kind not allowed to the metaphysician. What one has a right to protest against is the abuse of the freedom when the physicist says that this is what a "thing" really is, and that some traditional notion is refuted and proved false by the new physics. He is transcending physics, making a meta-physical statement, and assuming that it is proved by "physics." A good physicist has become a poor philosopher.

And so the mathematician has a freedom. He can take infinity to be a law or a kind of aggregate. Why can't he? Or better, why shouldn't he? It may be said that if he knew enough metaphysics he would not choose the latter. Perhaps so. But is one speaking of the present, or historically? If of the present, we are inclined to agree. But if one is speaking historically it is somewhat irrelevant to regret the fact that mathematicians have not been omniscient, that in exploring the details of quantity they have come up with results not always conformable with being. The error to protest against is not that which naturally flows from his freedom, but the kind of error that comes from its abuse, viz., when by arbitrary fiat he makes metaphysical the axioms and nominal definitions of a system constructed through postulational techniques. As a man he may be both mathematician and philosopher of mathematics, but he makes a serious error when he thinks that the difference between the two disciplines, and the evidence relevant to each, is a function of his "interests."

It has been pointed out that it is useful and a good "working" approach, to consider quantity in abstraction from being, although the end is to know quantitative being. What is wrong is to reify what can only be a distinction of reason. "Being" and "quantity" are not co-ordinate categories representing something which lie in juxtaposition to each other. If this is not clear in the mind of the mathematician the means and end (mathematics and the philosophy of mathematics) will become confused, with the result that he will not understand what evidence is relevant to each, what proves what. "Intuitionism" and "Formalism," for example, are not names of strict mathematical positions, but of positions in the philosophy of mathematics. Although Mr. Kattsoff, to whom reference has already been made, speaks quite to the contrary at times, he does admit the following: "The amazing thing about the Intuitionist-Formalist controversy is that it is really a problem not solvable mathematically, but logically and epistemologically." [13] We may overlook for the moment the use of the terms "logic" and "epistemology." What is of interest to note is the admission, and also that it is "amazing" that a philosophical problem is a philosophical problem!

In system *X* infinity is an entity, but only within the system. What infinity is, is what the system defines it to be. But it is metaphysics and not the system that determines what kind of being or existence it has. This follows from the nature of a positive science. In system *Y* infinity is a rule. The mathematical problem is finished, so to speak. If we say system *X* is true, i.e., it conforms to being, then it is because a metaphysical position is presupposed—let us say, nominalism. If realism is assumed, then system *Y* may be asserted as true. *X* implies nominalism (if it does, and for illustration we are so assuming) in the sense that it conforms to that view of being. *Y* implies realism for the same reason. But there must be independent evidence for the metaphysical position presupposed.

A final question may be asked. If propositions of both mathematics and metaphysics constitute the evidence for a proposition of the philosophy of mathematics, then why should the latter be more determining than the former? Since it is granted that neither mathematics nor metaphysics is constitutive of the other, it would seem that they share equally in determining the philosophy of mathematics. And so, again, is not the preference arbitrary, whether to change the metaphysics to conform to a mathematical system, or select the mathematical system to conform to the metaphysical? Have we not said that both are means to the philosophy of mathematics, and are not means always subject to change?

The term "means" is likely to obscure the relationship in the question. It is not like a social policy. Metaphysics is a means only for the logic of the argument we were trying to demonstrate, for one of the two premises required for a conclusion in the philosophy of mathematics is metaphysical. But a more relevant answer is that we are trying to know quantitative being, not "beingtative quantity," to coin a phrase. In the very effort to make being adjectival to quantity we are forced to create nonsense syllables. This is what we might expect, for the ultimate in nonsense is created when we make being a mode, and a mode being. Of course, a mode of being is a kind of being, but is not wholly identical with it.

Also a careful observation of arguments leading to conclusions in the philosophy of mathematics will disclose the fact that the middle terms are primarily metaphysical and not mathematical notions. The illustrations we have used have been too simplified to show this. Yet, in one example it was "quantity" that was the middle term. "Quantity" is a metaphysical (predicamental) category which is the foundation of mathematics. "Number" is primarily a mathematical notion. They are not on the same co-ordinate level. There is number because there is quantitative being, and not conversely. Therefore, the philosophy of mathematics is essentially philosophy and not mathematics, just as, for example, the philosophy of history is essentially philosophical. If the middle terms were mathematical (which, of course, is impossible), then we should have instead of the philosophy of mathematics something called the "mathematics of philosophy" or "mathematical philosophy." Taken literally, the "mathematics of metaphysics" has as much and no more meaning than "German race" or "perfumed triangle."

It is understandable, then, and not at all "amazing," why such problems as give rise to the names "Formalism" and "Intuitionism" are to be solved by coming to grips primarily with metaphysics. Mathematics creates the problems of the philosophy of mathematics; it cannot alone solve them. Without the metaphysical a person is doomed either to skepticism or to endless conjecture and commentary. Once this latter road is taken, the road to nonbeing, he must condemn that which is ever the judge of him. He must identify nonsense with sense, foolishness with wisdom, after having made a mode being, and being a mode. In fact, anything can happen, for there is nothing to stop the arbitrary will and interests that motivate, except perhaps fatigue, despair, or a lack of imagination.

However, the consistent nihilist is probably but a convenient fiction, a sort of philosophical asymptote toward which the curve of error moves. He who lives and writes is more likely than not to be simply confused. We have made a careful distinction between problems of the philosophy of mathematics, and the problem of the nature of the philosophy of mathematics as a kind of knowledge. Our concern has been with the latter, which is one of the order of knowledge. It has been pointed out that if there is unclarity about the nature of the kind of knowledge with which one is dealing, then that will be reflected in the pursuit of that kind of knowledge itself. If so, the solution is to clarify the order of knowledge. Confusion is only increased by supposing that endless manipulation of the concepts of the kind of knowledge in question can ever solve this kind of problem.

No better example of such confusion can be found than in

the following quotation from Bertrand Russell's *Introduction to Mathematical Philosophy:*

> Much of what is set forth in the following chapters is not properly to be called "philosophy," though the matters concerned were included in philosophy so long as no satisfactory science of them existed. The nature of infinity and continuity, for example, belonged in former days to philosophy, but belongs now to mathematics. Mathematical *philosophy,* in the strict sense, cannot, perhaps, be held to include such definite scientific results as have been obtained in this region; the philosophy of mathematics will naturally be expected to deal with questions on the frontier of knowledge, as to which comparative certainty is not yet attained. But speculation on such questions is hardly likely to be fruitful unless the more scientific parts of the principles of mathematics are known. A book dealing with those parts may, therefore, claim to be an *introduction* to mathematical philosophy, though it can hardly claim, except where it steps outside its province, to be actually dealing with a part of philosophy. It does deal, however, with a body of knowledge which, to those who accept it, appears to invalidate much traditional philosophy . . .[14]

Here in six sentences we have the purpose of a book defined. And yet it would be difficult to find anywhere six successive sentences that contain as many and as varied an assortment of errors. But the whole purpose of giving the quotation would be lost if it were thought that any of them were propositions of the philosophy of mathematics. He is talking *about* it, and hence the errors are those concerned with the order of knowledge. Those of the philosophy of mathematics, with which we are not now directly concerned, are derivative.

It will be sufficient by this time to give but a few hints as to what is involved in each sentence.

First and second sentences. By refusing to consider subject matter, that in terms of which a distinction can be made, the appearance can be created that philosophy and mathematics do the same thing, but mathematics does it better. The second sentence isn't even a proposition. Unqualified "infinity," as it is used, "belongs" to no knowledge whatsoever. The mathematician, natural scientist, and theologian may each be concerned with infinity in some respect.

Third sentence. Mr. Russell does not know whether he intends to talk about the "philosophy of mathematics" or "mathematical philosophy." If there is other than a linguistic difference, the latter is a nonsense phrase, as was shown.

Fourth sentence. Here we have the notion that mathematics is to prove something "philosophical." By "speculation" the philosopher tries to figure out what the mathematician is doing!

Fifth sentence. It is somewhat of a mystery how a book on mathematical philosophy can be philosophical only when it no longer deals with mathematical philosophy. The comment on the third sentence is relevant here.

Sixth sentence. What Mr. Russell really does is to posit a nontraditional philosophy and "interpret" mathematics accordingly. The mathematics is then said to be evidence for what was arbitrarily posited!

This confusion in his Preface on the matter of the order of knowledge is so great that immediately following it there is an "Editor's Note" on the terms "mathematical philosophy" and "philosophy of mathematics." The gist of it is that it is all rather unclear, that what Mr. Russell intends to talk about must be "the business of somebody," and that perhaps he knows what he is doing. At any rate, the distinction between mathematics and philosophy is clear in Mr. Russell's mind. On the second page we are informed that:

> The distinction between mathematics and mathematical philosophy is one which depends upon the interest inspiring the research, and upon the stage which the research has reached; not upon the propositions with which the research is concerned.[15]

Since mathematical philosophy is for him the same as the philosophy of mathematics, what he is saying is that the difference between mathematics and the philosophy of mathematics is a function of Mr. Russell's "interests" and "inspiration."

At this point intelligible communication ends on the order of knowledge. But such subjectivism does make understandable many things that are said. Anything can happen. Something called "epistemology" becomes a substitute for metaphysics. Existence is derived from "truth," and not conversely. Propositional functions, bare contentless forms, are "sometimes true." Were it not for the phenomenon of hermaphroditism, which might throw doubt on the principle of "excluded middle," Mr. Russell in his mathematical logic might just as well have used "male" and "female" as "true" and "false." In turn, the meaning of implication is reduced to that of disjunction: "The fact that 'implies' is capable of other meanings does not concern us; this is the meaning which is convenient for us." [16] The justification for this criterion of "convenience" is this: "Provided our use of words is consistent, it matters little how we define them." [17]

It is by this means and in this manner that Mr. Russell hopes to investigate "the traditional problems of philosophy," those which have been left to the metaphysician whose mental life is "foggy" like "that of children and animals." [18] It must be admitted that after four decades it is somewhat clear what is meant. At least the alternatives are understood.

8

Experimental Science as Knowledge

Experimental science is the name given to that kind of knowledge which has as its purpose the seeking of true generalizations. A generalization is a proposition that is descriptive, is general rather than singular, and constitutes one of the two domains of the phenomenological context. The object of experimental science is the "mobile" of mobile being insofar as there are regularities and uniformities. In contrast to history, which seeks to reconstruct the uniqueness of events, experimental science is concerned with repeatable associations of events. Whether a generalization is to be taken in an extensional or intensional manner is not relevant to the definition. The phenomenological context is a primitive notion as we are using it. It is the context of spatio-temporal phenomena, of that the description of which will be made in terms of concepts that fall under the "categories," Aristotelian or their equivalent in non-Aristotelian terms. As has been pointed out before, the term "descriptive" is to be thought of in its broadest sense, and is to be contrasted with "prescriptive" and "evaluational," not with "explanatory." Also, the terms "experimental science" and "natural science" have often been used interchangeably. For the purpose of economy this has been, and still is, convenient. We shall see later that they are not quite the same.

Historical Propositions as Evidence for Generalizations

Nature is neither an undifferentiated continuum, a homogeneous "blur," nor is it a chaos of particulars. Every event, thing, and property is unique. But there are also common features which may be described in terms of qualities and relations. These are the subject matter of generalizations. The "data" for generalizations are "facts." The latter term is used equivocally. Sometimes the conclusions or central propositions of a theory will be called "facts." As used here the more basic meaning is referred to, namely, what from the standpoint of the order of knowledge can be expressed as historical propositions. A historical proposition is singular, of the phenomenological context, and is descriptive of uniqueness. "Uniqueness" is to be contrasted with "generality," or "universality."

The data for experimental science are facts, but facts as expressed in historical propositions. There are no primitive forms for these facts other than those expressible in terms of historical propositions. Such historical propositions, as we have already shown, may be descriptive of immediate experience or of immediate experience as interpreted. Examples of such propositions are: "This is red," meaning "I am now (at a given date) having an experience of red"; "This (with a given referent) is an electron" (or, more exactly, "a photograph of an electron"); "This is potassium"; "This pointer-reading is 10." It may be well to point out again that "This book is red" and "I am now experiencing redness" are both historical propositions. The fact that one is descriptive of immediate experience, while the other proposition presumes to be descriptive of something independent of human experience, does not make any difference so far as the type of proposition is concerned. Both are descriptive of uniqueness, although the reference of one is subjective and of the other is objective.

Historical propositions are not merely instrumental to generalizations as they are to metaphysical propositions. Rather they constitute generalizations. "Generalizations presuppose historical propositions" here means that historical propositions are *constitutive of* generalizations. According to the meaning of "constitutive of" as already defined, for a given generalization to be true some *specific* historical propositions must be true. If the specific historical propositions are false, then the generalization is false. The question now arises as to whether historical propositions are sufficient as well as necessary as evidence for generalizations.

In saying that historical propositions are sufficient as evidence for generalizations we are simply referring to the well-recognized principle that all natural science ultimately rests upon "brute fact." This principle has been stated in many ways. If it is said that in the long run it is good scientific methodology always to modify scientific theories in the light of facts rather than to discard facts in order to uphold a given scientific theory, then what is said is simply that the facts expressed by the historical propositions are ultimately determining so far as the truth of generalizations is concerned. In our own terminology the principle could be rephrased as follows: Good methodology in the experimental science demands that in the long run theory should be changed in accordance with newly discovered facts expressed in terms of historical propositions; therefore, they are not only necessary, but also sufficient to establish the truth of generalizations. Mathematical, metaphysical, and even theological propositions may be instrumental to the search for true generalizations, but in no case can they possibly be constitutive as evidence. An experimental scientist may have metaphysical reasons or even theological reasons for his search for true generalizations, but it is impossible for such metaphysical or theological propositions to constitute even part of the evidence for any generalization. Also, the fact that the experimental scientist may use the propositions of mathematics does not mean that they constitute, even in part, evidence for the truth of any generalization. Undoubtedly it is the case that without some real, formal relations, there could not be generalizations. But the point here to be made is that whether any generalization is true or false is to be determined on other grounds than those which determine truth about formal relations. Mathematics may be useful in discovering the habits of nature because nature exemplifies the formal relations of a mathematical system, but what habit or habits nature has cannot be determined by any amount of knowledge of formal relations.

From the standpoint of the order of being it may be said that without the ontological neither the generalizations nor historical propositions would be possible. It does not follow, however, that in the order of knowing the ontological is constitutive as evidence for generalizations. To illustrate: From the truth that God created the world, and hence the actual order of nature from among possible orders, there is no enlightenment as to *what* that order is. The latter may be discovered whether or not one believes in God. This fact constitutes the element of truth in the statement attributed to Laplace, that experimental science has no need for God.

In any experimental science the aim is that of the coherence of a system. The coherence of a generalization with a system will be one test of its truth. This principle does not alter the fact that only historical propositions are constitutive, for every generalization with which a given generalization is consistent must itself rest ultimately upon historical propositions as evidence. Were this not so, then a generalization would become merely a theorem in a deductive system. Coherence implies not merely formal consistency, but also consistency with "facts" expressed in terms of historical propositions.

Actually there is an "interplay" between historical propositions and generalizations such that each is evidence for the other. However, in case of incompatibility between a generalization and a historical proposition, priority always must be given ultimately to the latter. That this must be so is easily understood. To know how it works in practice one would have to consider the logic (or technique) of experimental procedure. The key generalization *X* of a theory may be incompatible with certain historical propositions *a, b,* and *c* that have been found through experiment. If the incompatibility is genuine and does not turn out to be misconceived, then there are only two alternatives. (1) The generalization *X* is given up or modified. (2) The generalization *X* is held in spite of the incompatibility. Good experimental procedure demands, ultimately, the first alternative. But the second alternative may be a good procedure in the short run. It may be sensible, conservative experimental procedure to question the truth of facts expressed in terms of some historical propositions rather than to relinquish an apparently well-grounded generalization.

This conservative procedure is constantly practiced by the working scientist. A good example would be the use of the key generalization of Mendeleev's theory, that the properties of elements are periodic functions of their atomic weights. For some time after 1869 this generalization was incompatible with some "facts" presumably known. Rather than give up the generalization the "facts" were reinvestigated and found to be incorrect. It is only "in the long run" that historical propositions take priority as evidence over generalizations.

For other than the most primitive historical propositions resting upon intuitions, generalizations are necessary as evidence for the very historical propositions which also constitute evidence for *other* generalizations. This is the case because without uniformities in nature there could not be uniqueness; or to put it in another way, unless some properties were repeated there could not be any properties, and hence no world of nature at all.

Without the non-unique even the unique could not be known. By way of passing, we may note that this is true even in the ontological context. A miracle is a unique event, but without a world in which a miracle did not take place there could be no miracle. In other words, in the order of knowledge without the metaphysical there could not be the theological. Although the unique and the non-unique may be distinguished, that does not mean that they can be separated in fact or even in knowledge. A historical proposition such as "This is a meteorite" cannot be demonstrated without other propositions about the nature of matter.

Generalizations are partially constitutive of some, not all, historical propositions. Generalizations are necessary to establish knowledge of "history." History is that kind of knowledge in which the uniqueness of past events relevant to human affairs is the end to be sought. In seeking knowledge of human history part of the evidence of the specific activities and motives of historical characters rests upon assumptions as to how human beings generally act in given situations. Therefore, without the assumption that certain generalizations are true, propositions dealing with the reconstruction of historical events could not be obtained.

However, generalizations are not sufficient as evidence for historical propositions. This principle simply means that there is a brute-factness to events that cannot be exhausted by generalizations. Any event or act precisely because it exists is unique. There are generalizations because there are unique events. There are not unique events because there are uniformities in the world. Were it otherwise, nature would be a blur, or equivalent to nothing at all. Nature would be pure homogeneity and pure undifferentiation. Nature would be at best merely the matter of Plato without form, or Hegel's pure abstract being which equals nothing. It is for these reasons that there must be certain primitive historical propositions, the truth of which is immediately evident.

The manner in which a "fact" and a generalization may conflict. The fact that historical propositions ("facts") constitute evidence for generalizations is somewhat elementary. What it is important to understand is how they do so, the manner in which the one is evidence for the other. It is on this that confusion and misunderstanding arises. Clarity on this manner may be obtained through the concept of "incompatibility," which we have already used.

Whenever one type of proposition is evidence for another type there is the possibility of incompatibility. There are only two conditions under which historical propositions and generalizations can conflict.

(1) A class of historical propositions can conflict with a generalization.

(2) If the quantifier "all" of the subject of a generalization is taken literally, then it is possible that a historical proposition may be incompatible with the generalization. In the absence of these two conditions there can be no conflict between historical propositions and generalizations.

Given a series of events, there can be no generalization about them from the standpoint of their uniqueness. Consider the proposition "All social revolutions have idealistic beginnings."

It may be that on further study the historian might find some one social revolution that does not have an idealistic beginning. In this case, the original generalization would have to be modified quantitatively. Instead of saying "all," one would have to say that social revolutions generally, or for the most part, have idealistic beginnings. With a restricted quantifier, the incompatibility is removed.

No one historical proposition can be incompatible with any generalization with a restricted quantifier. In the case of an unrestricted quantifier and incompatibility, the historical proposition has priority over the generalization. This follows from the principle that all generalizations must rest upon "facts."

The question may be asked whether, for the propositions of the experimental sciences, anything more than restricted generalizations is ever necessary. If not, then it would be impossible for any one historical proposition to be incompatible with any generalization of experimental science, and hence any "law" of nature obtained by the experimental method. This would be the case if the statistical theory of generalization is held.

To illustrate the problem involved, let us consider the following example. Let us suppose that a Mr. Brown tosses a coin in the air. Instead of coming down to the floor according to the law of falling bodies, the coin does a dance in the air, sails around the room, does another erratic dance, and finally glides down to rest upon the floor. If Mr. Brown is healthy-minded, he will assume that he has had an illusion, and that the coin did not actually behave as apparently it did behave. On the other hand, if he believes that it was not an illusion, he will try to find reasons for the behavior of the coin. It might occur to him that it was a trick coin of some kind, or that someone was playing a trick upon him by causing the coin to move in the way in which it did, knowing perhaps that Mr. Brown would flip a coin in the air. Or it might even occur to him to investigate possible sudden changes in the atmospheric conditions in the room or wind currents. What Mr. Brown would do first, however, is throw the coin into the air again to see if the same strange behavior occurred. Now, let us assume that it does not occur again. No matter how often Mr. Brown throws the coin into the air, it behaves normally. After having eliminated the possibility of wind currents, atmospheric conditions, and so on, as accounting for such behavior, Mr. Brown would probably come to the conclusion that it was an illusion after all. His problem would shift from that of accounting for the behavior of the coin to that of attempting to account for the fact that he had such an illusion. As we have said, Mr. Brown is healthy-minded. He would probably accept the hypothesis of illusion and visit his family doctor!

There is, however, one other possible explanation, and that is that the coin actually behaved the way it seemed to behave. If such a hypothesis were considered, then there could be only two explanations. The behavior of the coin might be said to be an uncaused event, contrary to the usual behavior of natural objects, or the behavior is a caused event. The difficulty with the first explanation is that it is no explanation at all; it is really the kind of answer that one might give in absence of any rational explanation. If the second alternative is taken, namely, that there was some cause for such behavior, then the cause is either natural or supernatural. If the event was caused naturally, then it can be explained according to the uniformities of nature. We have already assumed that no uniformities of nature or natural laws known by man can account for such behavior. Mr. Brown, then, is left with the explanation that it was either caused by some act of spontaneity of nature or that it was a supernatural event, and hence a miracle.

The point to be made here is that even if the coin actually behaved in the way in which it apparently behaved, the proposition cannot be considered incompatible with Newton's formulation of the law of gravitation. The law still holds. It still holds true that natural phenomena occur according to the law of gravitation as described by the physicist's formula. Hence, it is possible to hold that the historical proposition is true and can be explained as a miracle, and yet have no incompatibility between this proposition and a law of natural science. It is still possible, at least theoretically, for Mr. Brown as well as his scientific colleagues to hold to the conclusion that the behavior of the coin was normal and that what was perceived was an illusion. Even though the coin really behaved in such a strange manner and its behavior really was a miracle, it would still be possible to hold the hypothesis that there was an illusion. Furthermore, whether it did or did not behave in such a strange manner, it would still be the case that the principle of gravitation is *generally* truly descriptive of the behavior of natural objects.

The only way in which Mr. Brown and his scientific colleagues can hold that the law of gravitation is incompatible with the historical propositions describing the uniqueness of the strange event is to say that the law of gravitation is not merely descriptive of the way in which natural phenomena usually behave, but is also prescriptive and defines the way such a phenomenon must behave. However, such an interpretation of the law of gravitation would have to be made on metaphysical grounds. The experimental method by which the propositions of physics are obtained can never demonstrate the metaphysical necessity of the law obtained. Such a method can demonstrate with some degree of plausibility that this or that in fact happens, or that in general a given type of object behaves in this or that manner. But the experimental method never demonstrates that a given material phenomenon *must* occur. It is generally the case that unsupported objects fall toward the earth. This is the most that the method of experimental science can demonstrate. A generalization is descriptive of contingent reality. The moment one leaps from contingency to necessity one has jumped from the phenomenological context to the ontological context. If the experimental scientist wishes to interpret the law of gravitation as prescribing the limits of possibility, then he may do so; but if he does so, he must make his assertion as a metaphysician and not as an experimental scientist.

If one historical proposition cannot be incompatible with a generalization, it is nevertheless true that a class of historical propositions *as a class* may be incompatible with a generalization. If, for example, to use the illustration, Mr. Brown, after repeatedly throwing the coin in the air, were to discover the conditions under which such apparently strange behavior occurs, then undoubtedly his discovery would be of interest to his scientific colleagues. If he were to go to his fellow physicists and tell them of the strange behavior of the coin, and on being requested to show them exactly what he did and to produce the same phenomenon again, he tried to do so and failed, then his scientific colleagues, being healthy skeptics and hence good experimental scientists, would immediately dismiss the act of the behavior of the coin either as a joke or as an illusion.

On the other hand, if Mr. Brown could describe clearly and exactly the conditions under which the strange behavior of the coin took place, and write up the matter carefully and have it published in a scientific journal, and other physicists over the world having read the article and having duplicated the same conditions would find that the same behavior as he describes takes place, then, of course, the situation as regards the respectability of Mr. Brown as a scientist would be quite different. Undoubtedly, some modification of the law of gravitation would be necessary, and Mr. Brown would go down in history as a great scientist. But the evidence that would require the modification of the law of gravitation is something more than *one* historical proposition. It is a class of historical propositions. A sum of historical propositions constitutes the data: this coin behaved in such and such a manner; that coin behaved in a similar manner; this coin in a similar manner; and so on.

When we say that one fact can disprove a scientific generalization, whereas a number of facts must constitute positive evidence for the generalization, we speak somewhat inexactly. The "one" fact that is necessary to disconfirm a generalization is not one historical proposition, even though that one historical proposition may be factually true. The "fact" necessary to disconfirm a generalization is not simple, but rather complex. It is the complex fact described by a class of historical propositions, each proposition as a member of the class describing in its own way some particular fact.

In the case of incompatibility between a class of historical propositions and a generalization, the class of historical propositions has priority. Once again, this is a recognition of the principle that if generalizations are to be descriptive of natural phenomena, the descriptive propositions must rest upon the simple facts of nature; otherwise a generalization could never be disconfirmed or confirmed.

To sum up, only a class of historical propositions can be incompatible with a generalization. On the other hand, no one historical proposition as such can be incompatible with a restricted generalization. Both could be false, although evidence may show the one to be true and the other false. However, it is theoretically possible for both to be true.

There is another way of handling this problem. Let us suppose that one insists that a generalization means "all," and that "some" merely refers to a summation of historical propositions and cannot be a quantifier of a real generalization. In this case one historical proposition could be incompatible with the generalization. Now one has the right to so insist only if responsibility as to implications is accepted. Let us consider the alternative.

The generalization will be interpreted either extensionally or intensionally. If the latter, then either there is evidence for it or there is not. If there is no evidence, then there is no problem. Its *a priori* nature is postulated, is merely imposed temporarily by the mind for *methodological* purposes. If there is evidence for its intensional interpretation, then the evidence cannot be merely from historical propositions, but must be metaphysical. The proposition ceases to be *merely* a generalization, and becomes a proposition of the "philosophy of nature"—as we shall see later when we study the nature of the latter discipline. In this case, then, the proposition would have to be challenged on metaphysical grounds; one historical proposition would still not be sufficient.

If the generalization is to be taken extensionally, and also as unrestricted, then it is necessary that the assumption be made that reference is only to events having purely natural causes. If this assumption is not understood, then one would in effect be taking the generalization intensionally and *arbitrarily* eliminating the possibility of one unique supernatural event which may also be historical. Whether or not there are such events is another matter. The point is that from the standpoint of the experimental scientist *qua* experimental scientist such a question is not within his jurisdiction. It is one on which he must remain agnostic, although as a *man* he may not do so.

The explanation of the *manner in which* historical propositions can and cannot be evidence for generalizations has now been given. It was the misunderstanding of this relation of evidence which has been partly responsible for untold confusion in relating such kinds of knowledge as experimental science and theology, thus giving rise in modern times to such pseudo-problems as the "warfare between science and theology." There can be warfare only when either or both are wrongly conceived.

Historical propositions wholly constitute generalizations. This inductive analysis of the relation between historical propositions and generalizations can now be expressed more formally in terms of the "constitutive" relation. Let "H" stand for "historical" propositions, "G" for generalizations, "g_1" for a specific generalization, and "h_1," "h_2," for specific historical propositions. Let us remember that "historical propositions" and "history" cannot be identified. Historians seek historical propositions, but if one seeks historical propositions, that does not necessarily define the historian. He seeks only a certain kind.

"H is wholly constitutive of G" means that "G presupposes (implies) H"; hence, "if G, then H." Or

(1) If g_1, then (h_1 and h_2 and h_3) . . . h_n

The parentheses denote a class of historical propositions. The unique case of "wholly constitutive" may now be stated. "Type *B* knowledge presupposes type *A* knowledge" means that "*A* is wholly constitutive of *B*" if the truth of a specific proposition of *B* requires the assertion of a class of propositions of *A*. "*A*" can only refer to historical propositions, "*B*" only to generalizations.

The so-called problem of induction arises because historical propositions *wholly* constitute generalizations. It is to be observed that whereas from a purely formal standpoint we can assert the antecedent of (1), nevertheless we can never really do so *because there is no evidence independent of the consequent which would allow one to do so.* Of course, what actually happens in practice is that the evidence is split up. The explanation has often been as follows. Some particular facts (h_7, h_8,

h_9 . . .) are observed. This gives rise to a generalization. Then one reasons that if the generalization, g_1, is true, then certain other facts (h_1, h_2, . . .) are true. The latter facts, if found to be true, then confirm g_1. This is all quite correct. However, the facts that give rise to g_1 and those that confirm it, constitute one and the same *kind* of evidence, such that logically the two sets of facts may be interchanged. They are but parts of the total sum expressed in the consequent of (1)—"h_1, h_2, . . . h_n."

If there are no grounds, independent of the consequent of (1), for asserting the antecedent, then where do we look for evidence? Only to the consequent, which we assert, and having done so we assert the antecedent. But logically this cannot be done. Hence we have the strange situation in which there are no (material) grounds for asserting what is (formally) logically permitted, and, on the other hand, where there are such grounds an assertion is logically prohibited. This predicament makes for the "problem" of induction—for which one must turn to metaphysics, since formal logic alone is not sufficient—and also partly explains why experimental science is experimental, or at least not wholly deductive. What creates the predicament is the fact that the relation of H to G is that of "*wholly* constitutive." The only way out is the one that is taken. The relation of "wholly constitutive" allows (1) to be converted by weakening both the antecedent and the consequent. We affirm the antecedent and assert not that g_1 *is* the case, but that *probably* it is. We can do this because the conversion—allowed not formally, but by the constitutive relation—gives us the following:

(2) If (h_1, h_2, h_3, . . .), then (probably) g_1.

Whereas in (1) the truth of g_1 presupposes an indefinite extension, in (2) the extension—except in perfect enumeration—must always be definite and limited, and hence also the consequent limited to "probable."

Some questions and explanations are now relevant at this point. Has our explanation not been too "empirical"? What of the confirming ability of a "powerful deduction"? Of theory? This is to be admitted, but is not relevant to the issue. Many generalizations can "strengthen" another, but they all rest ultimately upon "facts," historical propositions.

It has often been said that it is "easier" to be certain that a generalization is false than it is to be certain that it is true. The plausibility of this statement lies in the fact that the predicament of which we spoke does not hold if the consequent of (1) is denied, for in this case the (material) grounds for the denial happen to conform to what is also permitted (formally) logically. No further comment is necessary on the fact that it is a class of historical propositions that must be denied. Also, in (2), what gives probability is a class, not just one "h."

But what of the single "fact" that leads to a great discovery —e.g., Newton seeing the apple fall? The answer is that the single fact is actually a class of facts. The particular apple that presumably Newton saw falling represented for him a class of such objects falling. The *one* occurrence of the apple falling, *in itself and alone,* was not sufficient evidence. But it was *instrumental* to leading Newton to raise questions about a whole class of similar events, and thence to the discovery of the law of gravitation.

In seeking generalizations experimental science, by its very nature, is interested chiefly in repeatable phenomenon—or, more exactly, in the common features of unique events, since every event is unique. In the words of Mr. A. Castell, for a generalization "the evidence is always a repetition of particular instances or cases." The evidence is composed, not of a variety of facts (historical propositions) converging on another (historical proposition), but of repetitions of the same fact in different contexts.[1] We can now better understand what the "same fact" means, namely, a class of historical propositions.

The working scientist understands fairly well the demands of experimentation, that only phenomena that are repeatable, potentially or actually, can be the subject of study. Mr. Norman Campbell, in his *What Is Science?,* speaks as follows:

> The evidence for the invariable density of a new compound is not the single measurement of it, but the general law that all densi-

ties have invariable properties. This law is established by the observation, not of a single instance or of one or two, but of a very large number of instances, in none of which the relation has been found to fail.[2]

In describing the methodology of experimental science A. D'Abro says: "History tells us of events past and gone which, for all we care, may never reoccur; but in science a phenomenon which could never occur again would be of little interest." [3] Henri Poincaré also contrasts history and experimental science in the following way:

> Carlyle has written somewhere something after this fashion. "Nothing but facts are of importance. John Lackland passed by here. Here is something that is admirable. Here is a reality for which I would give all the theories in the world." . . . But Bacon would not have said that. That is the language of the historian. The physicist would most likely have said: "John Lackland passed by here. It is all the same to me, for he will not pass this way again." [4]

The historian finds generalizations necessary in order to discover and reconstruct the uniqueness of past events that are of particular relevance to human affairs. The experimental scientist finds it necessary to use historical propositions relevant to the particular subject matter he is studying in order to arrive at generalizations. It is for this reason that experiment is necessary in the latter case, while history is nonexperimental. The techniques of the historian and the experimental scientist cannot be the same.

We may now state formally the constitutive relation between generalizations and historical propositions. Generalizations only partially constitute evidence for historical propositions. "H presupposes G" may be expressed as

(3) If h_1, then g_1 *and* h_x.

In (3) "h" can stand for any historical proposition, including those sought for by the historian. Hence, the generalizations of science constitute part of the evidence of historical truth. When the historical propositions are not the kind the historian seeks, but are those which constitute facts for the experimental scientist, then it is readily understood how a generalization may constitute evidence for a fact.

The relation is that of "partially constitutive" because ultimately facts check generalizations, and not conversely, although there is an interplay of evidence between them. Second, two kinds of knowledge cannot each be wholly constitutive of the other, for otherwise they would be the same kind of knowledge. Third, in the definition of this kind of relation we have already seen that some other factor is involved. The definition was stated for a synthetic science, and we spoke of the other constitutive factor as "type C" knowledge. In the case of a non-synthetic discipline such as history, or even the "facts" which constitute data for experimental science, there is no other kind of knowledge. It is for this reason that we have denoted the other constitutive factor by "h_x," which may stand for a primitive historical proposition, or a complex one, the evidence for which may consist of other historical propositions and generalizations.

Since a complete analysis of the nature of history is not part of the present volume we must be content at present merely to point out that this must be so. The reference is of course to history as a phenomenological discipline, as a positive science, not to the philosophy of history, which is a synthetic science. In "historical criticism" part of the content of "h_x" would be the brute fact nature of what is reported by some "witness." In passing we may observe that the denial of the "h_x" factor would be equivalent to the reduction of history to an experimental science. Since this is rationally impossible, it must be done arbitrarily. The arbitrariness lies in the postulation of (usually) some kind of naturalism which supposedly implies that the only method of obtaining any kind of knowledge is by something called the "scientific method."

In (1) we saw that while we were formally permitted to assert the antecedent, there were no material grounds, independent of the consequent, for doing so. By contrast, in (3), while we are formally allowed to deny the consequent, there are no material grounds for doing so. Of course part of the consequent can be denied, namely, g_1. But the "h_x" factor cannot be denied on material grounds independent of h_1. Translated into simpler terms this means—what we have already explained—that in experimental science, in case of an incompatibility between a fact and a generalization *ultimately* the former has priority. The relevance of this for history as a positive discipline is this, that however much the evidence from experimental science may be for some historical propositions, such evidence can never be conclusive, can never be absolute. In other words, there may be evidence for an event that happened once and only once, and which because of that very fact is not amenable to experimental disconfirmation.

We can now understand more clearly the meaning of some notions that to begin with we took as undefined, e.g., why experimental science is phenomenological and not ontological. Something may have ontological being, or be ontologically true, and yet not be amenable to the methods and techniques of experimental science. The virtue of experimental science, as with anything else, lies in its limitations. If only one person in the world had a headache, and he had it only once, such a phenomenon could not be data for experimental medicine. And yet it would be a real existing fact. To delimit reality or being or the possible in terms of what can be evidence for experimental science is not itself experimental science. It is to make a metaphysics out of one domain of the phenomenological. But to reduce being to the phenomenological is to destroy both and understand neither.

The chief experimental sciences are physics, chemistry, biology, including their many subspecies, together with psychology. It is to be noted that in two sciences, astronomy and geology, there is also a historical emphasis. Instead of stars and solar systems in general, our sun and this particular solar system may be described as an end in itself. And so with specific rock formations, and with *this* earth. This fact has no significance for the order of knowledge. It merely calls attention to what is included as content under the *names* given to various disciplines. In the historical emphasis, to use the technical language of realism, attention is on a "material" object rather than on a "formal" object. Physics and chemistry are not restricted to this or that kind of material thing; biology is not restricted to this or that living, material thing. But geology is restricted to a part of this earth; and the part is physical and not that which is obtained by "abstraction."

The Relation of Mathematics to Experimental Science

In considering the relation of mathematics to experimental science we are asking about the relation between two positive sciences. A distinction must be made between mathematics and the philosophy of mathematics, experimental science and the philosophy of nature or natural science. We shall see presently what the philosophy of nature is. It is what natural science should properly be, the science of composite beings that have "natures," the science of mobile being. But just as quantity can, for a limited purpose, be treated in abstraction from being, so can motion and change, in which case we have experimental science. And so the question before us is the relation between the positive science of quantity *qua* quantity and the science of motion *qua* motion. Is mathematics constitutive of, regulative of, or instrumental to, experimental science?

Let us take a very simple bit of reasoning in an experimental science and find out how mathematics is used. Ohm's law states a relationship among three factors in any circuit—pressure, current strength, and resistance. Let E, R, and I stand respectively for electromotive force (volts), resistance (ohms), and current strength (amperes). In terms of what is known about direct currents one can reason that since the current in any electric circuit is equal to the electromotive force applied to the circuit, divided by the resistance of the circuit, therefore the resistance required to be inserted in any circuit, so that a given current will flow by reason of a known pressure, is equal to the pressure to be applied, divided by the current that is to be maintained. Expressed symbolically the argument is that "Since $I = E/R$, therefore $R = E/I$." Now, there is a premise presupposed which makes possible the implication and inference, although it might take an additional syllogism to obtain it. It is an axiom that allows one to multiply both sides of the equation by R/I. Also presupposed is the commutative law $RI = IR$.

It may seem that we have here a case of mathematics being constitutive of a generalization of experimental science. Mathematics as constitutive of experimental science is that interpretation of "presuppose" in which "if a specific proposition of experimental science is true, then a specific mathematical proposition must be true." And is it not the case that if the generalization "R = E/I" is true, then (say) the commutative law "RI = IR" must be true? There appears to be an additional reason. We know that if type A knowledge constitutes type B knowledge, then the evidence for type A must be other than, and independent of, the evidence for type B. If this were not so, arguments would cease to be arguments and become modes of question-begging. Mathematics satisfies this criterion, for we have already seen that historical propositions and generalizations cannot constitute evidence for the propositions of mathematics.

However, the constitutive relation exists only in appearance. The complex form "RI = IR" is *used,* but what does it mean to say that it is true? Just as there are non-Euclidean geometries, so there is a noncommutative algebra. In quantum physics, if the symbol R is taken to denote the motion referred to some frame of measurement, and the symbol I denotes location also referred to a frame, and further, if the symbols are not treated as ordinary numbers but as matrices, then RI ≠ IR. Instead of the difference between RI and IR being zero, it is now equal to something, a quantity which can be identified with a quantum constant already known.[5] The physicist tells us that the commutative law is satisfactory in dealing with the macroscopic, but not always in studying the microscopic, and that since 1925 (and Heisenberg) such a fact has "revolutionized" physics. For example, the "state" of a physical system is no longer to be thought of in terms of the accurate fixing of velocities at given points, but as consisting of a definite distribution of "probability" over a whole range of possible configurations of the system. In the example of Ohm's law the commutative law was presupposed. But it is not always presupposed. Therefore, the commutative law is sometimes true, and the noncommutative law is sometimes true. The nonphysicist dares not tell the physicist that he must not use a noncommutative algebra because it is not true. For the experimental scientist, if it proves useful for the purposes of prediction, manipulation, and control, then that is sufficient. So far as he is concerned that which is useful is true. In the Ohm's law example it has been convenient to use the commutative law. But it might be the case, however unlikely, that a noncommutative algebra is used, and that the difference between RI and IR is simply neglected for practical purposes because the quantity is so small that it always is under any amount that could possibly be discovered by experiment. It may be said that $R = E/I$, but it is at least possible for either the commutative law or the noncommutative law of multiplication to be presupposed. Therefore, it cannot be argued that the former is constitutive as evidence for the generalization.

A positive science is necessarily relativistic. And this is as it should be, for it is essentially concerned with a mode of being *qua* mode. The complete meaning of truth requires the notion of "conforming with being." Because of the special kind of abstraction that defines a positive science, there is a sense in which it is not concerned with truth as is the "philosophy" of that science. More exactly, a limited meaning of truth is implied. The philosophy of mathematics is concerned with what kind of being a quantitative form is *true to*. For mathematics as positive a theorem is true if it conforms with the axioms, and the axioms may simply be postulated and need not be considered as conforming to anything, although in fact they will do so. It is in this sense that it is sometimes said, and quite correctly, that truth in mathematics is simply "consistency." In dealing with quantity *qua* quantity one cannot give the same meaning to truth as if one were dealing with quantitative being, intelligible matter. Without the "matter" one is left with pure form and with consistency among forms.

Likewise, if the "mobile" is abstracted from "mobile being," then the experimental scientist may identify the "true" with the "useful." The only error would be to insist that this is all "truth" can mean. This would imply that by pure fiat a mode is identified with being; a metaphysics is made out of the positive science, and we have a kind of positiv*ism*. It is the "philosophy of nature" that is concerned with whether the "useful" is really the "true," and for this problem something more is required than experimental science.

So far as mathematics and experimental science are concerned as such, and in abstraction from the metaphysical, it is understandable that pure consistency is not sufficient to allow a mathematical proposition to be constitutive as evidence for a generalization. From the standpoint of experimental science, different mathematical systems may each be consistent, but one is more useful than another and hence "true." From the standpoint of the philosophy of nature something is useful because it is true, and not conversely.

Before moving on we may pause to answer a question. It may be remarked that we are assuming alternative mathematical systems to be on the same co-ordinate level, as if each in itself was a genus. Actually, the mathematician is seeking unity and coherence, and he conceives these so-called alternative systems to be stages of increased generality in vertical rank. Just as the circle can be said to be a limiting case of an ellipse, so does one geometry stand in relation to another. We confess to some uncertainty in answer, partly because of the different meanings of the terms "mathematics" and "geometries" as ordinarily used. There are those who think of geometry as an empirical science. The above remarks would be true if reference is either to the philosophy of mathematics or to mathematics conceived (falsely, we believe) as an empirical science. It would still seem that mathematics as a positive science is characterized by the possibility of alternative systems in the sense we have stated.

The nonconstitutive character of mathematics in relation to experimental science is what we might have expected, for we have already discovered that historical propositions are not only necessary but also sufficient for the generalizations of experimental science. But if mathematics is not constitutive, neither is it regulative—for the latter as much as the former would require some specific mathematical proposition to be true, and known to be true and not merely consistent, on mathematical grounds alone. That mathematics is not regulative may be best understood when we see why it is instrumental to experimental science.

Type *A* knowledge as instrumental to type *B* knowledge is that interpretation of "*B* presupposes *A*" in which "if some propositions of type *B* are true, then some propositions of type *A* are true." Experimental science presupposes mathematics. If some propositions of mathematics were not true, then experimental science would be impossible. With respect to experimental science mathematics remains hypothetical; a mathematical statement is categorical only with respect to the system of which it is a part. Two mathematical systems, *X* and *Y*, may both be consistent. One, both, or neither may be exemplified in the physical world. The range of possible forms is greater than that which is actual. Whether there are physical structures which are relatively isomorphic with *Y* can only be determined by experiment. If so, then we say that *Y* "fits" the data better. The data consist of historical propositions, together with generalizations. It is these that determine that *Y* is "true" to something in the world. *Y* is selected because it is a good instrument. Good experimental procedure requires that forms be fitted to "facts," and not vice versa. Although some forms are necessary, *what* forms fit *what* is a question independent of the truth (consistency) which the forms have.

Therefore, in an argument a mathematical major premise is instrumental in obtaining a conclusion, but is not constitutive as evidence. On the other hand, in an integrative science, such as either the philosophy of mathematics or the philosophy of nature, the metaphysical major premise is not merely instrumental in obtaining a conclusion, but also partially constitutes the truth of it. *To conceive of mathematics as constitutive is equivalent to making a metaphysics out of it.* This process occurred early in modern times and has created innumerable difficulties. It has spawned philosophies which reflect the very difficulties they were created to solve. When mathematics is made a metaphysics it means in practice that the reigning mathematics becomes absolutized. With Descartes (and even earlier) the Euclidean geometry becomes metaphysical, and even has theological implications, in Newton. More recently the relativity of mathematics as a positive science has quite correctly been recognized. When made a metaphysics, in the first case we have a false absolute; in the latter the false absolute is relativized. But there is little to choose between Descartes and Jeans or Eddington.

Neither metaphysics nor mathematics is constitutive of experimental science. Metaphysics is constitutive of the "philosophy of nature," for there we understand nature in its wholeness and in its true being. Historical propositions are constitutive of the generalizations of experimental science. Mathematical propositions are *instrumental* in discovering the generalizations which are constituted by historical propositions. To make mathematics constitutive is to make what is "useful" identical with the "true." In the philosophy of nature they are more often than not found to be the same. But when by nominal definition they are so identified, then we have a kind of positivism.

Yet, is there not something incongruous about the thesis being upheld? Several questions might be raised. Do not mathematical "forms" constitute things just as much as do the metaphysical? If so, why should metaphysics be constitutive in a conclusion predicating (say) potency of things, while mathematics is said not to be constitutive of a conclusion in which (say) triangularity is predicated of things? Both kinds of arguments can be set up in terms of premises and conclusions. And in both the major premises seem to be evidence for the conclusion; otherwise there is no argument. Furthermore, does not our thesis gain whatever plausibility it may have from the specially selected examples we have used? Is not the mathematical truth that two plus two equals four as absolute as any metaphysical truth? And therefore is not the "object" of mathematics real and in things? In answering these questions we must keep in mind the distinction between the order of knowledge and the order of being.

Let us consider the following two arguments. (1) The sum of the angles of this thing is 180° because it is a Euclidean triangle. What is presupposed is that the sum of the angles of a Euclidean triangle is 180°. (2) A line is potentially infinite in number of points because it is material. What is presupposed is that whatever is material is potentially infinite in number of points. Now, does "presuppose" mean the same thing in both cases? So far as the purely formal logic of the arguments is concerned, they do. Each enthymeme presupposes a premise that is suppressed. However, the question at issue is not one of "formal logic" but rather of the relation of kinds of knowledge to each other; and for this the content instead of the form of the argument is relevant. In form the two arguments are:

(1)
(*A*) Euclidean triangles are entities the sum of whose angles is 180°.
(*B*) This is a Euclidean triangle.
(*C*) This is an entity the sum . . .

(2)
(*a*) Whatever is material is potentially infinite in number of points.
(*b*) A line is material.
(*c*) A line is potentially . . .

In order to understand what is involved in (1) and (2), and also what is obscured by the purely formal structure, let us examine the consequences of denying the conclusion of each. In abstraction from all content the denial of the truth of a conclusion implies the denial of the truth of either one (indiscriminately) of the premises, or both. But when the content is considered, the matter is different.

Considering (2), if (*c*) is denied, does one intend to deny (*b*)? Hardly. The (*a*) is metaphysical, (*b*) is mathematical (for one is concerned with "intelligible matter"), and (*c*) is a proposition of the philosophy of mathematics. The (*c*) states what a line *really* is; (*b*) states what it is in the mathematical system *X*. What (*b*) states that is relative to a system may also be what a line really is. *But it is the argument, and not* (b), *that tells us that.* In another system *Y* a line may be conceived of as generated from unextended (actual) points which are the "individuals" of the system in contrast to *X* in which what is considered to be actual is the line itself and the points are abstractions. In (*b*) what a line is, is determined by the postulates and definitions of the system. Therefore, in denying the conclusion (*c*), which is a proposition of the philosophy of mathematics, one does not intend to deny that in system *X* a line is "material." If this is intended, then one makes the denial on purely mathematical grounds, showing that there is an inconsistency between such a meaning of "line" and the definitions and postulates. Otherwise it is quite possible for (*c*) to be denied, and (*b*) at the same time to be affirmed.

We must remember that in mathematics as a positive science the "truth" of (*b*) is "consistency," and as such in abstraction from being, in abstraction from the major premise which is metaphysical. The problem is to know whether the nominal meaning of "line" is also the real, true meaning. If the nominal meaning is given in (*b*), then in the light of (*a*) it can be asserted as something other than nominal in (*c*). But it does not at all follow that if (*c*) is denied, one denies also the nominal meaning. In fact the latter remains exactly what it is in system X. Rather, what is denied is the truth of (*a*). Both (*a*) and (*c*) are philosophical statements. What one is denying is the "philosophy" in (*c*), and this is what is found in (*a*). It was for this reason that in examining the nature of the philosophy of mathematics we pointed out that where there is disagreement it is essentially metaphysical.

If in (2) the major premise is true, it is because it conforms to being. Likewise, if the conclusion is true. But if the minor is true, it is so relative to the system. The problem of the philosophy of a positive science is to determine what kind of being or nonbeing the entities of the positive science have. The problem is not to determine the phenomenological relations between them, for that would be to commit the very grave error of making metaphysics constitutive of the positive science itself.

It may be pointed out that there are metaphysical systems as well as mathematical systems. Why should "relativity" be confined to mathematics? Well, in the first place mathematics is not metaphysics. Although the postulational method is never wholly arbitrary in intention, there is a conditionality about it that there is not in metaphysics. On the level of pure mathematics a system remains hypothetical. One is not forced to determine whether or not it is true to anything. It is in this sense, but only in this sense, that Russell's statement is correct, that in mathematics we never know whether what we are talking about is true. Instead of recognizing the very limited and restricted truth of Russell's statement—which to him was not clear—some realists have unfortunately opposed his view with one which appears to be a deduction from realistic metaphysics. If one should not make a metaphysics out of a positive science, neither should one deduce a positive science from metaphysics. Historically the one error has usually been a reaction from the other.

Metaphysical statements are not intended to be hypothetical. What conditionality there is, is psychological, and not intended objectively. For example, the priority of act over potency is either true or false. If it is false, it is also impossible; if it is true, it is necessary. Now the difference between mathematics and metaphysics, relative to the question raised, is this: What mathematical statement is true is a problem of the philosophy of mathematics, and hence is determined by metaphysics. On the other hand, which metaphysical proposition is true is itself a metaphysical problem. If there are different metaphysical systems, then someone is wrong. If there are different mathematical systems (say, geometries), then if each is consistent no one is "wrong." The question of wrongness arises when one answers the question as to which one is physically real.

Lest we lose sight of the purpose of this analysis we may recall that it was to show the different ways a major premise may be presupposed by an enthymeme. We have found that when metaphysics is constitutive of the philosophy of mathematics, as in example (2), the denial of the conclusion implies the denial of the truth of the major premise. If the example is phrased in terms of the so-called hypothetical proposition instead of a categorical syllogism, viz., "If *P*, then *Q*," it means that the denial of *Q* does not require the denial of *P* but rather the denial of the implication itself, namely, *P* implies *Q*. The denial of *P* follows upon the denial of *Q* only when the latter is compatible with the "truth" of the implication. As we shall now see, this is the case with argument (1). In passing we may observe that a nonintentional "formal" logic must of necessity obscure these distinctions.

In (1), if the conclusion is denied, it is the minor premise (*B*) that must be denied rather than (*A*). If the sum of the angles of this thing to which reference is made is not 180°, then it is not a Euclidean triangle. But it still remains true that all Euclidean triangles have 180° as the sum of the angles. The denial of both (*C*) and (*B*) is quite compatible with the assertion of (*A*). Both (*C*) and (*B*) are historical propositions; (*A*) is mathematical. "This" might not be a triangle of any kind; or it might be a non-Euclidean triangle if reference is to something on an astronomical scale. At any rate, from the standpoint of mathematics as positive, as a nonphysical science, what is asserted in (*A*) is the consistency of a theorem with its postulates. When the conclusion is denied, the truth of (*B*) is also denied. But with respect to (*A*) all that is denied *is its applicability, relevancy, and usefulness in a given case.*

The difference between (1) and (2) may be summed up in the following manner. The (*B*), a historical proposition, is that which determines if (*A*) is applicable and useful; (*a*), a metaphysical proposition, is that which determines if (*b*) is true as well as consistent. The (*A*) is presupposed as instrumental by (*B*) and (*C*); (*a*) is presupposed as constitutive by (*b*) and (*c*). Finally, and this is most important, *in (1) the argument gives us the new knowledge that what is existentially the same is related in a certain way through meanings; in* (2) *the argument tells us that what is related in a certain way through meanings is existentially the same.* The term "meanings" is used because of its neutrality, instead of "essences" or "properties." Perhaps a few words of explanation will be helpful.

We can know, independently of the argument, that the subject of (*B*) is existentially the same as the subject of (*C*). Without (*A*), which is presupposed, we can know that the referent of the "This" is the same in the minor and the conclusion. On the other hand, in (2) we cannot know independently of the argument that the subject of (*b*) is the same as the subject of (*c*). It is by means of (*a*), which is presupposed, that we know that "line" in (*b*) is the same as "line" in (*c*). This is what we might have expected, for we remember that metaphysics is above all a doctrine of existence and not merely essence, although neglecting neither. This will help one to understand what can be demonstrated on other grounds, that when the metaphysical is reduced to the mathematical, and at the same time there is a wish to escape positivism, there is a movement toward the relativism and radical "essentialism" that characterizes a mathematical idealism.

The forms that common, sensible matter may take are selections from all possible forms appropriate to "intelligible matter." The universality of the forms lies in their formal nature, not in their exemplification. On the other hand, in a metaphysical proposition such as (*a*) the universality of "matter" lies also in its "exemplifications." "Matter" and "potency" are not present in part of the world of nature and absent in other parts. There cannot be alternative metaphysical systems, one applicable here or now, another applicable there or then.

Historical propositions and generalizations may presuppose the mathematical. But, if so, the relation of mathematics to experimental science is that of "instrumentality." We have explained why, contrary to appearances, mathematics cannot be constitutive of experimental science. But even in abstraction from the details this should not be surprising. From the knowledge of the nature of a positive science it should be clear why one positive science cannot regulate or be constitutive as evidence of another. The relative can only be instrumental to the relative.

Is not the content of a mathematical concept in things just as much as the content of a metaphysical concept? Is not "triangularity" in a thing just as is "potency"? Why should a kind of knowledge representing the latter be constitutive, while the kind of knowledge representing the former be only instrumental? This question is now more easily answered. In the first place, one cannot argue directly from the order of being to the order of knowledge. In the second place, even in the order of knowledge, metaphysics is and is not constitutive depending upon whether reference is made to the philosophy of a positive science or to the positive science itself.

The distinction between "instrumental to" and "constitutive of" with respect to the way a premise may function in an argument, has not always been clear in classical realism. The contemporary positivist has not recognized it either, thus allowing himself to overstress the instrumental. We have not said that a positive science does not arrive at truth, nor that its "sentences" are not propositions. We have said simply that the truth cannot be determined by the positive science *alone*. We have not said that it does not contribute. It does. But the truth that is sought is never merely about "quantity" in abstraction from "being"; rather it is about quantitative being. Hence, the philosophy of mathematics is the end sought, and for which mathematics as a positive science is a means. The truth that is sought is never merely about the "mobile" in abstraction from "being"; rather it is about mobile being. Hence, the philosophy of nature is the end, and for which experimental science is a means.

The propositions of a positive science, therefore, have a hypothetical nature. In abstraction from the philosophy of that science they are eternally "candidates" for truth. When the positive science is absolutized and the metaphysical is denied, implicitly or explicitly, then of course we can never arrive at truth. All that we can ever obtain are the "candidates" in our "quest for certainty," to use a phrase of John Dewey. We are forever left with postulates *qua* postulates, with hypotheses and hypotheses about hypotheses. Since the metaphysical and philosophical have vanished, the "instrumental to" relation, which is valid when properly understood as restricted, now becomes unrestricted, with the result that we have "instrumental*ism*." Although the "satisfactory" in a utilitarian sense may also be true, in absence from the metaphysical "utility" and "truth" are now identified. The mode of being becomes being, the adjective becomes a noun, nonbeing becomes being. It was left for Hegel to justify such nihilism by creating a philosophy in which such contradiction, by dialectical movement, is identified with rationality. It was left for the Marxist to socialize it. Contemporary totalitarianism, whether fascistic or communistic, is partly defined by the fact that it accepts as ultimate "utility" and "consistency," which is as near to the meaning of "truth" as the positive sciences can get. American society and education was founded on a contrary notion which it is tragically and gradually repudiating.

The mathematical logician recognizes in his own way the instrumentality of mathematics to experimental science. However, Bertrand Russell would not call (1) an argument at all. The (*A*) would be a general proposition that is "always true," and which relates "propositional functions"; (*B*) and (*C*) represent values which satisfy the functions. The form of (*A*) is: "If x is a Euclidean triangle, then x has 180° as the sum of its angles." The "this" of (*B*) is then substituted for the x. Mathematical logic requires the identity of the element x as part of the logical structure independent of the content of the argument. This is possible when the values of x are subjects of historical propositions, as in argument (1). But the requirement eliminates *a priori* other possibilities, and hence other kinds of knowledge. As was shown a few paragraphs above, in (2) "line" in (*b*) and (*c*) cannot be known to be identical independently of the argument, and hence of (*a*). The requirement to the contrary means that there can be no philosophy of a positive science. There is only the positive science.

What is meant by "always true" is somewhat the same as what we have referred to as the consistency between a theorem and the axioms of the system. The proposition is applicable or not, depending upon what is substituted for x. The plausibility of this kind of interpretation rests upon the nature of mathematics as a positive science. The extension of it to all kinds of knowledge, together with the required identification of logic and mathematics, is that to which objection should be made. This leads to a type of pragmatism in which various kinds of knowledge are eliminated instead of related and explained. In addition to "facts," historical propositions and generalizations, there remain only logical propositions, and "logical propositions are such as can be known *a priori,* without study of the actual world." [6] The (*a*) in argument (2) must also be interpreted as a general proposition relating propositional functions. Not only is the distinction between "instrumental to" and "constitutive of" with respect to a premise eliminated; so also are the distinctions between metaphysics, a positive science, and the philosophy of a positive science.

Although essentially sound, realism has not always clearly distinguished a positive science from the "philosophy" of it, and in turn the relation of metaphysics to both of these. We are told that "$2 + 2 = 4$," and that "once the *meaning* of these concepts is understood, the necessary truth of these judgments becomes self-evident and needs no demonstration." By "self-evident" is meant the "immediate internal, objective evidence . . . of reality manifesting itself to the intellect." [7] This would seem to imply a view of mathematics somewhat different from the view we have been discussing as realistic. So far as "self-evidence" is concerned there seems to be no difference between mathematics and metaphysics, the difference being only in the nature of the object. Furthermore, the distinction between mathematics and the philosophy of mathematics seems to be negated, together with the analysis we have given of the different ways in which a premise may be instrumental or constitutive in an argument.

This meaning of self-evidence and mathematics rubs the intellectual fur of the modern positivist the wrong way. Why should "$2 + 2 = 4$" be so self-evident and not "$x^2 + y^2 = r^2$," the equation of a circle? Or a hundred and one other mathematical propositions? Objectively, the one requires demonstration just as much as do the others. The difference is subjective, the one being psychologically simpler than the other. It required over three hundred pages in the first volume of *Principia Mathematica* to arrive at the cardinal number "one," and even more to get to "two" and "four." Is it to be wondered at that the aforementioned realistic view, if such it be, is dismissed as a medieval innocence which at this late date can only be called ignorance? And have we not heard that sometimes two and two equal five; or one?

There can be some truth to the criticisms of the mathematical logician without it following at all that his solution is correct. The proposition "$2 + 2 = 4$" is certainly *evident,* but as such it is a proposition of the philosophy of mathematics rather than of mathematics as positive. The simplicity of its statement conceals the fact that there is a metaphysical presupposition about act and potentiality in relation to discrete and continuous quantity. The traditional realist tends to identify mathematics with quantitative being, the product of the second order of abstraction, just as he has also tended to identify natural science or the philosophy of nature with mobile being, the product of the first order of abstraction. And so far, so good. What was not recognized sufficiently was that peculiar form of abstraction which is the separation of a mode from being. It was not always recognized that, because it cannot be an end in itself, it does not follow that it cannot be a legitimate means if properly understood. Realism now tends to recognize experimental science as positive, but even today mathematics and the philosophy of mathematics often tend to be identified.

Of course this mistake tends to play directly into the hands of the mathematical positivist. If the realist insists that $2 + 2 = 4$ is a proposition of mathematics instead of the philosophy of mathematics, then the mathematical logician may oppose this notion with another. According to Russell, "Any mathematical equation is a propositional function." [8] If the matter is argued out on this level, we merely have a war situation. What we have tried to do is to show that, roughly speaking, when the mathematical logician talks about mathematics in terms of propositional functions he is considering what we have called mathematics as a positive science. And much of the time when the realist is speaking of mathematics he is really referring to the philosophy of mathematics.

If these distinctions are kept in mind most of the difficulties of which we have spoken can be clarified. Two apples plus two apples are four apples. This is what has been called an empirical or existential proposition. It is not a proposition of mathematics or of the philosophy of mathematics. If one were to attempt to prove the truth of such a proposition it would be found that mathematics enters into the argument only instrumentally. It is metaphysics that would enter constitutively. Apples are *actual* entities and in this application potentiality is irrelevant. But sometimes two waves plus two waves equal one wave. This does not mean that two *things* plus two *things* are *actually* equal to one *thing*. But they may through motion become one wave, i.e., they are *potentially* one.

At this point any further clarification must wait upon an analysis of what is meant by the philosophy of nature. Before turning to that problem let us examine the relation of metaphysics to experimental science.

The Relation of Metaphysics to Experimental Science

That metaphysics cannot be merely instrumental to experimental science follows from the very nature of metaphysics. Of course, if it is possible for some propositions of experimental science to be true, then some metaphysical propositions must be true. But we speak of one kind of knowledge being instrumental to another only when it is nothing more, i.e., when it can be neither regulative nor constitutive. Metaphysics is a kind of knowledge which must be regulative or constitutive. It cannot be merely instrumental.

We have also seen that by the very nature of a positive science it is impossible for metaphysics to be constitutive of it as evidence. If it were otherwise a positive science could not be what it is. Metaphysics is constitutive of the philosophy of nature, but even for this integrative discipline experimental science as independent, as a positive science, is necessary. If metaphysics were constitutive as evidence of experimental science, then even the philosophy of nature would be impossible. In fact there would be neither experimental science nor the philosophy of nature; there would be only metaphysics. No amount of knowledge of being can be evidence for the facts about the details of motion, about the relations between substances or events. If one's purpose is that kind of knowledge which is the philosophy of nature, namely, mobile being, then knowledge of both the "mobile" and "being" is necessary. Neither can be deduced from the other.

There are rights and duties connected with the pursuit of any kind of knowledge. These are easily misconceived, and an intellectual immoralism is the consequence if the nature of the kind of knowledge pursued is not understood. Unfortunately, those concerned with a mode and those concerned with being have quarreled down through the ages. When experimental science is denied its rights, there is "philosoph*ism*." When metaphysics is denied its rights there is "positiv*ism*." In both cases either there is the error of ignorance, or else the intellectual sin of pride overcomes the love of wisdom.

If the pressure is constant, the volume of a gas is proportional to the temperature. This is a generalization, found experimentally by Gay-Lussac. The evidence consisted of historical propositions, for he had to work with particular gases, and not gas "in general." As evidence metaphysics was and is irrelevant so far as the confirming or disconfirming of the generalizations concerned. In his own confused, intuitive way the experimental scientist knows this, even if he doesn't know *why* this is so. He rightly insists upon his freedom, his freedom *from* the metaphysical. *His right is the philosopher's duty not to interfere.*

The earth moves, or it does not. If it does, then it does—and metaphysics can never change the fact or make it a nonfact. It is the perversion of the function of metaphysics to attempt to do so. When it does do so, there are always those who are ready to identify the perversion with that which is perverted, thus allowing them a mask for their own species of perversion, the absolutizing of experimental science.

The orbit of a planet is elliptical, or it isn't. Kepler found that it was so. The evidence consisted of historical propositions in his "star" catalogue, first begun by Tycho Brahe. The ontological (metaphysical and theological) was not only irrelevant, but it was a handicap to overcome—one in which Copernicus was only partly successful. On ontological grounds the circle may or may not be the most perfect figure. To understand that this is irrelevant, and that the "facts," the historical propositions acquired through observations, are determining was a revolution in man's knowledge quite as important as the one in astronomy.

In this sense, but only in this sense, the scientist has been correct in the "warfare" between the scientist and the philosopher. It should be noted that we speak of men, not of kinds of knowledge. It is impossible for experimental science and metaphysics to be at war. "Positivism" is philosophy, not experimental science. And while the positivist is quite correct in insisting that metaphysics is not constitutive as evidence for experimental science, what he does not understand is that his protest has nothing to do with the essence of positivism, which is defined by the denial of the autonomy of metaphysics as a kind of knowledge.

The point need not be labored that metaphysics is not constitutive of experimental science. However, it is irrelevant to experimental science only in this sense, for it is regulative of it. Even the autonomy of experimental science is a relative one. Experimental science presupposes metaphysics in many ways. The very possibility of some propositions of experimental science being true presupposes the validity of perception, of logical principles. There is presupposed the existence of something, objective and independent of the power or will of the human being. These presuppositions are not constitutive; i.e., they are not constitutive of *what* is true experimentally.

It may be objected that what we have said demonstrates only that metaphysics is instrumental, but not that it is regulative. For it to be regulative experimental procedure must presuppose not merely some (indifferently), but specific metaphysical propositions as true. Now one experimental scientist may proceed on the assumption that the logical principle of excluded middle is absolute, another on the assumption of its limitation. It may be granted that logic rests upon metaphysics, and that some logic or metaphysics must be used; but no specific one is implied. Are there not alternative metaphysical systems just as there are alternative mathematical systems, the one chosen being the one most useful? Likewise with the assumption that there is something independent of the will of man. One person may say that it is sensation, another that it is nature consisting of individual substances. How can metaphysics be regulative when the experimental scientist can proceed apparently with indifference as to whether (say) idealism or realism is true?

In this objection there is a confusion between the structure of knowledge, the relation of two kinds of knowledge to each other, and the social situation of science involving different beliefs of scientists. Socially, we do have the situation in which scientists apparently assume different metaphysical positions. Of course, whether or not a scientist is aware of what he is assuming is a psychological matter, and is irrelevant to the order of knowledge. But when one says that (say) an idealism is presupposed, he must mean that a contradictory position such as realism is false. He cannot possibly mean that both idealism and realism are "sometimes true," the one here and then, the other there and now. Being metaphysical positions the kind of universality asserted is such that if the one is true the other is not. A theorem in Euclidean geometry does not contradict a theorem in a non-Euclidean geometry, for the contradiction can only exist between the theorem and postulates *within* a system. With respect to physical existence they might both be true because both are exemplified. On the other hand, while any metaphysical proposition will be a member of a metaphysical system, because it is believed by human beings, what is intended is its existential truth in its universality relative to being and not relative to the system. This kind of intention is not demanded of a mathematical statement, although it *is* in asserting a proposition of the philosophy of mathematics.

Therefore, if one says that experimental science presupposes a nature composed of individual substances rather than sensations to be co-ordinated, he means to assert not some (indifferently) metaphysical propositions, but a specific one. He must hold that one who asserts the contrary is wrong. Which is correct is another matter. The thesis that metaphysics is regulative of experimental science requires only that some (not all) specific metaphysical propositions are presupposed as true. It is not asserted that no "mistakes" are possible. The regulative function of metaphysics is independent of whether a proposition *is* true. A false metaphysical proposition that is mistakenly assumed to be true regulates just as much as one that is actually true.

How metaphysics is regulative of experimental science may be understood by an illustration. We choose an example from biology.

Whether acquired characteristics are or are not inherited is a matter to be discovered through the experimental science of biology. The evidence will consist of facts in the form of historical propositions and generalizations. No evidence will be forthcoming from metaphysics. Metaphysics will, however, function as regulative, whether the biologist recognizes it or not. That is, some metaphysical propositions will be presupposed.

Consider the different metaphysical positions: (a_1) that there are only internal relations, (a_2) only external relations, or (a_3) that there are instances of both. The inheritance of acquired characteristics in terms of a_1 and a_3 is possible, in terms of a_2 is impossible. For an external relation the nature of the term is essentially independent of the relations it has. This is not true for terms related internally. For experimental procedure the genes might be considered atomically, in the fashion of the old notion of the atom as something relatively self-sufficient and unchangeable. The analogy is imperfect, but it has been approached in the "mechanistic concept of life." In this case a_2 would be presupposed. Not only are there no known cases of the inheritance of acquired characteristics but such is impossible. The truth or falsity of the metaphysical positions are not in question here. The point is that any experimental procedure of this kind presupposes some metaphysical propositions.

The experimental biologist finds no evidence for the inheritance of acquired characteristics, and hence rejects neo-Lamarckism or any similar view. He does this on experimental grounds. The presupposition is a_3. Such inheritance might be possible but there is no reason to believe that it is actual. Since this possibility is presupposed the results of experimentation, even though they be negative, do not prove the impossibility of such inheritance. And since a_3 is not constitutive it implies nothing as to whether acquired characters are inherited or not. But unless a_3 were regulative, allowing the possibility, there would be no reason to experiment in order to find out whether what was possible is or is not actual.

It may seem that whether metaphysics is regulative, or, on the other hand, is substantiated by experimental science, depends upon the kind of metaphysics in question. In the example given the metaphysics used for illustrative purposes was regulative, and, of course, that which is regulative cannot be proven or disproven by the kind of knowledge regulated. But let us suppose that an experimenter proceeded on the assumption that inheritance of acquired characteristics is impossible, not merely nonactual, and suppose further that in the near future some cases of such inheritance were found by his colleagues. What was said to be impossible is now found to be not only possible, but actual. Have we not here a case in which the metaphysics that is supposed to regulate not only does not do so, but is actually disproved by experimentation? If so, then contrary to all that has been said before, a positive science can prove something metaphysically.

It would be begging the question if, in answer, we should point out that such a metaphysical position as a_2 is a "bad" one to begin with, and that it is inadequate for experimental purposes. Undoubtedly, this is true, but it does not answer the question. It still leaves the appearance that it is experimental science that shows it to be a "bad" metaphysics. A more relevant answer is that just as an experimental fact is not evidence for a_2, so a different experimental fact cannot be evidence against it. This means that the presumed facts discovered about inheritance simply are not facts. Of course this answer is not very satisfactory. We seem to be faced with an unpleasant dilemma. In the case at hand, either metaphysics (a_2) is regulative, or it is not. If it is, then we have the worst kind of *a priorism,* that which not only hinders but rejects the work of the experimenter. If a_2 is not regulative, then it is a metaphysical position which can be proved false on experimental grounds. Generalizing, we may say that we can have either metaphysics or experimental science, but not both. If the term "metaphysics" must still be used, then it can only refer to the speculation that comes from generalizing the notions of the positive sciences, the latter constituting the evidence for whatever "metaphysical" truth there may be.

Let us re-examine the problem. While there is no evidence of the inheritance of acquired characteristics, good experimental procedure must allow for the possibility that some evidence may be found. Let us designate the two possible facts as non-IAC and IAC. There are at least two persons involved, A and B. A "knows" that non-IAC is true, because in terms of a_2 it is impossible for IAC to be true. According to our supposition B finds that IAC is true. a_3 is regulative for B, for unless the possibility of IAC was presupposed there would have been no reason to experiment in order to find out if it is actual. A is forced into either denying IAC or "reinterpreting" the experimental results of A so that they are compatible with a_2. Thus far A and B are "logical," and for both metaphysics is regulative. But who is correct, and how is the problem to be resolved?

It is B who is correct. But it is important to understand why he is. It is not because IAC disproves a_2. If a_2 is false, and undoubtedly it is, then there must be independent evidence of its falsity. This means that there must be metaphysical evidence for the falsity of a_2, which is a metaphysical position. Now if a metaphysics is false, then it is to be expected that as regulative it will lead to experimental difficulties. Either it will be incompatible with the "spirit" of experimental procedure, or it will continually force *ad hoc* reinterpretations of the results of experiments. The appearance of IAC would then be a *sign* of the falsity of a_2. But IAC would not disprove a_2.

The situation is this. If a_2 is false, then it is false on metaphysical grounds, and hence leads to experimental difficulties. *The a_2 leads to experimental difficulties because it is false; it is not false because it leads to experimental difficulties.* Any metaphysics will be regulative whether it be true or false. Hence, its truth or falsity is irrelevant to its regulative function. If the metaphysics is false, then it follows that difficulties will occur in experimental science. It would be the fallacy of "undistributed middle" to argue that because there are difficulties in experimental science, therefore the metaphysics must be false.

The formal fallacy may be avoided by converting the major premise of the argument. But then one would have to assert that if certain difficulties arise in experimental science, then it necessarily follows that the regulative metaphysics is false. However, this is a plain contradiction, for that which regulates cannot be disproven by that which is regulated. This contradiction can be avoided only by absolutizing experimental science. It is unregulated because it becomes a metaphysics itself, in which case we have positivism. And also, in which case there is really no metaphysics. Either metaphysics as knowledge exists, or it does not. If it does not, then there is no problem as to the relation of metaphysics to experimental science. If it does, then it must be regulative of experimental science.

The nature of the possible incompatibility between a metaphysical proposition and a proposition of experimental science. The laws of incompatibility must be stated exactly. This may be accomplished now by formalizing what has been considered discursively. We have been considering IAC in an "all or none" sense. More accurately, let "b_1" refer to IAC "in any and every respect"; "b_2" refer to IAC "in some, but not all, respects." We have said that the assertion of IAC presupposes (a_3) that some relations are internal. Hence, (1) if b_1 or b_2, then a_3.

It should be observed that the converse cannot be meant, for that would mean that contingent fact is deducible from metaphysics. Of course the converse may be asserted in a "weak" form, e.g., if a_3, then b_1 or b_2 is *possible.* This is true, and known to be so on metaphysical grounds, but in the weakening we have lost the relationship between generalizations and metaphysical propositions. What we can say is this, that if the propositions of type *B* knowledge are taken as a group, it is the metaphysical proposition, a_3, which establishes the possibility of their truth; but it is experimental evidence that establishes *which* is true, b_1 or b_2. Now let us suppose that b_2 is experimentally confirmed in the future. What happens when there are possible material grounds for either asserting the antecedent or denying the consequent? What if the metaphysician denies a_3? On metaphysical grounds one would be denying the possibility of b_2, the actuality of which is being asserted on experimental grounds.

The fact of possible conflict is not to be denied; what must be understood is its nature.

There are three erroneous "solutions," erroneous because each "solves" the problem of conflict by reducing one kind of knowledge to another. It might be said that a_3 is simply a "postulate," useful for a period, and cannot be denied on grounds independent of the antecedent. The a_3, a_2, or a_1 may be asserted or denied at different times, but always depending upon the latest experimental developments. This way in effect reduces metaphysics to a purely formal discipline like mathematics; also it ceases to be regulative and becomes merely instrumental.

The second "solution" is to say that experimental science proves what is true metaphysically. That is, the only ground on which a_3 can be asserted is the same as that upon which b_1 or b_2 is asserted. There are two reasons why this cannot be so. If there is no independent evidence for a_3, then there is no metaphysics that can be regulative. A metaphysical proposition cannot be regulative if it is wholly "proved" by what it regulates. In the second place, if the truth of b_1 or b_2 were to "prove" a_3, then the falsity of either or both would tend to "disprove" a_3. Not only is this logically impossible (denial of antecedent), but it so happens that whether b_1 or b_2 are true or false, either or both, is irrelevant to the truth of a_3. The "presupposition" relation still remains.

If it is wrong to solve the problem by reducing metaphysics to either mathematics or experimental science, the third error is even worse. It may be said that in case of incompatibility between a generalization and a metaphysical proposition, the matter is always to be settled in favor of the latter. Historically, when this is done, all attempts imply the reduction of a generalization to a metaphysical proposition. Time need not now be wasted on showing why this is an error. At any rate the regulative function of metaphysics is destroyed.

There is an argument for this third alternative that appears to be nonreductive. In case of conflict the metaphysical has priority for the reason that the necessary has priority over the contingent. But actually there is no argument because these statements are irrelevant. If b_1 and a_3 are not both true, then there is no problem. On the other hand, if they are, then a difference in the kind or mode of truth cannot be used as evidence of the denial of the truth of either.

None of these ways solves the problem. What is the answer, then, to the problem of resolving a possible conflict between experimental science and the metaphysics that is regulative of it? The answer may be given in two parts.

First, the possibility of conflict must be admitted. There is no use denying it. What must be understood is the nature of it. A false metaphysical proposition can be incompatible with a true proposition of experimental science. Moreover, as we have said before, a metaphysics need not be true to be regulative.

Second, a true metaphysical proposition may be the *sign of* the falsity of a proposition of experimental science; also, a proposition of the latter may be a *sign of* the falsity of a proposition of metaphysics. But "sign of" is not equivalent to "proof of." A true proposition of one kind of knowledge can be the sign of the falsity of a proposition of another kind of knowledge *only if the truth and falsity of each can be determined independently of the other. Propositions representing two kinds of knowledge can conflict only if each is relatively autonomous.*

There can be no incompatibility between metaphysics and experimental science *as such*. It can show up, however, in the *work* of the experimental scientist if he assumes a false metaphysic as regulative. Whether he is aware of it or not, he will make, and work upon, some metaphysical assumptions. Conflict will be minimized to the degree that he understands metaphysics and becomes a "philosopher" of his special science. It will be maximized to the extent that he tries to "make" a philosophy out of his speciality.

In terms of these principles of the order of knowledge we may understand the protest of some years ago by American and British biologists against the neo-Lamarckism of Lysenko, a Soviet scientist. The Americans were correct, but in some quarters, as is so often the case, they did not thoroughly understand why they were correct, and consequently gave the wrong reasons. Some said that the Soviets were wrong because they held to an "*a priori* and philosophical" position, whereas the Americans were "scientific" and "experimental."

What was the actual situation? In both cases metaphysics was presupposed. Most of the American protesters held to a view which presupposed a metaphysical position similar to a_3 as regulative. Inheritance of acquired characteristics may or may not be possible. By experiment there is no evidence for their actuality. The Soviets held to a_1. The triadic dialectic of their materialism implies that relations are internal quite as much as does the dialectical idealism of Hegel. Now it is characteristic of the latter kind of metaphysics—although we cannot develop the point here—that kinds of knowledge tend to be blurred together, especially experimental science and philosophy. It is not always clear where the one ends and the other begins. Hegel stressed the philosophical and unfortunately made some deductions about matters that properly belong to experimental science. In the process of turning Hegel upside-down Marx identified his dialectical materialism with "science," and his followers have done so ever since. If "science" is identified with a metaphysics (Marxists do not like the term) in which only internal relations are allowed, then it follows that there must be inheritance of acquired characteristics. At this point Soviet philosophy became constitutive of experimental science.

What the American biologists should have pointed out is that the Soviets erred in making metaphysics constitutive of experimental science. And further, that even if it were merely regulative it would still give rise to experimental difficulties. It then could be pointed out that although biology is in no sense evidence for or against any metaphysics, nevertheless whether a metaphysics is true or not is of utmost importance for the existence and development of biology as an experimental science. We need, therefore, to become more conscious of the whole philosophical question, understand the nature of the independent evidence for the truth of the one metaphysics and the falsity of dialectical materialism, and thereby become more appreciative of a metaphysical heritage we have taken for granted, one which we are now refusing to perpetuate intellectually in our universities. It might have been pointed out that when physical science is made into a metaphysics, and scientism gets hold of a society, there is much other than experimental science that suffers.

All this might have been done. But some of those who were most vocal argued against the Soviets with their own peculiar brand of pragmatic scientism, with the implication that it was "philosophy" as such that was at fault. The question was also begged in some quarters by assuming that the issue was a biological one. Actually, the whole problem was philosophical, one having to do with the "order of knowledge." *Biology was merely the occasion, the circumstance that gave rise to the philosophical problem.*

9

Natural Science: The Philosophy of Nature

The problem of the philosophy of nature is: What is nature? Insofar as man is part of nature "philosophical psychology" is a part of the philosophy of nature. Philosophical psychology is also called "the philosophy of human nature."

In order to understand what the philosophy of nature is we must know "how to get it." To know how to obtain it we must know the kind of evidence relevant to it. But to know the kind of evidence that is relevant we must know what kind of object it is that we are studying. We have said that the object is nature. Are there, then, two kinds of knowledge about nature, the one that of experimental science and the other philosophical? In a sense there are. And yet how can there be? That part of metaphysics which is cosmology is concerned with nature. And of course we were concerned with the metaphysics of knowledge as well as that of nature when we tried to understand what "knowing" means. But is there not something strange and almost unreal about a "philosophical approach" to nature in comparison with that of experimental science? Some think so. Let us see why they do.

The critic speaks. In metaphysics there is talk of qualities and of essences; in the experimental sciences, especially in the more advanced ones, the emphasis is on relations, measurement, and quantities. Is not "knowing" in experimental science quite different from the kind of "metaphysical knowing" which we have described? According to the account that has been given a person looks at a creature and by some kind of abstraction grasps the "essence" of horse, and having done so now presumably knows *what* a horse is. In contrast, biologists will study such creatures for years and sum up the knowledge gathered in volumes. Not only will we be told about the horse as it is now, but also about its development through the ages from a small, fox-sized creature. Is it to be maintained that all these volumes tell us nothing about *what* a horse is, but that the "what," some mysterious essence, is rather to be grasped "philosophically" by some kind of "looking" plus "abstraction"? When we ask what such an essence is, all that can be discovered is that a horse is a material, living, sensible being with certain properties that define its specific nature. Even if true, this seems to tell us very little.

The chemist may use the term "substance." But what has that got to do with the metaphysical notion? Which gives us the true meaning of the term? Again, consider the difference between the categories of physics and metaphysics. In the latter we hear about matter, form, act, potentiality, existence, possibility, essence, substance, accident, and cause. What have these to do with the concepts of physics? Physics cannot use the metaphysical notion of "matter." What have "field," "factor," "divergence operator," "probability amplitude," and innumerable other physical concepts, to do with metaphysical concepts? Even in the "logic" of knowing in physics one speaks of "function," "operators," "matrices," "signals," and not of "formal sign," "subject," and "predicate."

Furthermore, note the difference in method. The method of metaphysics is deductive plus something called "rational induction" and/or "intelligible induction." To the metaphysical skeptic these seem to be but fancy names for "either-you-see-it-or-you-don't." On the other hand, the method of experimental science is hypothetico-deductive together with sense verification. Definitions are framed cautiously and are constantly revised in the light of new evidence. This is in contrast to the way of the metaphysician, especially the realist, who takes (for example) "matter" and "man" as defined two thousand years ago as a "real" definition. Such definitions would seem to be either empty formulas or, if they have definite content, are positive handicaps in the acquisition of new knowledge. Insofar as the metaphysician's favorite statement that "man is a rational animal" is true, it is empty; insofar as it has some specific meaning it would seem to be furnished by the various experimental (empirical!) sciences of man.

The metaphysical approach to nature, the critic continues, was an understandable one in the prescientific ages. It was a relatively simple, cozy universe made up of earth, air, fire, and water. A thing remained at rest until it was moved. The essences of things were supposed to be directly intuited. Anyone could know what a horse is. But today we know that motion is primary and not rest. And the scientist will find little meaning in the notion of intuiting the essence of electrons. The electron is what it does; it is relations, rather than some presumably qualitative core, with which the scientist is concerned. Metaphysical ideas still persist, however, but scientific progress seems to be proportional to their liquidation. For example, the notion of "substance" persisted even when excuse for it had vanished. It is well-known that even false ideas "work" sometimes in science, although in the long run their inadequacy may retard the development of a science. Such was the case with the idea of material substances describable by the laws of mechanics. It took some time to overcome the metaphysical idea of substance and substitute the more adequate notions of "field," "energy," "event."

The Greeks and the medievals knew nothing, for example, of invisible radiation, the Doppler effect, or interference bands. Also, electrons are material but are not "hot," do not have the "quality" of heat. Radiation is a carrier of energy in complete absence of any substance between here and the sun. Yet it has mass and momentum. "Substance" seems to have vanished; if the term is still to be used it is to be conceived of as derivative from energy. Again, what happens to "substance" when we now know that a material thing can alter with the time-rates of alteration of spatial position? Does a horse still have the same "essence" and "exist in itself" if it should approach the speed of light, or if its motion should be radically altered to the contrary?

The matter is even more serious when we leave substance and consider qualities. Even in Newton's day the vibratory nature of light was unknown. Consider the consequences of Fresnel's discovery together with what is called the Doppler-Fizeau effect by which may be determined the radial speed of approach or recession of the stars. If we were to approach a red object with sufficient speed it would appear green, with greater speed it would appear violet, and with still greater speed it would be invisible. Now what is the *real* color of the red horse—ontologically? What does it mean now to say that a quality is the foundation of the relation of similarity? It would seem that velocity can be equally or even more relevant in the determination of similarity. At any rate, these considerations, together with a great many others, cause the question to be raised: Which is the real world—that revealed metaphysically through "common sense" and direct intuition, or that revealed by modern science?

When the question is put in this way there are only two answers. The one is that experimental science is all there is. That is the more extreme positivist answer. The more recent form, neo-positivism, admits the legitimacy of "philosophical" questions and answers, but holds that they are determined by experimental science. This way leads to some kind of "postulational metaphysics" which we have already studied. This cannot be identified with the philosophy of nature because there is no philosophical truth independent of experimental science in terms of which the latter can be interpreted. One positivist, Moritz Schlick, did use "philosophy of nature" as a name of his last brief essay. However, even for him "the philosophy of nature is not itself a science, but an activity which is directed to the consideration of the meaning of the laws of nature." [1] And such "meaning" ultimately resolves itself into a "logical analysis of language." [2]

More often the substitute for the philosophy of nature is something called "the philosophy of science." As usually found the name stands for no definite object of study but rather for bits of several: (1) Philosophy of science sometimes includes a "logical analysis of language," the aim being to find out what scientific concepts and propositions "mean." (2) Included are epistemological analyses of "scientific knowing." Epistemology is here conceived to be independent of, or a substitute for, metaphysics. (3) Philosophy of science includes also speculations on the subject matter of the various experimental sciences, the aim being to "stretch" the concepts of the sciences to make them metaphysical elements in postulational systems.[3] The subject matter of the various experimental sciences do constitute part of the data of the philosophy of nature. But it is something quite different to consider "science" as a kind of knowledge. The subject matter now is a kind of knowledge, and the discipline considering it is the metaphysics of knowledge and not the philosophy of nature. The difference here is that represented by the distinction between first and second intentions. It is a sign of confusion to think of the philosophy of science as one homogeneous kind of knowledge when it is actually composed of fragments of other kinds.

As we have said before, in order to understand what the philosophy of nature is we must know what its object is. If we know what its object is we can know what kind of evidence is and is not relevant to the demonstration of a proposition of the philosophy of nature. If there is not clarity on these matters, then the philosophy of nature becomes almost anything anyone claims it to be. There is endless quarreling and fruitless speculation, with the consequence that the philosophy of nature becomes nothing at all. Speculation about nature can be fruitful only if we already know what it means to do this. In other words, such speculation presupposes an order of knowledge. If there is no such order, then there is merely blind speculation about "speculation about nature." There are then not only private guesses about nature, but also about the guesses themselves. However ingenious these may be the outcome is despair, and skepticism, for it will occur to some that there really can be neither the philosophy of nature nor metaphysics.

Before defining the kind of knowledge which the philosophy of nature is we may comment briefly on some of the criticisms that have been given. When one objects that there cannot be two sciences of nature, one experimental and the other philosophical, it is not always clear what is being denied. It is true but irrelevant to point out that the metaphysician or the philosopher of nature has little to say about the essence of horse, while the biologist writes a volume on the subject. An essence may be vaguely or "generally" grasped, and at the same time it be left to an experimental science to furnish the details. Strictly speaking such an "essence" is not an affair of metaphysics at all, but rather that of the philosophy of nature. And, as we shall see, experimental science does make its contribution to a philosophy of nature. The problem of the philosophy of nature is that concerned with a natural thing as a whole, and this involves the problem of the relation between essence, property, and accident. This is not a problem of experimental science, but it can and does furnish part of the data. Similarly with the philosophy of human nature, which is a part of the philosophy of nature. That man is a rational animal was known long before the development of experimental psychology. It is not the function of experimental psychology to prove that man is rational or that he is an animal. Nor can it disprove it. But it can help us to understand better the sense in which man is a rational animal and a creature of nature.

What is complementary to experimental science is not the philosophy of nature but metaphysics, specifically that part called "cosmology." Whether or not metaphysics tells us very much about, say, man, depends upon what may be meant by "very much." Undoubtedly, experimental psychology can produce a greater quantity of true propositions about man than can metaphysics. Matter pulverizes and pluralizes, and hence the more material the subject matter the greater the possible number of facts. But if by "very much" we refer to the importance of a proposition, then the case is different. The difference between the moral foundation of democracy and the moral nihilism of a totalitarianism rests upon the assertion or negation of the truth of such propositions as that man is a substantial unity or that man is a rational animal. For morality one true metaphysical proposition may be of more worth than any or all propositions of experimental psychology.

Further misunderstandings may perhaps better be met after

an analysis of the structure of the reasoning by which propositions of the philosophy of nature are obtained.

Consider these three propositions:

(1) An atom is composed of physical parts.

(2) An atom is a substance.

(3) The physical world is finite.

What kinds of knowledge-claims do these propositions represent? *What kind of evidence is relevant in the demonstration of each?* In terms of an order of knowledge an answer can be given. Otherwise one must make guesses according to appearances. Are not (1) and (2) propositions of experimental science, since it is that kind of knowledge that deals with atoms? Of course, experimental science may give us knowledge about atoms, but it does not follow that any proposition about atoms is a proposition of experimental science. It may seem that (3) is obviously a proposition of experimental science, one that is now proved by relativity physics. But when we turn away from appearances the answers are different. The (1) is a proposition of experimental science. The evidence for its truth consists of historical (singular) propositions together with other generalizations. One may know on nonexperimental grounds, i.e., metaphysical, that the atom is divisible. But only experiment can tell us that it *is in fact* divided, is composed of physical parts.

The Evidence for a Proposition of the Philosophy of Nature

"An atom is a substance" is a proposition of the philosophy of nature. The evidence for it cannot come alone from either experimental science or metaphysics. It must come from both. If it were not for experimental science either we would not know that atoms exist, or our knowledge would be so little that we could not say whether or not the atom is a substantial unity. Moreover, it is not the function of metaphysics to describe atoms. Yet "substance" is a metaphysical predicate. Were it not possible to have metaphysical knowledge independent of experimental science the statement that the atom is a substance could not be a proposition and hence capable of truth or falsehood. And so, in giving the evidence one would turn to physics, which shows the atom to have a relative independence. An atom can remain itself while undergoing certain kinds of change, can take upon itself various qualities and relations. If we may call this a sort of condensed minor premise of what might be quite a long argument, the major would consist of a statement of what a substance is, or perhaps of the properties which any substance has. The reasoning would begin with the notion of substance as that which exists in itself. A material substance will have the (deducible) property of "relative independence in action," phenomenologically expressed. Experimental science may furnish us with the evidence that an atom has such a characteristic, and then the conclusion is drawn that the atom is a substance.

Summing up an argument in a condensed form, in a syllogism, has the virtue of making clear the kinds of evidence necessary to draw a conclusion. But it hardly does justice to the subtleties of the argument, which usually requires some lengthy dialectical analysis of the relation between the concepts of experimental science and metaphysics. In an integrative kind of knowledge, which the philosophy of nature is, there is a lack of homogeneity in concepts. Assuming for the purpose of illustration that the form of the reasoning is *Barbara,* the object that one is talking about is the subject of both the conclusion and the minor premise. Since the minor is a proposition of experimental science the predicate must be nonmetaphysical, one of the phenomenological context. Yet this predicate will be the middle term which constitutes the link between the two premises, and hence will also be the subject of the major premise. But since the major is a metaphysical proposition the common term must here be metaphysical. In the example used the middle term (one of them, at least) was "independence."

But how can a term be a phenomenological concept in one premise, metaphysical in another, and allow a conclusion to be drawn without there being either a four-term fallacy or merely a "verbal" connection? It is sufficient for our purposes in this study to point out *that* it must be so. The full understanding of the fact is a matter for further research. But the problem can be understood. In any nonintegrative science the concepts are homogeneous with respect to kinds of knowledge. This is true of metaphysics, mathematics, and the experimental sciences. The evidence for each is confined to one context. In the case of an integrative science such as the philosophy of nature its context is defined and constituted by the union of two contexts, the phenomenological and the ontological. What is distinguished on the level of knowing for the purpose of understanding the real must be integrated for the very same reason. But such integration involves the relating of the concepts of the two contexts. This means that some of the concepts of each context, while not the same, cannot be wholly different. When two kinds of knowledge are related by means of such concepts we have the problem that has been called the "analogy of knowledge," which is not the same thing as the analogy of proportionality, although not wholly different from it.

If, to use our example, an atom is to be known wholly (insofar as it is possible), and not merely in an aspect, then both the phenomenological and the ontological must play a constitutive role. If either is neglected, then an aspect is identified with the whole. In terms of material logic this would require the elimination of one or the other of, or the breaking down of the distinction between, substance and accident, and also essence, property, and accident. But these distinctions are required. If the philosophy of nature is approached from the standpoint of experimental science one works from accidents to properties in the direction of essence, the latter never being obtained except nominally. The most that experimental science can do is to grasp an essence in terms of those properties which are sometimes called "dispositional." However, a property is a phenomenological expression of an ontological essence. From the standpoint of metaphysics the most that one can do in a problem of the philosophy of nature is to work from essence to property in the direction of accident. But one cannot reach accidents in this way any more than can one reach essence by means of experimental science.

Just as metaphysics requires the "analogy of being," so an

integrative knowledge such as the philosophy of nature requires an "analogy of knowledge."

The Function of a Cosmological Proposition in a Science of Nature

Let us now consider the last of the three kinds of propositions mentioned. The statement that the physical world is finite is neither a proposition of experimental science nor of the philosophy of nature. It is a metaphysical proposition, a proposition of that kind of special metaphysics called "cosmology," the study of the mobile as being. The physical world is that of a multiplicity of things composed of matter and form. The infinity of matter is purely potential. Hence, as actual the physical world is limited, is finite.

The kind of data, consisting of historical propositions, which would be constitutive as evidence of generalizations, would not be constitutive of such a cosmological proposition. However, historical propositions are instrumental to the cosmological proposition. That is, while no amount of evidence of the kind used in experimental science can demonstrate conclusively that the physical world is or is not finite, nevertheless, as we have already seen, unless it were possible to have some true knowledge such as that which can be expressed in the form of historical propositions, it would be impossible to have cosmological knowledge because abstraction would not be possible. It is in this manner that we understand what otherwise would be a plain contradiction, viz., that the data that leads to experimental science must be, and yet cannot be, necessary to metaphysics. There is no contradiction when we see that the propositions of sense experience must be instrumental to, but cannot be constitutive of, metaphysical propositions.

If all this is denied, then in effect one is denying that the metaphysical proposition is really a proposition. It is a pseudo-proposition, a sentence without the possibility of truth or falsity. The only other alternative that could be implied by the denial is that the proposition is really not metaphysical at all, but is a generalization. But this would be to misconceive the nature of a generalization. The proposition in question is not of the same order as, say, Boyle's law of gases. The latter is experimentally proved in a sense in which the proposition that the physical world is finite could never be. Experimental science requires the notion of limited, relatively closed systems. But the system of limited, relatively closed systems is not itself that kind of a system.

Why, then, are there those who suppose that the cosmological proposition in question is really a proposition of "science" (meaning, "experimental science")? There may be innumerable psychological reasons, but ultimately the actual reason is that in the absence of clarity about the order of knowledge, i.e., the metaphysics of knowledge, there is no limit to the acquisitiveness of a science—or, more exactly, of a human being who identifies himself professionally with a science. There are only two alternatives. In terms of an order of knowledge one can understand what one's professional subject is and what it is not. A discipline is seen in the light of knowledge as a whole. The other alternative is to interpret, to some degree or other, the whole in the light of the limited kind of knowledge with which one happens to be familiar or connected professionally. If one is a "scientist," then there is no clear reason why "science" should end here rather than there. Since there is a certain degree of arbitrariness in conceiving what experimental science *is,* the scientist is accordingly convinced of the arbitrariness of a non-scientist saying what science *is not.* The "verbal," then, apparently would be determining; for if experimental science is concerned with the physical world, then is not any proposition about the world a proposition of experimental science? For example, why cannot the scientist talk about the system of limited, closed systems? Of course, he can. But it does not follow that everything the experimental scientist talks about is experimental science simply for that reason. He may talk about mathematics, but mathematics does not for that reason become experimental science.

But there are those who, while admitting all this as abstractly true, would nevertheless insist that such a proposition as that stating the physical world to be finite is one belonging to experimental science and not to that part of metaphysics which is cosmology. The argument is as follows. Natural science is theoretical as well as experimental. Laws are verified experimentally. But there is also "physical theory" which has the function of explaining the laws. A proposition constituting an explanatory theory may not itself be a "law," and hence is not confirmed in the manner of a law. Such a proposition may be a "postulate," something required by physical laws. Such laws, which are experimentally confirmed, themselves confirm the postulates which explain them, and hence the postulates are not entirely arbitrary. That the physical world is finite is such a proposition, a postulate. (Its specific meaning in physical theory is assumed; for the purpose of illustration such meaning need not be elaborated.) The Newtonian physics had a certain postulate, one which was verified at that stage of the science. The new physics requires a different postulate, the physical universe is "closed." If, so the argument goes, one wishes to call such a postulate "cosmological" or "metaphysical," then one may do so. The metaphysical will then be constituted by speculation on experimental science. It is the "theoretical" science which explains "experimental" science, but as such it has no autonomy; its "truth" is a function of the experimental science of any given period.

In this kind of reasoning we meet again the position with which we have become familiar, namely, "postulational metaphysics." However, as we have seen, metaphysics must be autonomous. If it isn't, there can be no cosmology, for the latter is a part of the former. Nor can there be any philosophy of nature, for there is no "philosophy" independent of experimental science by which the latter can be "interpreted." What is in general false is manifested in different ways when found presupposed in arguments. This may be seen in the argument in question by a specific analysis.

Consider a law that has been experimentally verified. As regards "implication" or "presupposition" the following three distinctions may be made: (1) what is implied *by means of* the law; (2) what implies the law; (3) what the law *directly* implies. In demonstrative arguments these correspond respectively to the following positions in which the law may be found, major premise, conclusion, or minor premise. For example, what is implied by means of a law is some specific value. If, say, using the law of gases, values for a specific gas are substituted for pressure and temperature, then *by means of* the law a certain value is determined for the volume. As regards (2) we can say that what implies a law are a group of historical propositions. Of course this needs interpretation, for on purely formal grounds one cannot leap from "some" to "all." Yet there is a sense in which the historical propositions constituting (for example) the data for Tycho Brahe and Kepler implied that the orbit of the earth was elliptical rather than circular. Another interpretation of (2) is this: What implies a law may be another law. For example, we can say that the first law of Kepler's three laws implies the second.

It should be clear that the cosmological proposition that the physical world is finite is not required or implied in experimental science in the sense of (1). Nor is it an example of (2). It is not one law among others from which one or more laws are deducible, although it may be and undoubtedly is, compatible with all known laws of nature. But "deducible from" and "compatible with" are not the same thing. There are no laws in relativity physics that can be deduced from the proposition in question. If there is to be any kind of implication at all, it would be more plausible to maintain that relativity laws "require" or imply that the physical world is finite. This possibility leads us to the third distinction that was made. But first, a word about "theory" and the meaning of "postulate." There is no such thing as theoretical science in separation from experimentation. One can speak of an experimental scientist and a theoretical scientist. Professor Bridgeman of Harvard might be said to be an example of the former, Einstein of the latter. The reference here is to a division of labor. But there is no experiment, only blind trial and error, without theory. Such blind action cannot be found, except perhaps at the very beginnings of an experimental science.

The term "theory" is sometimes used to stand for the "postulates" which "explain" laws in experimental science. Science is conceived to be advanced to the degree that it is postulational, i.e., deductive, although it can never be merely that because experimental confirmation is always necessary. At any rate a powerful deduction is often more fruitful than an inductive generalization from data. Now it might be argued that a proposition stating that the physical world is finite is a proposition of experimental physics, not a law, but rather a proposition that functions as a postulate. The Newtonian physics was based on a postulate derived from a Euclidean notion of the world. The Einsteinian laws require non-Euclidean postulates, the notion of a universe that is endless but not infinite.

It will require some analysis to understand why, in spite of its apparent obviousness, this interpretation is false. We may assume that this case is not one of the two previously analyzed, viz., that in which a law may be said to imply another, or that which is implied by means of a law. Apparently, this is a case in which a law implies something which is a theory or a postulate, and at the same time the theoretical proposition is conceived to be required and to explain a law. However, if this is to be the distinction between theory and law in science, it is not clear as to what implies what or why there is the implication. Does a theory imply a law, or a law the theory? If the latter, then we have a strange use of the notion of "postulate" when it is identified with theory. In mathematics, for example, a theorem may be said to be implied by postulates, but can it be said *in the same sense* to imply them? In the case on hand is it meant that the laws of relativity physics imply or are implied by the postulate or theory that the physical universe is finite? We shall show that the kind of unclarity of which we have spoken is the consequence of confusion of kinds of knowledge in their relation to each other, and specifically of the attempt to interpret the nature of experimental science in terms of itself. For analysis we shall use as an example of this attempt Norman Campbell's explanation of the nature of "theory" in his book called *What Is Science?* [4]

Mr. Campbell does not believe that the laws of experimental

science can ever be explained by inclusion in more general laws, and that even if it were possible to include all scientific laws as particular instances of one extremely general and universal law the purpose of science would not be completely achieved. The laws must be explained, and therefore "theory" is necessary. A theory is not a law, but is "closely related" to it.[5] The laws of gases, relating volume, temperature, and pressure, have been explained by the Dynamical Theory of Gases. According to this theory a gas consists of an immense number of very small particles, molecules, flying about in all directions, colliding with each other and with the wall of the containing vessel. The speed of these molecules increases with temperature, etc. How does a theory explain? In two ways. "The first is that if we assume the theory to be true we can prove that the laws that are to be explained are true." [6] We may symbolize this as follows: If T (theory), then L_1 (any particular law of gases). By "explanation" is meant that L_1 is "deducible from" T. L_1 has already been experimentally discovered and verified. But a good theory should also be such that some law, say, L_2, which has not been discovered, can be deduced. After having been deduced, if it is verified experimentally, then it partially confirms the theory. The theory, in turn, explains what confirms it. For example, in terms of the theory, if molecules exist, have a definite size, and are not mathematical points, then it can be deduced that their behavior would be different under very high pressures, when the space actually occupied by the molecules constitutes almost wholly the space of the vessel.

Now, of course, this exposition of "scientific explanation" is no different from that of any other scientist trying to explain experimental science in terms of itself. It seems simple. We have the following implication:

I. If molecules have a definite size, then their behavior varies with volume. This may be symbolized as: If T (theory), then L_2 (a law).

If experiment confirms the consequent, then it is asserted and also the antecedent is asserted. But logically this cannot be done. Since it is done, evidently the actual implication is the converse:

II. If molecular behavior varies with volume, then molecules have a definite size. As symbolized: If L_2, then T.

Now the question is: Just what is it that implies what? Does T imply L_2, or L_2 imply T? The problem here is that which gives rise to the modern problem of "induction." In passing we observe that this problem is one deserving a great deal of study. It is sufficient for our purpose to call attention to the direction we believe it should take. The problem cannot be solved if the order of knowledge is broken down, e.g., if logic is reduced to mathematics, or metaphysics is reduced to physical science, or formal signs are reduced to instrumental signs, or cognition is reduced to "action," or intentionality is reduced to "intension" or "prediction."

Also demanded by the general problem is clarity as to the meaning of "postulate" and "implication." We have already observed how a hypothetical proposition in mere logical appearance may obscure the actual logic involved. If implication is reduced to conjunction, there is no answer to scientific explanation. In analyzing the example of Mr. Campbell we shall find that either three or five kinds of propositions are assumed, depending upon what it is conceived to explain. Specifically the problem is this: How from "if T, then L_2" can we confirm T by asserting L_2? No "new logic" need be created if one makes use of the natural order among kinds of knowledge. The following analysis aims to indicate the direction in which a solution is to be sought, although in doing so we shall have to make assumptions about "modality," and "probability" in particular, which would require further elaboration for adequacy.

Every proposition must assert something. Now the question is: What is asserted in (I)? The second question is: If something is asserted, what is the evidence of it? There must be some reason even for what one "postulates"; otherwise, one could say literally anything. Is it asserted that molecular behavior *in fact* varies with volume? No, this could not have been meant *before* the experimental confirmation which then became the *grounds* for the assertion. Otherwise, one would have to say that scientific truth is obtained by first assuming "propositions" for which there is no evidence whatsoever! Furthermore, the consequence is not asserted because it is conditional upon the antecedent. It should be noted here that the particular stage of the time of the reasoning is of importance. For if we are considering how a theory leads to new knowledge, we must not assume in the analysis that very knowledge. Such knowledge was potential at one time, and is actual and "old" at the time of this writing. Of course, once knowledge has become actual it can be formalized deductively into a system and an argument.

We call attention again to the fact that to say a theory is assumed or postulated is legitimate only if it is clear what is actually being done. There must be some grounds, some evidence, for what is postulated; otherwise there would be no reason for one postulate as against innumerable others. Keeping this in mind we may ask if the antecedent is asserted. No, for there is no evidence, and this is made manifest by the "if." Moreover, if the antecedent is asserted, then there would be no need for experimental confirmation of the consequent since its truth could be deduced from the antecedent! Thus far all this is rather obvious, and no difficulties are presented. The form of the reasoning is "If A is B, then A is C." What is asserted is neither that A is B nor that A is C. What is asserted is, then, some connection between B and C. There is an "implicative relation." But the understanding of what is asserted is made impossible if the relation is conceived of as "material implication." So interpreted what is asserted is "It is false 'that molecules have a definite size is true and that their behavior varies with volume is false.' " Of course this much at least is meant, but it is not sufficient for it does not tell us *what* is asserted. When the logic of the reasoning is conceived of intentionally we see that there is a suppressed premise: The behavior of all entities of a definite size is the function of volume. (Such a vague and awkward statement is sufficient for use as an example. For scientific theory it requires exact interpretation.) Apparently, we have an answer to what is asserted in (I)—neither the antecedent nor consequent but a connection between them which is implied, but which as explicit is suppressed.

But again, if we remember that there must be some grounds for an assertion, we must conclude that even this presumed major premise cannot be asserted, for there is no evidence. All we can say is that it is merely *formally* presupposed. The reason for this is that the major premise is a much "stronger" statement than even the consequent or the antecedent, which latter in the reasoning would constitute the minor premise. In short, if there is as yet no evidence to assert either that molecules have a definite size or that their behavior varies with volume, there is even less (than no!) evidence for asserting that the behavior of all entities of a definite size *is* a function of volume. It would not help to say that the implied major premise is not really asserted but only hypothetically postulated, for that does not solve but only pushes the matter back a step. *To avoid an infinite regress of postulations for which there is no evidence, something must be asserted for which there is some evidence.* If so, this puts us (and the experimental scientist) in quite a predicament. For if the suppressed major premise of (I) cannot be asserted, but is only formally required, then neither can the hypothetical proposition which is (I) be asserted. But if (I) cannot be asserted in any sense, then it would seem that we have reduced the analysis to an absurdity, for it would make experimental science impossible. If a choice has to be made between the fact of experimental science and such an analysis as the foregoing, surely it is reasonable to say "so much the worse" for the latter.

And there the matter would stand if it were not for something that is usually overlooked by experimental scientists, and even others, who are unaware of an order of knowledge and of the function of different kinds of knowledge in relation to each other. It is true that (I) cannot be asserted (except arbitrarily, of course). But it so happens that for experimental science it is not necessary to assert it. All that is required, fortunately, is a much milder statement in which "is probably" is substituted for "is." The reasoning now becomes as follows:

(1) The behavior of all entities of a definite size is probably a function of volume.

A (2) Molecular behavior is that of entities of a definite size.

(3) Molecular behavior is probably a function of volume.

It is understandable why (1) can now be asserted, and yet

could not be asserted if "probably" is not a part of the copula. Experimental science does not require that the connection between subject and predicate be asserted as an existential fact. All that is required is the assertion of its plausibility or likelihood. By an analysis of each proposition in the argument we can understand the meaning of "construct," "postulate," and how "methodological" and "logical" propositions function in reasoning in experimental science.

What is the evidence for the assertion of (1)? The evidence is not existential but logical. That is, (1) can be asserted on the grounds of "analogy"; not the analogy of proportionality but that of "resemblance." There is an analogical deduction from the total physical theory existing at the time. But such a deduction does not allow one to say "is," but only "is probably." It is for this reason that (1) is not a proposition of experimental science, i.e., the kind of proposition experimental science seeks, but is a logical proposition, a being of reason. All propositions as entities are beings of reason. But here we are referring to what is intended by the proposition as a whole. When we say that "*A* is probably *B*" we do not mean that in reality, independent of the mind, such "probability" exists. Rather the probability is logical, and is that which is appropriate to the weak form of analogy based on resemblance.

The concept of "probability" requires an analysis more thorough than is necessary for our purpose. It will be sufficient to take note of the distinction between this kind of probability and that which we speak of when we say that a proposition of experimental science is "probably true." The two statements "'*A* is probably *B*' is true" and "'*A* is *B*' is probably true" are not the same. This may be seen in the following manner. A statement of the form "'*A* is not *B*' is probably true" is compatible with "'*A* is *B*' is probably true"; but if "probably true" means "more likely or more plausible than not," and not merely—to use the mathematical meaning—some infinitely small fraction above zero, then it is not compatible with the assertion that "'*A* is probably *B*' is true." To put the difference in another way, in "*A* is probably *B*" the "probability" is part of the copula which relates subject and predicate, whereas in

" '*A* is *B*' is probably true" the probability is concerned with the relation between the whole proposition "*A* is *B*" and the incomplete evidence for it.

The (2) is a proposition of experimental science, that is, the kind experimental science seeks. It is not a logical proposition because the existence of molecules is asserted. It is also asserted that they have a definite size and are not mathematical points. The evidence for the latter assertion rests upon the analogy of resemblance. But this does not make the proposition logical, because the existence of molecules is asserted. What are the grounds for this assertion? None! The theory is merely postulated. But have we not said that there must be some evidence even for a postulate? Yes, a short time ago we were deliberately inexact because we did not want to jump ahead too far. What we said is still correct if limited to the context of the analysis of (I). But if generalized it might occur to one that if there must always be evidence for a proposition to be postulated, then there would be no reason to postulate it. This is correct. The revised and more exact statement is that a proposition for which there is as yet no evidence may be postulated if it clearly presupposes one or more propositions for which there is evidence and which are not postulated.

With this in mind let us note that in the reasoning about the nature of gases what is postulated as "theory" is the existence of molecules, not that they have a definite size. This is admitted by Mr. Campbell in his exposition. He says that "the most important feature of the theory is . . . that which states that there are such things as molecules, and that gases are made up of them. It is that feature of the theory which makes it a real explanation." [7] We may note in passing the problem posed for us, and one which Mr. Campbell does not succeed in answering. How can the one thing that is postulated without any evidence be the key feature of real explanation? Surely this is strange, and we shall see presently that the answer is not as simple as Mr. Campbell supposes.

In (3) what is asserted is that the behavior of these existing molecules *is probably* a function of volume. The evidence consists in what is asserted in the two premises. We can now see why, in the revised statement of (I), the consequent must contain "is probably" rather than "is." What kind of proposition is (3)? It is not a proposition of experimental science, for it is not asserted that the certain kind of behavior *is* a function of volume. It is not a purely logical proposition, a being of reason intending merely objects of second intentions because, as in (2) so in (3), the real existence of molecules is intended. Here we have a kind of knowledge which is that of the context of "material logic," for first and second intentions, the real and the logical are linked together. When logic is purely formal it is the science of mutual relations, the determination of which is independent of the content of the concepts. Material logic is concerned with the relating of the formal to the real, the nonlogical. And this demands that *what* one is talking about be taken into account. Hence, material logic is synthetic, an integrative discipline, and in this respect similar to the philosophy of nature. But there is a difference. Whereas the philosophy of nature is always constituted by an ontological and a phenomenological proposition, there is a variable factor in material logic. The constant constitutive factor is formally logical. But since the logical may be applied to any kind of object of knowledge, the variable constituent factor may be a proposition of any kind of knowledge. In the example used the nonlogical proposition happens to be a proposition of experimental science.

Thus far we are only part way through our account of scientific explanation. But we may pause for a moment to see how "constructs" may have a function and yet subjectivism be avoided. Psychologically, one may intend the existence of the subject of (1). The point to be made is that it is not necessary for the purpose of the reasoning. Since (1) is a logical proposition, if the scientist wishes to insist that the "middle term" is only a "logical construct," then he may do so. After all, as we shall soon see, the whole argument is only *instrumental* to what is really sought, namely, the grounds for asserting that molecules *do* have a certain size—for this is the theory that is to be confirmed. But even in this instrumental argument (1) functions instrumentally in obtaining (3). Hence, the scientist may think of the middle term as a "construct," which means that, to understand it realistically, it is conceived to be merely in the order of nominal essence and not of existence. What the scientist *qua* scientist dare not do is to assert that the middle term can be nothing but the construct. There is no *reason* for saying so. But once it is arbitrarily done the scientist now turned "philosopher" finds himself on the way to a subjectivism from which a desperate and futile attempt to escape is made through such notions as "isomorphism" or "epistemic correlations." Subjectivism is avoided by seeing the function of a "logical construct" through a realistic view of knowledge. Existence is intended for the objects of the subject of (2) and (3). The middle term, which *may* be conceived of as in the order of essence, connects the two premises, (1) and (2). In the conclusion, (3), essence and existence are brought together.

But we have some distance to go before we reach our final end, which is the confirmation of the "theory"; this theory when confirmed, we may anticipate, must be a statement about the real world and not formally or materially logical. We now see the problem. How can we get to the real if in the instrumental argument thus far the middle term is in the order of essence and at the same time the existential element is only the result of postulation? Although it is true that existence is *intended,* the fact remains that we have not got beyond the subjective to the real, for postulation in abstraction from evidence is but a psychological act full of hope.

In (3) the existence of molecules is definitely intended—in contrast to the content of the subject of (1), the existence of which *need not* be intended in order for (1) to perform its instrumental function. But (3), the proposition as such, does not intend to link existential behavior actually with "function of volume." The significance of the word "probably" (or its equivalent) is that what is intended is not wholly logical, nor wholly real, but a connection between the two. However, this is not the kind of proposition the experimental scientist seeks, *but is only instrumental to the search.* It is through experiment that evidence is obtained giving the grounds for asserting "is" rather than "is probably." It is then that one can say *therefore* molecules have a definite size. But in this argument, which we shall call *B*, just as in the former argument *A*, there is a suppressed premise. The argument is as follows.

(4) All entities whose behavior is a function of volume are those having a definite size.

B (5) Molecules are entities whose behavior is a function of volume.

(6) Molecules are entities having a definite size.

Now (5) can be asserted independently on experimental evidence. But (6) requires for evidence (4) as well as (5). What is the difference between (3) and (5)? The (5) is a proposition of experimental science. The (3) functions as regulative with respect to the experimental procedure by which evidence is obtained to assert (5). These relations between kinds of knowledge are not affected by the fact that (5) may be said to be only "probably true." This has already been explained in contrasting (2) and (1). The "probability" of (5) is not part of the proposition as it is in (3). In (5) probability is not concerned with the relation between subject and predicate, but refers to a relation between the proposition and the degree of evidence upon which it is asserted.

What kind of proposition is (4), and what is the evidence for it? It is a proposition of special metaphysics, of cosmology, that which is concerned not with being *qua* being but with being *qua* mobile. An immediate reaction might be that obviously this is not so, that (4) is a proposition of experimental science. Are not "behavior," "volume," and "size" all phenomenological concepts? But the obviousness comes from judging by appearance. Such terms can be found in a proposition of experimental science, the relations between them being determined by experimental evidence. But they can also be concepts derivative from, and hence presupposing, the "categories"—"behavior," "volume," and "size" being subsumed, respectively, under "motion," "space," and "quantity."

Such is the case in (4). The truth of (4) can be obtained through a metaphysical analysis of "material substance" (entity), "space," and "quantity." No knowledge of molecules is necessary; or, for that matter, no knowledge of anything in experimental science is necessary. It is true that that common experience on which even experimental science is based is necessary, but, as we have already seen, such experience is purely instrumental to, and not constitutive of, the metaphysical.

The (6) is neither a proposition of metaphysics nor experimental science, but one of the philosophy of nature; for here a metaphysical predicate is applied not to a purely metaphysical entity, but to a very definite and particular type of entity about which there is experimental evidence in (5). "Molecule," no more than "dog," is a metaphysical concept, although both kinds of entities have metaphysical aspects. In the philosophy of nature we seek to understand things in their wholeness. This demands that the phenomenological and ontological be brought together. When that is done a proposition emerges which is neither purely phenomenological nor metaphysical. In this manner propositions constituting the philosophy of nature are obtained.

A short time ago we mentioned the importance of the "analogy of knowledge," which must not be confused with the "analogy of being." We refer to it again in order to understand the nature of the argument. The middle term of *B* must be interpreted metaphysically in (4) and phenomenologically in (5); or, in more specific terms, in (4) reference is to the mobile *qua* being, and in (5) to the mobile *qua* mobile. The middle term is one and the same in order to perform its function, and yet not quite the same in order that there be a "movement of thought."

We have suggested that the analogy of knowledge is a subject requiring much investigation. If realism is not clear about it, substitutes will be created to account for that which faces any philosophy. There must be a "movement of thought," to use an idealistic phrase. Let us consider the alternatives. Either the middle term in the two premises is absolutely the same or it is not. If it is, then either it must be interpreted metaphysically or phenomenologically, but not both. If interpreted metaphysically, then the philosophy of nature is merely deduced from metaphysics. In effect this is to say either that experimental science has no contribution to make to a knowledge of nature, or that a science made up of such metaphysical deductions supplements, competes with, or tries to do the same thing as, experimental science—but in a different way. This error is that of a certain kind of extreme realism—more exactly, a kind of neo-Platonic idealism—of which Christian Wolff would be a good example. It may be called the "Wolffian error." Instead of leading to an understanding of nature it makes for a misunderstanding of metaphysics, rendering its pretensions rather absurd in comparison with experimental science.

This perversion of the function of metaphysics, trying to make it do the impossible, merely reinforces the opinion of those of a nominalistic bent that the phenomenological interpretation of the middle term is the only sensible one. With the phenomenological absolutized there can be no metaphysics or philosophy of nature. A study of the methodology of experimental science becomes a substitute for the philosophy of nature.

Neo-Hegelianism quite correctly denied that the middle term can be absolutely the same. But it began with the phenomenological and attempted to transcend it by a "movement of thought" which was called "dialectical." Both Platonism and nominalism were condemned as "linear thinking," to use Bosanquet's term. The middle term is the same in the two premises, and yet it is not the same. The "conclusion" was to differ from the premises in degree of depth, a fullness of thought which was identified with concreteness. However, there was no guidance for the dialectic, no way of knowing what it must do; that is, there was no "check" through experience on that content over and above the phenomenological, which was supposed to be generated by the dialectic. A metaphysics was created from the epistemological, and not by abstraction from *things;* hence there was a tendency toward a monism of knowledge in which there is a breakdown and confusion between kinds of knowledge. The consequence was sterility so far as a philosophy of nature is concerned.

These are the alternatives to moderate realism, alternatives which practically define what is unique in modern philosophy. It is little wonder that the philosophy of nature is a neglected discipline and that there are those who know only of the "philosophy of science," which is perhaps best classified as a part of material logic.

We began with an analysis of Mr. Campbell's exposition of "scientific explanation," using his own example of the behavior of gases. We were concerned with his particular exposition only because it is typical of what physical scientists do when they attempt to explain "scientific explanation" in terms of "science." "If we assume the theory to be true we can prove that the laws that are to be explained are true." Of course, this is not quite so. "Material truth" is not obtained by deduction from a postulate. Either there is a confusion of "formal" and "material" truth, or what is said is simply this: Whatever is deducible from an assumption can be proved to be deducible from the assumption.

But there is another question. Granting for the moment the hypothetical proposition, how can we know that the theory postulated is true, that molecules exist? "We only know that they exist by inference; what we actually observe are gases, varying in temperature and pressure; . . ." [8] In short, "If *A*, then *B*." On what grounds can we assert and know *A* is true? By "inferring" it from *B!* Since this is fallacious reasoning or, at best, arguing in a circle, the whole modern problem of "induction" arises—the last word of which (in perhaps more senses than one!) may be seen in the works of R. Carnap.

What we have tried to show is that various kinds of knowledge are involved in the reasoning of experimental science, that if experimental science is to make its contribution to our knowledge of nature—and not merely the manipulation and control of what we do not understand—then some kinds of knowledge serve as regulative and instrumental to the kind of proposition the experimental scientist seeks. And further, if the trend toward subjectivism which the merely logical invites—in itself legitimately instrumental—is to be avoided, then the propositions of experimental science must be interpreted in the light of the metaphysical to produce propositions about *real natures.*

Having completed the analysis we must now relate it to the purpose for which it was made. We said that the proposition

"The physical world is finite" is metaphysical (cosmological). It is not a proposition of the philosophy of nature because its truth or falsity can be known without the benefit of experimental science. For the same reason it is not a proposition of experimental science. Yet in some manner or other it seemed to imply, or be implied by (it was not clear which), relativity physics. Now the answer can be given. The proposition stands in the same relation to relativity theory as proposition (4) does in the theory of gases. Just as (4) is a cosmological proposition constituting part of the evidence of some proposition of the philosophy of nature, which argument is a final one after an instrumental argument involving both logical propositions and propositions of experimental science, so does the proposition to the effect that the physical world is finite constitute part of the evidence for one or more propositions of the philosophy of nature, the rest of the evidence deriving from relativity physics as an experimental science.

At this point we can answer specifically a question that has already been answered generally. An objection might be made that, granted the instrumental argument *A*, our interpretation of argument *B* is wholly unnecessary. Instead of (6) being a proposition of the philosophy of nature and (4) a metaphysical proposition, why cannot both be interpreted as propositions of experimental science? The whole of argument *B* then consists of one kind of knowledge, experimental science. We then have only two kinds of knowledge in the study of nature, experimental science and the "logical" which is instrumental to it.

Now so far from this being an objection it is something which must be insisted upon. What is necessary is that one must be clear as to exactly what is asserted, and on what grounds. From the standpoint of pure experimental science (4) and (6) can be interpreted as propositions of experimental science. If one's purpose be not to understand things which have "natures," but rather to predict, manipulate, control—in short, to "handle" things—then *B* not only can but must be so interpreted as the objector wishes. But if one's purpose be primarily *cognitive,* then prediction and control, while necessary, are not sufficient.

They become not the end, but rather are instrumental to the purpose of cognition. To assert otherwise is to identify the necessary means with the end. To insist that it *must* be that way is simply "cognitive nihilism."

If all that is meant is "can" and not "must," then one is simply asserting a minimum methodological procedure for experimental science. From this standpoint, experimental science as *purely positive,* one can postulate and experiment and experiment and postulate some more—*ad infinitum.* A proposition such as (4) in argument *B* then becomes one kind of postulate among others, one which is necessary, as the scientists say, in order to render the theory of gases "intelligible." The point is that from the standpoint of experimental science *as such,* that is all one will ever get—*an infinite regress of postulates.* One is eternally confined to the phenomenological. It is for this reason that Maritain called such science "empiriological"—"empirio" (propositions of experimental science) and "logical" (propositions of logic as instrumental). But if an infinite regress of postulates is to be avoided, if the phenomenological is ever to be transcended and real existence understood, then there must be ontological (metaphysical) evidence for what from the standpoint of experimental methodology is merely postulated. Once again, the only error that can be made is to assert that the requirements of experimental science are absolute, and that there is nothing more. In that case experimental science as positive is arbitrarily and dogmatically made into a philosophy, namely, positiv*ism.*

In summary, in the course of explanation in experimental science a theory implies a law in a hybrid form involving "is probably," but by means of a logical proposition. Through experimentation the law as a proposition of experimental science implies theory by means of a metaphysical proposition. This latter proposition, for purely methodological purposes, *can* be taken as a proposition of experimental science. That the physical world is finite may be taken in either one of these ways. It is really a cosmological proposition, but it may be taken "as if" it were a proposition of experimental science.

What Is Natural Science?

Having examined the nature of "scientific" explanation, let us return to the consideration of what kind of knowledge the philosophy of nature is. Explanation in natural science is both inductive and deductive, as we have seen, but it is not merely the simple process of "going up and down." Various kinds of knowledge are involved. It is to be observed that in the last sentence we spoke of explanation in "natural science" rather than "experimental science." Earlier in the volume we said that there was a difference, but that for convenience sometimes they would be used synonymously. There is a difference, though we can now see that natural science, in its proper meaning, is simply the philosophy of nature. Natural science is the science of nature, of the "natures" of things in their wholeness, not just some one "aspect" of things. Of course the "wholeness" referred to is that which it is possible to obtain by means of a "science." Insofar as things are individuals they always possess private natures which are never wholly accessible to any science.

The science of nature is concerned with mobile being, which is the object of the philosophy of nature. The identification of "experimental science" with "science" or with "natural science" is historically relatively a recent phenomenon, one which represents the victory of positivism in universities. Previously, "the philosophy of nature" was the same as "natural philosophy," "science of nature" or "natural science," at least in content. For example, Newton's work was called *The Mathematical Principles of Natural Philosophy*. Only in recent times has there been a conscious separation of what is really only a distinct aspect of a whole. The science of nature is "one." We do not, historically or psychologically, begin with metaphysics and then apply it to something called "experimental science" to obtain the philosophy of nature. The "temporal" is irrelevant to the order of knowledge. But in the order of time we begin with changing things, the world of common sense experience. In order to understand nature we separate intellectually the mobile from being, and being from the mobile. The latter leads us to cosmology, and by further abstraction we reach being *qua* being, which is pure metaphysics. The former leads us in the direction of the details of mobile being, of the mobile *qua* mobile. When we put the "aspects" together again we get mobile being. We begin with it, and we end with it. We begin with natural science (the philosophy of nature), and we end with it. What is distinguished for the purpose of understanding must not be separated in reality. But this has been done. It is a serious error even in physical science; it is much worse in connection with the science of man. The philosophy of human nature, which is really a part of the philosophy of nature, has almost ceased to exist. In its place we find experimental psychology, a part that is assumed often to be the whole.

Let us sum up what is involved in the knowledge of nature, with reference to the "formal object," not just existential object. The condensed argument may be put in the form of two premises and conclusion.

Premise, metaphysical (cosmological), mobile *qua* being.

Premise, generalization of experimental science, mobile *qua* mobile.

Conclusion, of the philosophy of nature, mobile being.

We may understand why it has been said that human thought begins and ends in philosophy. It begins in "wonderment" and ends with whatever degree of wisdom and understanding the lover of the "logos" can acquire. Referring to "philosophy" in the limited sense of the philosophy of nature, one begins and ends with mobile being, progressing from vagueness and confusion to detail and clarity. But the process demands various kinds of abstraction. And knowledge proceeds from the general to the specific. Light was known long before the concept of "photon." An object at a distance may be merely a thing until on closer inspection we know it to be a kitten. And so the most general, the philosophical categories, are the most familiar. But on important matters humans will not wait upon the details. Guesses will be made, the specific deduced from the general without the benefit of verificatory techniques. In terms of our analysis a leap will be made from major premise to conclusion. Propositions about mobile being will be deduced from knowledge about the mobile *qua* being alone. Then the time comes when the mobile is considered merely in itself, a special kind of abstraction in part legitimate when conceived as a "means" only. However, this occurred historically without full consciousness of what was being done. In becoming conscious it is understandable, though regrettable, that the developing experimental science was considered to be a rival of, and finally the substitute for, the metaphysical.

There is a dialectic of error such that one error produces its opposite. If there are those who wrongly suppose that the orbit of a planet can be deduced from the ontological—the circle as "perfect," together with the goodness of God—then when the error is exposed by experimental science there are those who in the name of such science are willing to make pronouncements about the ontological, or wholly deny it. But of the two errors the more modern one is by far the more dangerous. In deducing the mobile from being, at the worst one achieves but the unfruitful comedy of mythology and falsehood. In deducing being from the mobile one produces the pathetic tragedy of both mythology and nonsense. There is no more awful notion in any human language than "nonbeing." The formula for generating it is to identify a mode of being with being itself, a part with a whole. When acted upon a practical nihilism results. Such action is exactly that, regardless of its form—whether it be a group absolutizing itself as a modern totalitarian state, or the more respectable but less spectacular procedure of identifying experimental science with natural science or the philosophy of nature. Both are forms of the sin of pride.

Is the philosophy of nature complementary to experimental science? Understanding the philosophy of nature makes possible the answering of several questions about "science." For example: Is the philosophy of nature complementary to experimental science? No, the former is partly constituted by the latter. It is cosmology that is complementary to experimental science. A whole cannot be complementary with a part.

If the parts of the philosophy of nature, as a kind of knowledge, are independent of each other, and hence relatively autonomous with respect to constitutive evidence, wherein lies the synthesis which the philosophy of nature is supposed to represent? Have we not an external relation between two kinds of knowledge, a mere juxtaposition; in which case the conclusion which pretends to be a proposition of the philosophy of nature is really nothing but a summation, and hence there is nothing "new"? An affirmative answer would be impossible because a contradiction would be asserted. If there is no foundation in things for the conceptual unity of "mobile being," then there can be no knowledge of either being or the mobile. What is distinct in knowledge need not be distinct in reality. For example, the independence of mobile *qua* mobile is logical and not real. Mobile being is real, but the "parts" that constitute knowledge of it are not thus real, although they have a foundation in reality. The synthesis on the level of knowledge is necessary to obtain the oneness of the real.

It is at this point that the notion of "community of knowledge," or "analogy of knowledge," is absolutely necessary in order to understand the nature of a synthetic discipline. As we have seen, the categories of "same" and "different" apply to middle terms in demonstrative arguments. And to such arguments as a whole apply also the categories of "actuality" and "potentiality." If what is actually in a conclusion is actually, and not merely potentially, in the premises, then there is no "new" knowledge. The argument is not really an argument. *It becomes merely a formal structure summing up what is already known independent of the argument.* This nominalistic view of the syllogism would make any kind of knowledge impossible that involves demonstration.

What is the nature of the integration? If the philosophy of nature is synthetic, integrating cosmology and experimental science as "parts," then would not there have to be some knowledge of the philosophy of nature not so constituted in order that in terms of it the integration may be accomplished? The answer must be negative for the simple reason that there is no evidence to the contrary. Implied in the question is the assumption that knowledge must conform in *a priori* fashion to a certain view of "whole," "part," and "relation." A whole may be more than the sum of its parts. Or it may not, in which case it is either an aggregate or a unity of parts in relation. The philosophy of nature has the latter kind of unity, a unity of kinds of knowledge in relation. The kind of wholeness and unity implied in the question is that which is conceived to be the only alternative to the nominalistic view of two kinds of knowledge in mere juxtaposition to each other. Actually, the former presupposes the latter—just as, for example, a political totalitarianism, in which the nation is thought to be something real over and above its parts, presupposes the anarchistic view of human beings against which it is opposed. In a synthetic or integrative discipline the nature of a part is not absorbed and modified. In the philosophy of nature, for example, the nature of experimental science is not lost but *fully revealed.*

If this is true, then it means that neither a nominalism nor an idealism can adequately account for the philosophy of nature as a kind of knowledge. Only realism is compatible with the notion of the analogy of knowledge, without which a kind of knowledge cannot be "related" without being modified or destroyed. An examination of the protests of physical scientists in the last century and a half against philosophical pronouncements on nature would probably disclose that much of the reference is to the post-Kantian idealism. Hegel's criticism, not his solution, was correct:

> What has in modern times been called the philosophy of nature consists principally in a frivolous play with empty and external analogies, which, however, claim to be considered profound results. The natural consequence has been to discredit the philosophical study of nature.[9]

But this is correct only against a nominalism, in which one speculates *because he can't know;* or, perhaps against the Wolffian error of attempting to deduce the philosophy of nature from the metaphysical. However, the Hegelian solution is even worse:

> The philosophy of nature takes up the material, prepared for it by physics out of experience, at the point to which physics has brought it, and again transforms it, without basing it ultimately on the authority of experience.[10]

Now "transforms" is "making," which implies that the function of the philosophy of nature is to make over or change experimental science. This is one of the most serious errors in the history of thought. Behind it is the breakdown of the distinction between first and second intentions, between *what* is intended and *that which* is intended, between the real and the logical. Hegel says: "The syllogistic form is a universal form of all things . . . but nature is weak and fails to exhibit the logical forms in their purity. Such a feeble exemplification of the syllogism may be seen in the magnet." [11]

That the principle of the magnet failing to exemplify the syllogism illustrates the weakness of nature—it is of such under the name of philosophy that has practically destroyed the discipline. Metaphysics is reduced to logic, and the philosophy of nature then becomes "applied logic." "We have merely to let the thought-forms follow the impulse of their own organic life." [12] And out comes the philosophy of nature! And with experimental science "transformed." The scientist quite correctly pursues his task without worrying about the syllogism. The idealistic error is to suppose "knowing" to be a kind of mental "digestion." The philosophy of nature does not transform or digest experimental science. Rather the latter is more fully revealed and understood, for the mobile is no longer seen in abstraction but as it really is, as a mode of *being*.

Although the original question must be answered in the negative, there is still a relevant question with regard to the integrating nature of the philosophy of nature: Wherein does the integration lie? If there is mere juxtaposition of metaphysics and experimental science, then there is no integration. On the other hand, there is no knowledge of the philosophy of nature independent of the two disciplines in terms of which the two are integrated. This means that the philosophy of nature is not a "cause" but an "effect." *It is not a discipline that integrates other kinds of knowledge; rather it* is *the integration.* Hence the question: Wherein does the integration lie?

There is only one alternative left for an answer. One of the kinds of knowledge integrated must be responsible for the integration. This kind of knowledge is metaphysics. The reason for this is that it is nature, or the "natures" of things, which we seek to understand, the "real," the "being" of things. The "philosophy" in the philosophy of nature derives from metaphysics, not from the experimental science. The latter, in itself and alone, is founded upon an abstraction from being. The nature of things is understood when a mode of being is integrated with a being of which it is a mode. The denial of this, the attempt to do the impossible, namely, to integrate in terms of experimental science, is philosophical nihilism, the movement toward nonbeing, nothingness.

There is nothing strange about metaphysics being an integrative factor and at the same time one of the kinds of knowledge integrated. The reflexive function is found in other respects. For example, knowledge about the order of knowledge is itself one of the kinds of knowledge that is ordered. The order of knowledge is a problem of the metaphysics of knowledge. With the exception of metaphysics, the problem of the kind of knowledge which any discipline is, is not itself a problem of that discipline. For instance, the nature of experimental science or of history as kinds of knowledge is not itself a problem of experimental science or of history. But the problem of the nature of metaphysics as a kind of knowledge is also a problem of metaphysics, the metaphysics of knowledge.

How do we know the essential nature of things? Is it metaphysics or the philosophy of nature that gives us knowledge of the essences of things? There would seem to be difficulties in answering one way or the other. If it is metaphysics, then the philosophy of nature would be rendered superfluous. If it is the philosophy of nature, then it would seem that metaphysics and experimental science vie with each other in giving information about the nature of things, and this would contradict the very meaning of the philosophy of nature as described. As a way out one might be tempted to say that we know essence through metaphysics, existence through experimental science, and that the two are seen together in the philosophy of nature. But this would be worse than no answer at all. Existence and essence can be correlated neither with kinds of knowledge nor with "mobile" and "being." The problem is a most difficult one, and the following pretends to be only partial and inadequate, though indicating, perhaps, the correct direction in which a solution is to be found.

The philosophy of nature, experimental science, and metaphysics are all concerned with the essences of things, but not in the same way. Part of the difficulty lies in the ambiguity of the notion of "essence," for one may think of it as contrasted with either "accident" or "existence." To correlate metaphysics and experimental science with the knowledge of the essence and accidents of things would be to define the error of "essentialism." Experimental science may be said to deal with essences, but as such and alone it can never get beyond nominal essences. Of course, a nominal essence may be a real essence. But whether this is so in any given case is the function of the philosophy of nature to determine. It cannot be determined by experimental science *qua* experimental science. The same may be said for metaphysics, but with one qualification. Metaphysics is concerned with "type" essences, e.g., what makes a material thing *what* it is. Now, a dog is a material thing, but it is not strictly a metaphysical (cosmological) problem to determine what a dog is. For that one needs the help of biology. The qualification is as follows. Insofar as any creature represents a metaphysical type, and not something subsumed under the type, then the metaphysical is sufficient. The "metaphysical types" referred to are the metaphysical levels of being, such as material, vegetable, living, rational. If the qualification is not made, then the error would be committed of thinking of an atom, a rose, a dog, and a man as on the same co-ordinate level as regards being. Any metaphysics except an extreme reductive materialism must avoid this error, and hence the avoidance is not peculiar to realism. Now, while an atom, a rose, and a dog represent only one kind among innumerable others of a given type, there is only one kind of natural thing that is "rational," namely, the human being. For this reason there can be a "metaphysics of man" in abstraction from experimental science in the sense that there cannot be, say, a "metaphysics of the atom." In other words, we can know more about the essential nature of man in abstraction from experimental psychology than we can know about any other creature in abstraction from an experimental science. In passing we may note that there is an additional reason to the one given—a creature that knows happens to be its own object.

The qualification has further implications, and also has a certain foundation. It has been recognized that in the case of creatures other than man it is very difficult to determine the specific essence or specific properties. We say that a man laughs *because* he is rational; he is not rational because he laughs. But as we go down further in the levels below man the relation between property and specific essence is increasingly more difficult to determine. For example "laughter" is to "rational" as the "negative charge" of an electron is to "what"? The "what" almost becomes an unknown "X."

What is the foundation or explanation of this fact? It is this. As one moves from man to lower levels of reality one encounters less form and more of matter—the potential, the inert. As one moves from the barest forms of (secondary) matter up to man, the converse is the case. If one moves on beyond the man he finally encounters the wholly nonmaterial, non-inert, pure act. It is the middle part of this scale of being that man can know best in a purely natural way. So far as essence is concerned humility demands that man admit to an agnosticism of a degree at both ends—but for quite different reasons. As one moves from man to the increasingly material there is also a movement from the intelligible to the relatively unintelligible, for one approaches the formless, always asymptotically, however. As we have seen, pure primary matter, although it does not exist as such, can only be known analogously. Even the formless can be known only by means of form. On the other hand, as we move from man finally to God the foundation of relative agnosticism as to essence is that of such pure intelligibility as to be above man's comprehension. This fact has been illustrated by comparison with the sun. The sun is the source of light. Yet if we look at it we are blinded. So God is the source of whatever is intelligible. Yet when we try to know God's essence we are blinded.

Insofar as man is part of nature the philosophy of human

nature is part of the philosophy of nature. Insofar as man is not to be understood as merely a part of nature, then man's essential nature can be grasped metaphysically, and hence independent of *some* of the evidence normally constituting a synthetic discipline. So far as constitutive evidence is concerned knowledge of God does not come from any synthetic discipline, but only from metaphysics and theology based on revelation. However, as we go to levels below human nature the philosophy of nature depends more and more upon experimental science and less upon metaphysics. But again this tendency is asymptotic and can never be anything else. To illustrate, if we want to know what an electron is we have to depend almost entirely upon experimental physics, however meager that may be. Metaphysics tells us little. It is in light of these qualifications, explanations, and clarifications that the philosophy of nature is to be understood.

A mathematical analogy may be helpful. Let the two axes, X and Y, represent respectively metaphysics and experimental science. However far one may proceed along either axis the value of the other is zero. This represents the relative independence of the two kinds of knowledge. Now the curve of the philosophy of nature may be represented by the simple hyperbola, the asymptotes of which are the two axes. The philosophy of human nature would be represented by that part of the curve which gradually approaches the X axis, and where the value of y is progressively small. The rest of the curve represents the various phases of the philosophy of nature. The attempt to understand the real natures of subatomic entities, as over and above the pragmatic and nominal essences given us by experimental science, would be represented by the other extreme part of the curve approaching asymptotically the Y axis, and where the value of x (metaphysics) is progressively less. The middle part of the curve, where the value of x and y are more nearly the same, would represent that part of the philosophy of nature which considers "living things." For example, it is much easier to understand the living in terms of the various kinds of causes than it is to understand what goes on in the interior of the atom. More specifically, final causation has an applicability here that it would be most difficult to find for subatomic entities—

although one would dare not infer from that fact alone the impossibility of application.

The analogy may be continued in pointing out two errors. It would be wrong to conceive of the "curve of knowledge" which is the philosophy of nature as a straight line with a slope having the numerical value of one, as if all conclusions of the philosophy of nature were to be obtained by adding equal parts of metaphysics and experimental science. The second error would be to identify the curve with either axis—which, if done, of course eliminates the curve. But it is understandable how this latter error can occur if only a partial perspective is obtained. Consider the historical periods before the rise of experimental science. The emphasis was upon man and man's relation to God. The part of the curve way out upon the *X* axis could not be seen to be different from the axis itself. Hence, the philosophy of human nature was simply the same as the "metaphysics of man." And there was a tendency to deduce the philosophy of nature from metaphysics alone. After several centuries in which experimental science has developed and matured the contemporary tendency is to see no difference between the philosophy of nature and the *Y* axis, for the further one goes into, say, recent experimental physics the more remote it is from metaphysics. And so the philosophy of human nature is denied through identification with experimental psychology.

In this day and age, when everything must be three dimensional to be "up-to-date," it would be a shame to limit our analogy to two dimensions. But it is sufficient for our purpose. Nevertheless, we should like to point out that even the philosophical is not to be left behind in such matters. It must be left for a later work to show that the *Z* axis is the "theological," and that "depth," and hence the true curve of the knowledge which is the philosophy of nature and the philosophy of human nature, cannot be obtained without it.

The Contribution of Experimental Psychology to the Philosophy of Human Nature

It may be asked: If it is true that the philosophy of human nature approaches the metaphysics of man, then insofar as there is a difference, wherein lies the contribution of experimental psychology? When we speak of the essence of anything we may have either one or both of two things in mind. First, there is the problem of determining that something has this nature rather than that. Second, there is the problem of understanding more fully what the "nature" is. As we approach the subatomic we rely more and more, but never wholly, upon experimental science for the answers to both problems. If, to use a previous example, we say that an atom is a substantial unity, although the proposition is one of the philosophy of nature the evidence comes chiefly from experimental physics. If we ask whether an electron is a substantial unity, perhaps the best answer is that it is difficult to say yes or no. Why? Whatever metaphysical knowledge we may have remains the same regardless of which question is asked, or what answer is given. The difficulty in answering the last lies in the fact that there is a lack of evidence from experimental physics.

On the other hand, it can be known on metaphysical grounds, independent of experimental psychology, i.e., constitutively, not necessarily instrumentally, that man is rational. No equivalent metaphysical knowledge can be had of an atom. However, in the philosophy of human nature it is not the function of experimental psychology to determine *that* man is rational or even what rationality is "in general." That is the function of metaphysics. Experimental psychology has the function of helping us to understand more fully just what it means, specifically, for man to be rational, and just how this is accomplished. It is to be understood that this does not exhaust experimental psychology, that it is quite a "broad" subject, and that much of its concern is with matters other than what man's essential nature is. Also, "rational" cannot be identified with "intelligence" in recent psychology.

This is also in part an explanation of why it is possible to have a philosophy of human nature in a sense in which it is impossible to have a philosophy of "atom nature." The latter is a part of the philosophy of nature in a sense in which the philosophy of human nature is not.

Some errors that are to be avoided. Further understanding of how metaphysics, experimental science, and the philosophy of nature each makes its contribution to discovering what are the essential natures of things must come through actually practicing the discipline of the philosophy of nature. Understanding the nature of "the philosophy of nature" as a kind of knowledge can never be a substitute for this. A few hints in the form of warnings may illustrate what we have in mind.

An error that must be avoided in the philosophy of nature is that of the reification of all logical or cognitive distinctions. From the standpoint of the order of being a thing has only one essence, one nature. It is the purpose of the philosophy of nature to discover it. But in so doing it may be necessary to divide mentally (a sort of epistemological "division of labor") what is really one. Such notions as nominal essence, phenomenological and ontological context, and the domain of experimental science have a foundation in reality but do not represent real things themselves. If this is overlooked, then there is a tendency to oppose one kind of knowledge to another on the false assumption that each attempts to do the same thing but that one does it better than another. This is a recipe for intellectual chaos, the kind which characterizes much of the so-called liberal education of the present century. After the Middle Ages the attempted compromise with this error, which was expressed as the doctrine of "two-fold knowledge," was short-lived. It was said that something could be true in one kind of knowledge, but false in another. This solves nothing, but rather reflects the breakdown of the order of knowledge. It is impossible for metaphysics and experimental science to be incompatible with one another in the long run. "War" occurs only when either attempts to be a substitute for the other.

Another kind of difficulty in the philosophy of nature, having to do with understanding concrete essences, the "natures" of things, derives directly from a metaphysical error. The nature which the philosophy of nature seeks to understand is *dynamic*. If this fact is not reflected in metaphysics (cosmology), then one can never get it in the conclusions which constitute the philosophy of nature; for it will never be found in experimental science, as Bergson and others have so often pointed out. The metaphysical error is to conceive of essences as static. The temptation is strong because *as abstracted and as objects of second intentions they are static.* This way leads inevitably to some kind of "essentialism" in which metaphysics and logic are confused. "Natures" are reduced to structures. When this happens there is an additional temptation simply to posit "existence," or perhaps make it one predicate among others. In the latter case existence becomes merely another essence. The dynamic nature which one expects to find and understand in the synthetic discipline will consequently never be found. This difficulty, which stems from metaphysics, is then easily transferred to the philosophy of nature. The trouble is eliminated if, in the words of John Wild, we "recognize active tendency as a third *ontological principle* correlated with essence and existence, and necessarily constitutive of any finite being." [13]

The third error to be avoided is that of confusing a methodological requirement with a metaphysical truth. It may be pointed out that the scientist studies "nature," but that in doing so he constructs his own concepts accordingly as they enable him to predict and verify his theories. He does not need metaphysical "notions." He prefers not to speak of "essences," or "natures," or even "things," but if such terms are to be used they must be interpreted in terms of "mental constructs"; that is, categories are not "imposed" upon the mind at all, but are freely created according to "need." This requirement is sufficient for the work of the scientist. For example, if one speaks of the "nature of a thing," then a reinterpretation must take place. The scientist knows nothing of "essence"; hence the interpretation must be in terms of "properties." According to Wilfred Sellars:

> . . . the concept of the nature of a thing, insofar as it is a coherent one, can be analyzed in terms of the concept of a dovetailing set of dispositional properties which specify both the states by which it has responded to its historical circumstances, and the states by which it would have responded to other circumstances.[14]

Thus far what is pointed out is quite true. So far from it being incompatible with anything that has been said about the order of knowledge, we would insist that it is necessarily implied. The word "scientist" is likely to be ambiguous, but in context we take it to mean "experimental scientist." The "needs" which he has are methodological demands as required by his objects. As an experimental scientist he can never find real being as such, for the mobile *qua* mobile is defined by its abstraction from being. The freedom to "construct" that he says he needs is a freedom he quite legitimately has. This freedom, which is often described phenomenologically in volumes, but is seldom explained, follows necessarily once the "object" of experimental science is understood. Since the object is the mobile abstracted from being, of course the experimental scientist *qua* experimental scientist is *free from* any responsibilities which might be "imposed" by being.

But most of these volumes referred to do not point this out. Rather the conclusion is drawn either that the real nature of things cannot be known or that they are identical with the scientist's "constructs" at any given time. Such a conclusion does not follow at all from the evidence given. It follows rather from a suppressed premise to the effect that experimental science exhausts the meaning of "science," or that the "scientific method" is the only method, or some such thought. What is the evidence for this? None whatsoever. It is a philosophical dogma which prevents once and for all any rational philosophy. What is defended, namely, the phenomenological description of experimental science, happens to be irrelevant to the conclusion for the simple reason that its truth may be granted and is not an issue at all. On the other hand, the suppressed premise that is relevant is posited dogmatically, and sometimes explicitly.[15]

When the scientist protests against "medieval" occult qualities, powers, and potencies his argument is not always clear. The ground on which he has been justified, and the sense in which he has always been correct is this: Metaphysical deductions about the natures of things can never be a substitute for experimental science. Consider an example. It makes some sense to the astronomer if he is asked whether or not the sun is spherical. He will say that the sun is spherical. This is a historical proposition, one that is a part of astronomy because of its historical interest in our particular solar system. As a hypothesis it accounts for much—the brilliancy of the planets when illuminated edgewise, the continued circular aspect of the solar disc, the passage of sun spots, and so on. Now, let us suppose he is asked what the "essence" of the sun is. The form of his answer may depend upon his temperament, but the substance of it will be clear. He doesn't seek essences. He may recall his history and remember the struggle, slow and gradual, to cast off such ideas. He remembers Kepler's statement:

> . . . lest perchance a blind man might deny it to you, of all the bodies in the universe the most excellent is the sun, whose whole essence is nothing else than the purest light, than which there is no greater star; which singly and alone is the producer, conserver, and warmer of all things; it is a fountain of light, rich in fruitful heat, most fair, limpid, and pure to the sight, the source of vision, portrayer of all colors . . .[16]

Kepler goes on to correlate astronomical entities with the members of the Trinity. It is not this, but the three laws experimentally obtained, which are of lasting value in Kepler's works. The astronomer is thankful that those days are over.

And quite correctly. But his protest is wholly exhausted when he points out that one should not give an astronomical locus to ontological entities, that it is a perversion of both metaphysics and theology to do so, and that the phenomenological must not be deduced from the ontological. However, his knowledge of experimental science does not guarantee against an error he may make, that of identifying metaphysics with a perverted version of it.

Like anyone else the experimental scientist pays a price for his freedom. If he has the freedom to deal with the mobile in abstraction from being, then he has the responsibility to not make pronouncements about being in the name of his speciality. When he does so he becomes a "philosopher," but a philosopher of nonbeing rather than of being. The "average man" cannot very well distinguish between the two kinds. He knows only that both he and "they" are confused, and he consoles himself with a defeatist agnosticism—for if "they" don't know, how can he be expected to know?

The philosopher of nature is the same as the natural scientist, for the philosophy of nature is the science of nature or "natural science." The experimental scientist as such is free from metaphysics as constitutive evidence. The natural scientist is not, for metaphysics is partially constitutive as evidence of the philosophy of nature. One may now understand why there is very little natural science responsibly taught in much of higher education. What is taught is chiefly experimental science. The tragedy is that the experimental scientist seldom, if ever, knows the difference, for his "Doctor of Philosophy" degree has long since ceased to demand that he know the "philosophy" of his special discipline.

Another question can now be answered. Experimental science constantly changes, and progresses through accumulation. Is this the case with the philosophy of nature also? The implication of this question is usually derogatory, whether answered yes or no. If the philosophy of nature changes as does experimental science, then it would seem to be a "function" of the latter. In short, experimental science provides whatever progress there is in philosophy. If the philosophy of nature does not change, then it does not progress and therefore is of little worth. It should now be seen the sense in which the philosophy of nature does and does not change. There is both a constant and a variable factor to the philosophy of nature, represented respectively by metaphysics and experimental science. In metaphysics, assuming the change is not merely from the false to the true—or conversely—change takes place as depth of understanding. In the philosophy of nature, because of the contribution of the variable factor which is experimental science, there is not only change in depth but also in accumulation. For example, while time may be required, both for the individual and for the race, for metaphysical understanding, waiting upon the development of experimental science at any stage is not necessary for the knowledge of many metaphysical propositions. On the other hand, to know some (not all) propositions of the philosophy of nature one must patiently await the development of experimental science. There was a time when it could not be known that the atom is a substantial unity because experimental science had not as yet given us knowledge about the atom.

The distinction between experimental science and natural science is necessary in order to understand what is done in practice by scientists. But it would be wrong to suppose that this distinction, "part" from "whole," is to be found sharply throughout history. Whether he knows it or not the aim of the scientist is always natural science, not merely experimental science. But because he is uniquely concerned with a "means," and because he often lacks philosophical knowledge, he may easily mistake a part of the quest for the whole. But in some sense or other he will be concerned with the "philosophy" of his subject, even though he may call it by some other name. It will also be understood by now that while any proposition must be examined in the light of the distinctions made, it is impossible to know whether it is a proposition of experimental science or natural science in complete abstraction from a careful statement of its meaning and the argument which supports it.

Summary of Principles

(1) Experimental science is necessary as evidence for the philosophy of nature.

(2) Metaphysics is necessary as evidence for the philosophy of nature.

(3) The philosophy of nature is not potentially a part of metaphysics; rather metaphysics is actually a part of the philosophy of nature.

(4) What are "complementary" with respect to each other are metaphysics and experimental science.

(5) In the philosophy of nature there is "applied metaphysics," but the application is to experimental science to obtain propositions of the philosophy of nature.

(6) It is in cosmology that there is no applied metaphysics, for it *is* a part of metaphysics, since its object is the mobile *qua* being in contradistinction to the object of the philosophy of nature which is mobile being.

(7) It is in an integrative science such as the philosophy of nature that there is established a "community of knowledge," and which requires a doctrine of "analogy of knowledge."

(8) The problem of analogy in connection with the community of knowledge arises in understanding the middle term which links major and minor and also relates two kinds of knowledge.

(9) Without a doctrine of analogy one is forever locked up univocally within a given kind of knowledge. This means each kind becomes "imperialistic" in relation to some other, institutionally speaking.

(10) Hence, there is the attempt to deduce the philosophy of nature from metaphysics.

(11) Or there is the attempt to generate the philosophy of nature from experimental science.

(12) If the following qualification is made, all of the aforementioned principles hold for the philosophy of human nature as well as the philosophy of nature: The contribution of metaphysics and experimental psychology to the philosophy of human nature is not to be thought of in terms of arithmetical equality. The evidence for the philosophy of human nature stems chiefly from metaphysics.

A Certain Difficulty in Contemporary Realism

It is not easy to contrast the thesis presented in this volume with the thought of other moderate realists. In a sense there is no essential contrast. And yet if there were really no difference at all one would be merely repeating and summing up the thought of others. But if there is a difference one assumes an obligation to point out what it is.

In his *Degrees of Knowledge* and *Philosophy of Nature,* as well as in other writings, J. Maritain has established himself as a contemporary master of the subject of the order of knowledge. Certainly in spirit there is not much difference between his analysis and ours. However, so far as the philosophy of nature is concerned we believe that he does not sufficiently distinguish between it and what we have called cosmology. We have gone to some length to show what the difference is. Second, we have used the term "metaphysics" to include cosmology, the study of being *qua* mobile, and not merely the study of being *qua* being. Third, we have tried to explore further than Maritain and others the relations between kinds of knowledge in terms of evidence. A careful analysis would disclose the fact that Maritain's notions of "subordination" and "subalternation" are not adequate substitutes for the distinctions we have made, namely, "instrumental to," "regulative of," and "constitutive of." In this sense Maritain reflects the inadequacy of much of past realism, and which it is the aim of this work to correct.

An example may illustrate in part. Maritain says that "the philosophy of nature needs the sciences for its completion . . ." [17] Also, a function of the philosophy of nature is to "transmit rulings from above to the world of the natural sciences . . ." [18] This establishes the philosophy of nature as regulative of the experimental sciences. This is consistent with the notion of the philosophy of nature as being "fundamentally distinct" from the sciences. But if so, we suggest that the philosophy of nature is being confused with cosmology. It is the metaphysical that is regulative—always. This is admitted by Maritain. But if so, then both the philosophy of nature and metaphysics compete in their regulative function over the experimental sciences. And this is hardly possible.

At other times Maritain means by the philosophy of nature more nearly what we have found it to be. It actually depends partly upon the experimental sciences. In fact, it has such an "intimate contact with the natural sciences" that they can force a change in the philosophy of nature, although not a "substantial change." [19] A philosophy of nature may only "last a man's lifetime, 50 years, 70 years . . . and this provided that its successive editions, if it has them, be periodically brought up-to-date." [20] Now this view is incompatible with the former. The philosophy of nature cannot be regulative of the experimental sciences and at the same time change as they change.

Perhaps it will now be better understood why we took some trouble to distinguish between a cosmological proposition (e.g., the physical world is finite) and a proposition of the philosophy of nature (e.g., the atom is a substantial unity). Both have to do with "becoming," and with the "mobile." But the facts of sense experience are only *instrumental* to the knowledge of the former, while *constitutive* of the knowledge of the latter. Once a cosmological proposition is known *by means of* sense experience its truth will remain forever untouched by the accumulated knowledge of the experimental sciences. Such knowledge can be "regulative." On the other hand, what may change every fifty years is that kind of knowledge, the philosophy of nature, which is partly constituted by the experimental sciences. Cosmology is concerned with *being* insofar as it is mobile. Experimental science is concerned with the *mobile* insofar as it is mobile. Here the "details" are furnished. To the extent they are furnished—and every fifty years or so may bring new "furnishings"—then by synthesis we can know the mobile (in some detail) insofar as it (in such detail) has being. And this is the philosophy of nature.

In terms of formal objects there is a difference between (1) general metaphysics: being *qua* being; (2) cosmology: being *qua* mobile (in general); (3) experimental science: mobile *qua* mobile (in detail); (4) the philosophy of nature: mobile (in detail) being. Facts of sense experience are instrumental to, but not constitutive of, (1) and (2); are wholly constitutive of (3); and are partly constitutive of (4). The (1) and (2) are regulative of (3), but partly constitutive of (4).

The confusion of the philosophy of nature with cosmology, which is a part of metaphysics, is of course not peculiar to Maritain. The matter is of sufficient importance that the criticism should not rest upon a few quotations. To make clear what we mean we may turn to a treatise, *The Philosophy of Human Nature,* by George P. Klubertanz.[21] Although the volume is on that part of the philosophy of nature which is the philosophy of human nature, the example will be all the more important for that reason. We shall see that just as the philosophy of nature can be confused with the metaphysics of nature (cosmology), so the philosophy of human nature can be confused with the "metaphysics of man."

The confusion of the philosophy of human nature with the

metaphysics of man. The problem of the philosophy of human nature is: What is man? The importance of the problem cannot be overemphasized. All of the practical sciences presuppose some answer. Mr. Klubertanz presents us with a well-reasoned answer. It is a reasoned answer because there is an argument. It isn't composed of happy guesses produced by generalizing in a conjectural fashion the limited categories of experimental psychology. At the beginning evidence is presented showing that man is a substantial unity. At the end evidence is presented demonstrating that man has a soul and, to a limited extent, what its nature is. In between, the "activities" and "powers" of man are considered—internal and external sensations, habits, the sensory appetites, the nature of the will and the intellect.

The author recognizes the problem of the order of knowledge by devoting a good number of pages to clarifying the relations between the philosophy of human nature, experimental psychology, and metaphysics. It is this thesis that we wish to question. We shall first present some of the difficulties that give rise to the problem. Then we shall attempt to demonstrate that in the body of his work the kind of knowledge represented is that of the "metaphysics of man" and not the "philosophy of human nature."

What is the difference between the philosophy of human na ture and experimental psychology? The two are contrasted in terms of "starting point," "methods," and "type of conclusion." Experimental psychology begins with

> specific facts that are precise and detailed. They are demonstrated to be universal in fact by techniques that more or less closely involve laboratory testing of many individuals. For example, this science investigates the various conditions that can have an influence on memory; it considers how much different persons forget after a week, a month, a year; it tests the advantages and disadvantages of various techniques of remembering.[22]

On the other hand, the philosophy of human nature begins with

> facts that need not be specific, but must be very accurately determined. They are ideally demonstrated to be universal by a proof

that gives the reason for their being universal. For example, the philosopher tries to see as clearly as possible what 'to remember' means; he investigates this action to see what he can learn about the nature of man from it; he relates this action to other actions of man in terms of the nature thus revealed.[23]

The experimental scientist is interested in measurement and verifying techniques. For the philosopher "measurement in itself is usually irrelevant." [24] "The technique of the philosopher is usually a rigorous use of reflection and/or analysis. From an experience, he passes by means of reflection-analysis to consideration of what it is that he has observed and of its mode of being." [25]

What kind of conclusion does experimental psychology obtain?

As far as possible the scientist states his conclusions quantitatively. In general, what he is looking for is the connections between various facts, the conditions that modify the fact, and the consequences this fact may have in relation to other facts.[26]

On the other hand:

The philosopher states his conclusions in terms of nature and mode of being. What he is looking for is the answer to these questions: What kind of activities are these? What kind of being is man? [27]

It is not at all clear to us what the contrast is. Are the "facts" different for experimental psychology and the philosophy of human nature? What are the "specific facts" of experimental psychology in contrast to nonspecific facts of the philosophy of human nature? In a note we are told that "by 'specific facts' are meant the very specialized results characteristic of the sciences." [28] But this is question-begging, for the term "specific facts" has already been used to define *that* which is now used to define *it*.

Experimental psychology investigates the "conditions" of memory, the philosophy of human nature tries to see what it "means." The distinction is real, but it cannot significantly be used to separate two disciplines. It would make the work of the experimental psychologist impossible. If he cannot investigate what memory means, how can he know its conditions? This difficulty might be surmounted if we could say that experimental psychology presupposes the philosophy of human nature. This possibility is eliminated, however, for we are told that "there can be no real direct dependence of either form of knowledge upon the other." [29] Perhaps experimental psychology measures what the philosophy of human nature is talking about? Measurement, it is said, is "usually" irrelevant for the philosopher. However, the word "usually" breaks down the distinction. Furthermore, what does it mean to say that the technique of the philosopher is "usually" a rigorous use of reflection and analysis as opposed to the scientist's technique of measurement? Doesn't the scientist reflect and analyze as well as measure?

There is reason to believe that the author is not completely satisfied with the distinction between experimental psychology and the philosophy of human nature, for in one of the *appendixes* he returns to the problem. However, the term now used is "scientific psychology." The "starting point" of scientific psychology is "experience and experimental or scientifically observed data," while that of the philosophy of human nature is "experiential, . . ." [30] To understand this a "note" refers us back to the material we have already quoted, and which we have not found clear. But another distinction is introduced. The "material object" of scientific psychology is "behavior, human and animal," while that of the philosophy of human nature is "man as revealed through his activities." [31] Now either the material object is the same or it is not. If it is not, then the psychologist and the philosopher are not talking about the same "thing" at all. One is talking about "man" and the other isn't. If the material object is the same, then not it, but rather the notion of "formal object," would be relevant in contrasting the two disciplines.

Again we return to the question as to the "facts" which presumably make the starting point of experimental psychology and the philosophy of human nature different. Are there two kinds of "behavior," two different kinds of "activities," the one the property of experimental psychology, the other of the philosophy of human nature? Perhaps what is meant is that the facts for experimental psychology are those of external observation, while those of the philosophy of human nature are the facts obtained from "internal observation" or introspection. If so, this would make impossible the aim of the philosophy of human nature, which is to understand the nature of man as a whole being, not just his subjectivity. Presumably this is not what is meant for the experimental psychologist can deal with introspection. " 'Behavior' means all 'nonautomatic' or modifiable activity which can be observed, admitting both external and self-observation." [32] Sometimes Mr. Klubertanz speaks as if instruments are used in getting facts in experimental psychology but not in the philosophy of human nature.[33] If this is to be the distinction between "special" and "nonspecial" facts, then a most unsatisfactory conclusion follows—the philosophy of human nature becomes the crude, prescientific stage of experimental psychology.

Well, are the starting points of experimental psychology and the philosophy of human nature the same, or are they not? Finally, the author says that they are the same "to some extent," though "not entirely." [34] Some of the evidence for scientific psychology is, and some is not, "meaningful" for the philosophy of human nature.[35] This does not help very much, for this would imply that experimental psychology and the philosophy of human nature could conflict with each other. Yet we are told that such conflict is impossible.[36] Some will "solve" this problem by simply taking a stand one way or another. For example, R. E. Brennan states flatly that "both disciplines have the same subject matter and the same starting point, namely, the acts, powers, and habits of man." [37] Furthermore, Mr. Brennan makes the following distinction: "The science of psychology studies chiefly what a man does. The philosophy of psychology studies chiefly what a man is." [38] But Mr. Klubertanz says that "both investigators strive to see what man is. . . ." Also both want "to know what man does," although the philosophy of human nature is not interested in measuring.[39]

Let us now sum up and define briefly our difficulties in understanding Mr. Klubertanz. A positivist might say that the philosophy of human nature is simply the name given to a speculative synthesis of the various experimental sciences of man, the philosophical categories being arrived at by generalizing some of the concepts of experimental science. The critic might say that this is impossible. But at least one knows what it is that is impossible, and what it is of which one is critical. It is this "what" of the author's conception of the philosophy of human nature that we find unclear. Or, one might have said that there is only one science of man, and it is called the philosophy of human nature. The experimental sciences of man are but phases, parts, of this one science. It is not difficult to distinguish among the various experimental sciences of man. But what our author conceives of is a science, the philosophy of human nature, which parallels or supplements experimental psychology, which "seems to be most closely related to experimental psychology," and yet is in some manner different from it.[40] And both "have true forms of organized knowledge about man." [41] What we have tried to show is that this conception is not at all clear. In fact, in this sense, we doubt whether there is any such thing as the philosophy of human nature. What supplements or complements experimental science is metaphysics, not the philosophy of human nature.

Now it may be objected that the whole matter can be cleared up if we take account of everything our author says. Have we not created our problem by selection of passages? Why not say that the philosophy of human nature is the *metaphysics of man?* Is this not made clear in one of the appendixes? The formal object of experimental psychology is "the observable and/or measureable behavior of human and animal organisms, insofar as this behavior manifests the integrated dynamic interrelationships within the organism or between the organism and its environment," while that of the philosophy of human nature is "the nature of man in relation to his being and activities." [42] The organizing principles of experimental psychology are physical, mechanical, and mathematical concepts, while those of the philosophy of human nature are "metaphysical." [43] Finally, the method of experimental psychology, or scientific psychology, is "rational induction," while that of the philosophy of human nature is "intelligible induction." [44] The former is that which is mediated by experiment, reflection, and analysis; the latter kind of induction is immediate, e.g., seeing that a part is necessarily less than the whole.[45] It appears, then, that the philosophy of human nature is a part of metaphysics. For both the formal object is being. The philosophy of human nature is a kind of *special* metaphysics, having to do with *human* being; *general* metaphysics is concerned with being *qua* being. Since the philosophy of human nature is the metaphysics of man, we would expect that the method of the philosophy of human nature and metaphysics is the same; and so Mr. Klubertanz says that both use "the method of intelligible induction, reflection, and analysis." [46] Now we can understand why the author says that in experimental psychology we find that "man acts thus and so," while in the philosophy of human nature we discover that "having such a nature, man must act thus." [47] The "must" is obtained metaphysically. Explained also is such a statement as this: "This course does not presuppose a course in experimental psychology." [48]

We would be willing to settle on the identification of what the author is doing in this book with part of metaphysics. But however much this seems to be the case, we cannot rest easily with this answer. And for several reasons. (1) If the philosophy of human nature is metaphysics it would be false to say that "it seems to be most closely related to experimental psychology." [49] It would be the "contrasts" and not the "parallels" that would have to be emphasized. (2) In considering the "evidence" for the unity of man as a composite substance the author appeals to the data of anatomy, neurology, including the effects of drugs, brain injuries, and glandular disfunction.[50] Now we have already been told that the philosophy of human nature is independent of the experimental sciences for its nature and evidence —". . . there is no biology or scientific psychology in the philosophical study of man." [51] Here we seem to have a plain contradiction. At any rate the philosophy of human nature cannot be metaphysical, for the experimental sciences can prove nothing in metaphysics. (3) The philosophy of human nature cannot be part of metaphysics because its function is to understand man in his wholeness. But even metaphysics deals only with an aspect of man, however important it may be. The philosophy of human nature would be concerned with "noumenal" man, experimental psychology with "phenomenal" man. If the philosophy of human nature is identified with metaphysics, then there could be no discipline which unites these two aspects of man in order that he may be understood as he *really* is. On the other hand, if the philosophy of human nature is the discipline which so unites, then it cannot be metaphysical. (4) Finally, the author eliminates any doubt that we may have had by bluntly saying that: "It would be totally incorrect to think of the philosophy of human nature as 'applied metaphysics,' and it would be almost as great an error to think of it as a branch of metaphysics." [52]

And so the philosophy of nature is not metaphysics. The author is aware again in an appendix that there are very real difficulties in saying what the philosophy of human nature is. He finally says we must "meet this problem squarely," and suggests that while the philosophy of human nature is not actually a part of metaphysics, it does depend upon metaphysics. In fact, "The best name for expressing such a relationship is that the philosophy of nature is a 'potential part' of metaphysics." [53] In a "note" it is suggested that if we are to understand what "potential part" means here it will have to be understood in terms of "analogy." [54] But it is not the analogy of proportionality; rather it is "an analogy of dependence or participation," a "community" of one kind of knowledge with another.

Now this community of knowledge is both relevant and important. But we would suggest in the light of our study that the relation of kinds of knowledge is just the reverse of what Mr. Klubertanz conceives it to be; that is, from the standpoint of the philosophy of nature, but only from this standpoint, metaphysics is a potential part of it. And hence, the metaphysics of man would be a potential part of the philosophy of human nature.

The point of this analysis is this, that what Mr. Klubertanz conceives the philosophy of human nature to be is really the metaphysics of man. This mistake is very understandable, and also difficult to avoid. For in our exposition we have seen that when we try to understand what human nature is, most of the evidence comes from metaphysics. The philosophy of human nature approaches the metaphysics of man asymptotically, with the value of experimental psychology being small. The converse would be true in understanding the nature of an electron. But however close the philosophy of human nature and the metaphysics of man are the distinction must be maintained. Otherwise there is an implicit denial of the former.

The proof that Mr. Klubertanz's treatise is essentially the metaphysics of man rather than the philosophy of human nature would require showing that the propositions of experimental psychology enter instrumentally and not constitutively into the key propositions which he proves in his book. This lengthy task cannot be done at present. A sample analysis may be sufficient.

Consider the following propositions.

(*a*) "The will is not subject to any efficient causality except from God, and so is not subject to external necessity." [55]

(*b*) "The proper object of conscious appetite is the known good." [56]

(*c*) "The soul is really distinct from the body." [57]

(*d*) "The human soul is immortal." [58]

In the proof of such propositions historical propositions and generalizations are not constitutive as evidence. Now the experimental psychologist will write a book also proving certain propositions about the "will," "intelligence" (if not "intellect"), about "appetite" and "internal and external sensations." But in this book the proposition will be proved by appealing to historical propositions and generalizations previously obtained. What is the relation between the two systems of concepts and propositions? This is the problem of the philosophy of human nature, but it is not essentially the problem of our author. In saying this we do not mean to play down the importance of what the author does. His problem, which is really the metaphysics of man, is a prior one, and so important that it must be solved in order to have the philosophy of human nature. But it is not the philosophy of human nature. The latter problem remains to be considered. Otherwise we merely have two systems, the metaphysics of man and experimental psychology, each supplementing the other. But if the problems of the philosophy of human nature are not solved correctly in the theoretical order, they will be improperly handled in practice. In short, judgments presuming to be the philosophy of human nature will be made in any case. This means that deductions about the philosophy of human nature will be made from metaphysics without the benefit of experimental psychology, or "speculative" statements about the philosophy of human nature will be made simply by "generalizing" the notions of experimental psychology, and without the benefit of metaphysical knowledge. In the first place we have an unfortunate kind of metaphysical *a priorism;* in the second case, positivism. In neither case do we really have the philosophy of human nature, but only an appearance. It is interesting to observe that both parties are absolutely correct in saying that the other cannot do what he is doing!

To illustrate: The author devotes a chapter to "habits." Two fundamental propositions are proved, that "habits are found only in the intellect and will and in the powers subject to their imperium," and that "animals can have no habits." [59] Compare this with a chapter on "habits" in a book on experimental psychology. By the mutual agreement of both writers their courses (in the university) are independent of each other. The metaphysics of man does not enter constitutively into the proof of the propositions of experimental psychology; and conversely. On one side of the campus the habits of animals are studied. On the other side is a professor (without any experimental apparatus!) denying that animals have habits, who says that only humans have them, and who insists on defining habit in terms of "operative power," "act," and "potency."

Let us grant that the professor without any apparatus is correct and that what he is saying is infinitely more important. The problem still remains: What is the relation between the two meanings of "habits"? In what sense are both correct? These are the problems of the philosophy of human nature. What the professor is talking about is necessary, but not sufficient for their solution. We know well what happens when this is not understood. Each view of man, having wrongly been conceived as total, is put in opposition to the other. The consequence is academic war. And for reasons which need not be mentioned, the party with the gadgets will win. And it will be said that the one way is medieval, prescientific, but still lingers on in some universities as a concession to the past and because of the slowness of change.

It is difficult wholly to escape the philosophy of nature or the philosophy of human nature. Mr. Klubertanz doesn't. In fact he gives a very penetrating analysis and solution to a most important problem: What is the relation between the metaphysical knowledge of man and the evolutionary conception of man obtained through the experimental sciences? Also, the "intellect" of metaphysics is related to the concept "intelligence" as used in experimental science. But where do we find such problems of the philosophy of human nature considered? Not in the body of his work, but in the appendixes under the general topic of "Related Issues." We intend to demonstrate that such "Related Issues" constitute the philosophy of human nature, in contrast to the body of his work, which is the metaphysics of man. The first example in this paragraph is chosen for analysis.

In the language of moderate realism evolution in biology seems to require the notion "effects are higher than their causes." How is this notion to be related to fundamental ontological (metaphysical) principles? The author gives a brief review of the evidence for biological evolution, and makes the following distinction:

> When inherited non-essential traits are changed in the series of generations, we shall call this change 'inter-racial evolution.' If essential perfections are gained or lost in the series of generations, we shall call this 'essential evolution.' [60]

There can be both kinds of evolution. When essential evolution occurs there is a "chance" interference of "lines of causality." From the standpoint of empiriological (experimental) science this interference is uncaused and contingent. "But what is chance with regard to creatures is planned by God." "Thus chance + providence can explain the origin of effects that are higher than their created causes." [61]

Our interest is not now in the truth or falsity of the propositions, but rather in the structure of the argument and the kinds of knowledge involved. The argument may be laid bare and condensed in the form of a syllogism. Let *a, b, c* . . . be the phenomena referred to in evolution theory.

(*A*) All effects higher than their causes are effects of God's intervention through secondary causes.

(*B*) *a, b, c* . . . are effects higher than their causes.

(*C*) *a, b, c* . . . are effects of God's intervention . . .

The conclusion (*C*) is a proposition of the philosophy of nature. The (*A*) is metaphysical. The (*B*) is a proposition of experimental science. Both metaphysics and experimental psychology are constitutive of the philosophy of nature. The philosophy of nature is an integrative discipline, and as such is essentially deductive. "Rational induction" is used to obtain (*B*); "intelligible induction" is used to obtain (*A*).

We have now concluded our demonstration. It is here in an appendix that Mr. Klubertanz comes to grips with the problems of the philosophy of human nature, in contrast to the body of his work which is really the metaphysics of man. Even the example we have used is strictly speaking one of the philosophy of nature and only indirectly that of the philosophy of human nature. Actually the number of propositions of the philosophy of human nature to be found are very few. An example would be—again under "Related Issues"—"It is quite probable that the human soul is created at the moment when the new individual is formed by the unison of ovum and sperm." [62] It is to be observed that the evidence for this proposition must come from both metaphysics *and* biology. A specific proposition of biology must be true if the proposition of the philosophy of human nature is true. On the other hand, for the proposition "The human soul is spiritual" to be true all that is required is that some (indifferently) phenomenological or empiriological propositions (or propositions actually or potentially of experimental science) be true. This means, to put it in other terms, that sense knowledge is necessary in order that through abstraction and induction the intelligible may be revealed.

Some practical implications. We wish to stress the importance of understanding what the philosophy of human nature is in relation to the metaphysics of man and experimental psychology. It would be trivial if it were merely a matter of "naming." Instead it is a matter of *what* is evidence for *what*. The barrier of the uncommunicable is not to be looked for, say, in the relation of mathematics to physics. Where it is to be found is in the sciences of man; specifically in understanding the evidence necessary for propositions of the philosophy of human nature, and the relation of that subject to the ethical. There are those who, while rejecting modern tendencies toward nonbeing (nihilism) to be found in certain forms of pragmatic relativism, believe that certain kinds of realism have also erred in attempting to base ethics on a metaphysics of man rather than on a philosophy of human nature. But this raises a most interesting question. What would be the effect of the identification of the metaphysics of man and the philosophy of human nature on "natural law theory" for ethics? Is it not possible that we may have here the key to some ethical disagreements? It is a serious question for many who are quite realistic metaphysically, and yet who believe, correctly or incorrectly, that certain particular ethical evaluations cannot be deduced from the metaphysics of natural law alone.

10

History and Theology, with a Summary of Principles Indicating Loci of Possible Conflicting Truth-Claims

There can be no incompatibility between true propositions, regardless of their domains or contexts. But knowledge is potential as well as actual, and in the process of acquiring truth different subject matters may make truth-claims that are incompatible, not merely in the formal sense as contraries or as contradictories, but in the sense that a proposition of one kind of knowledge is incompatible with the implications that follow from a proposition of another kind of knowledge because of the content of each. The loci of these possible incompatibilities should be known by scholars in various fields of study in order that the co-operative search for truth may proceed intelligently and fruitfully. But such can only be known in terms of the order of knowledge. In the absence of this is substituted the subjectivity of individuals, which means that knowledge-categories become name-weapons, instruments to satisfy personal pride.

Since, as we shall presently see, incompatibilities in the synthetic sciences are reducible to those among the autonomous sciences, it may be helpful for the purpose of summarizing to construct a chart. The large letters or abbreviations at the top and by the side of the chart stand for the propositions of the various kinds of autonomous sciences: historical propositions (H), metaphysical propositions (Meta), theological propositions (T), formal logical propositions (FL), mathematical propositions (Math), and the generalizations of experimental science (G).

Specific propositions of each in later analysis will be referred to by small letters, e.g., h_1 is a specific historical proposition. "Inst," "Reg," and "Con" refer respectively to the relations "instrumental to," "regulative of," and "constitutive of." These relations, the signs of which are in the squares, relate the letters or abbreviations in the following manner: the first term is the letter or abbreviation at the side; the second term related is at the top. For example, in the second square under "H" and in the first column of squares on the left is the sign "Reg." This sign is also immediately opposite "Meta." Reading horizontally from "Meta" to the relation "Reg," and then vertically to the top "H," we have the following statement: metaphysical propositions are regulative of historical propositions. The word "None" in a square means that, in the case at hand, no one of the three relations is present.

	H	Meta	T	FL	Math	G
H	X	Inst	Con of Some	Inst	Inst	Con
Meta	Reg	X	Con of Some	Reg	Reg	Reg
T	None	None	X	None	None	None
FL	Inst	Inst	Inst	X	Inst	Inst
Math	Inst	Inst	Inst	Inst	X	Inst
G	Con of Some	Inst	Inst	Inst	Inst	X

Historical Propositions and History

History, as positive, is that kind of knowledge which has as its purpose the seeking of true historical propositions about human events, and about natural events that have occurred which are considered relevant to human affairs. History as "nonpositive" is the philosophy of history, a synthetic discipline. Value-judgments are not constitutive of historical propositions but are relevant in their selection for historical writings.

The terms "history" and "historical" are equivocal. Reference may be to

(1) What is factually known (potentially or actually) of the process of historical events.

(2) The actual process of historical events as a whole.

(3) The method of arriving at historical truths.

(4) The historical writings themselves.

(5) A philosophical study of the historical process.

When speaking of "historical propositions" reference is to meaning (1).

Historical propositions are instrumental in a general sense to propositions of metaphysics, formal logic, and mathematics. This principle recognizes the necessity of sense experience as a source of knowledge. Because of the instrumental relation there can be no incompatibility between historical propositions and the propositions of the kinds of knowledge named.

Because of the manner in which historical propositions constitute generalizations, only a class of historical propositions can be incompatible with a specific generalization. In this case the historical takes priority, for "fact" is both *necessary and sufficient* to disprove any generalization.

Some historical propositions may be incompatible with some theological propositions, namely, a theological proposition that relates God to the world in a certain manner, e.g., the actuality or possibility of a miracle, or any causal action direct from God and incapable of explanation in terms of proximate causes. Historical propositions are not constitutive of theological propositions descriptive of God's intrinsic nature.

In the case of incompatibility the historical proposition has priority because its falsity is sufficient to reject the theological proposition based upon it. But a caveat is necessary. In the formulation "if t_1, then h_1," and given a case of incompatibility in which the evidence seems to be in favor of "not-h_1," from the standpoint of the order of being, i.e., from the standpoint of the absoluteness of theology, the antecedent must be asserted even against the evidence of "not-h_1." This simply means that the knowledge which is faith, and which transcends reason, has, because of its nature, a prerogative that is unique. And hence it transcends, but does not contradict, the order of knowledge *qua* order of knowledge.

How the principles of the order of knowledge can help clarify certain theological problems. A word of explanation before proceeding further. Although the detailed relation of theology to other kinds of knowledge is not to be a part of the present volume, an outline of the relation of the theological proposition to others may be given. A theological proposition is descriptive of ontological uniqueness, either of the intrinsic nature of God or of a specific act of God in relation to the world. Because of the singularity expressed the theological proposition is similar to the historical proposition. The difference is in context. But whereas the source of all propositions composed of concepts obtained directly or indirectly by abstraction (including the metaphysical) is in sense experience, the source of the strictly theological proposition is in special revealed experience.

In the discussion of any theological problem or related problem, one is doomed to failure from the start if the principles of the order of knowledge are violated or forgotten. What is called a theological problem may be merely such, or partially a historical problem. What kind of a question is it that is being asked? What kind of knowledge is relevant? If this is not clear, then one does not know what kind of evidence bears upon what kind of conclusion; nor can one very well distinguish primary problems from derivative ones. To illustrate, let us consider briefly two problems. One of the causes of the estrangement between the Orthodox Eastern and the Roman Catholic churches is the creedal "Filioque" clause. The former believes that the Holy Ghost proceeds from the Father only, and not also from the Son, as the latter holds. This problem is essentially one concerning the relation subsisting among the three Persons of the Trinity. Hence, the problem is purely a theological one in which the historical cannot enter constitutively as evidence. This conclusion is not altered at all by the fact that the Orthodox Church takes its stand on John 15:26, and that the Book of John is a historical document. The content of the verse is theological, not historical.

The second example illustrates a problem which is essentially historical, although not obviously so. Consider the problem of the Mosaic authorship of the Pentateuch. There is a prior problem of clarifying exactly what is meant by the proposition (h_1) "Moses wrote the Pentateuch," especially with regard to the question of all, most, or some. Given such clarification, and referring to the revealed content as $t_1 \ldots t_n$, three alternatives may seem possible. It might be held that "if h_1, then $t_1 \ldots t_n$." This would mean that theological propositions are constitutive of historical propositions. Some pages later we shall find this not to be the case. At any rate, it is difficult to see how the truth of a historical proposition could be evidence for revealed truth without having to hold also that such revealed truth is such merely *because* some man said so.

Another alternative is "if $t_1 \ldots t_n$, then h_1," a historical proposition being constitutive of theological propositions with respect to evidence. Now such an argument is possible in principle, and does not violate the order of knowledge. The only issue here is whether or not the content of revelation requires the historical proposition as constitutive. If it does, then the problem is historical. If it does not, then we have the third alternative, namely, that the problem is essentially historical because there is no constitutive relation between the historical and theological propositions. In short, the truth of the content of revelation can be known and accepted independent of the question of the truth or falsity of the purely historical question of authorship.

It may not be obvious at all that the second alternative resolves itself into a historical problem. Given the formulation "if $t_1 \ldots t_n$, then h_1," and given a century or so of historical criticism which seems to cast grave doubt on the Mosaic authorship, then does it not logically follow that doubt is cast on the truth of $t_1 \ldots t_n$? In which case surely there would seem to be a theological problem. Furthermore, it has already been stated that in case of a conflict between a historical proposition and a theological proposition, priority goes to the historical. In which case, again, there would seem to be a theological problem, if not a crisis.

In answering, the following considerations are relevant. Man cannot restrict the possible content of revelation. For the order of knowledge, if a proposition is theological, then the source of evidence must be in revelation. But from this it does not follow that a historical proposition cannot be revealed. For a proposition to be historical what is required is that its truth be capable of discovery through sense experience and reason. And h_1 is thus capable. However, it can be held on the grounds of revelation, which is what the formulation seems to require. But how is this to be reconciled with the notion of the priority of the historical proposition in case of potential conflict? In the first place, the conflict between history and theology can only be potential, thus creating a tension. The conflict is not absolute because history is a positive discipline and its evidence variable and accumulative. In the long run one expects tension to be reduced between faith and reason. Smith knows that he murdered Brown. However, from the standpoint of the detectives, the law and the courts, the evidence is that Jones murdered Brown. Because of Smith's peculiar relation to the order of being he will not be convinced by such evidence. Nevertheless, in the long run he may reasonably expect (whether it happens or not) that the truth will be discovered. And so, likewise, theologians who are responsible for the mediation of revelation may know that a certain historical proposition is true because it is required by revelation, although at some given period reason may furnish evidence to the contrary.

In the case at hand, our problem is not a theological one concerned with whether or not revelation demands the Mosaic authorship of the Pentateuch. What we are saying is that *if* it does, then the problem ceases to be theological. The problem remaining is historical, that of finding evidence through sense experience and reason for something accepted on other grounds. And even though historical evidence at a given period may lead to the temptation to deny the consequent (not—h_1), nevertheless because of the theologian's peculiar relationship to the order of being he insists on asserting the antecedent ($t_1 \ldots t_n$).

Further explanation would require part of another volume. This work has been concerned with the order of knowledge. We have distinguished it from the order of being, but it is not the problem of this volume to relate the two orders. In discovering such relations one would encounter a problem such as we have been discussing. A hint in the direction of its solution is this. From the standpoint of the order of knowledge the historical proposition has priority over the theological when the former is constitutive of the latter. However, the order of knowledge is a discipline on the level of reason, not of faith and revelation. And from its standpoint *alone* it does not provide any grounds for transcending itself. But in the tension between history and theology a commitment must be made. From the standpoint of the order of being, to which theology stands in a very special relationship, priority must go to the theological in case of conflict. Here is a unique case in which the order of knowledge is transcended, though not refuted, because faith transcends reason. And faith is concerned, in part, with the relationship between the two orders of being and knowledge. It is to be noted that the question of priority as to evidence between types of propositions incompatible within the order of knowledge is not the same kind of question as that of the priority of an order when, in the case of a potential incompatibility between the orders of knowledge and being, a commitment must be made.

Either the theological as knowledge is admitted, or it is not. If not, then there is no problem of the relation of historical and theological propositions. If it is admitted, then because of the peculiar nature of theology and its relationship to history, the order of being has priority for commitment over the order of knowledge. The tension remains, and effort should be directed toward its reduction. But the problem is not solved by eliminating either faith or reason, either theology or a positive science such as history. It may be that theology does not require the proposition as to the Mosaic authorship of the Pentateuch. If it does, then the problem remaining is purely historical, not theological. And if it does not, then, too, the only problem is historical.

It should also be noted in passing that what is essentially a metaphysical problem may be disguised and argued as if it were the historical problem of the Mosaic authorship. A brief outline may illustrate. Because of metaphysical difficulties there is a breakdown of the distinction between intentional and real being, with the consequent reduction of the order of being to the order of knowledge, of faith to reason. Hegelian idealism is a good example. Then there can be no unique case in which the order of knowledge can be transcended in terms of the order of being. Hence, the priority of the historical proposition to the theological becomes absolute. This leads to a type of historicism which requires the denial of the consequent (h_1), and hence, logically, the theological. The twentieth century has inherited, therefore, this problem: How much of the historical criticism of the Bible derives from history as a positive science, and how much is really a deduction from a metaphysics which is incompatible with the Christian revelation?

In summary, some one historical proposition can be incompatible with some one theological proposition expressing a relation between God and the world. From the standpoint of the order of being the historical fact exists because of the ontological. But from the standpoint of the order of knowledge the ontological truth in question may be known because first the historical fact is known. Although no one historical proposition, or group of such, is sufficient to constitute the truth of a theological proposition, it is possible for the assertion of the truth of some one historical proposition to be incompatible with the assertion of the truth of some one theological proposition.

This principle of the order of knowledge helps to explain why the theologian as such is always more concerned with history than with experimental science, whereas the converse is the case for the theologian who is primarily concerned with the metaphysical.

Metaphysical Propositions and Metaphysics

Metaphysics is regulative of all the positive sciences. If it were constitutive, then a science would not be positive but integrative, as is natural science or the philosophy of nature. Metaphysics is partly constitutive of theology, which is autonomous but not positive. Let us consider metaphysics first in relation to positive science, and then in relation to theology. Since whatever is true of any one positive science will be true for the rest, let us choose for analysis the relation of metaphysics to the generalizations of experimental science.

Metaphysics as regulative of positive science. The regulative relation means that if (indifferently) some generalizations g_1 or g_2, or g_3 . . . g_{10} are true, then a specific metaphysical proposition m_1 is true. On the other hand, if g_{11} or g_{12} or g_{13} . . . g_{20} is true, then m_2—a specific metaphysical proposition which is, let us say, incompatible with m_1—is true. Whether g_1 or g_2 is true or not cannot be determined by m_1. It allows only their possible truth. But as regulative m_1 implies that none of the generalizations g_{11} . . . g_{20} is actually true because none can possibly be true. Hence, the assertion of, say, g_{15} is incompatible with the assertion of the truth of m_1. It is in this manner that there is the possibility of incompatibility between experimental science and metaphysics—not between the types of knowledge as such, but between certain possible propositions of each.

This kind of incompatibility has always been subject to misinterpretation. Such has occurred whenever it has been thought that the one *proves* the other false or impossible. But this cannot be the case. Assertion of the truth of generalizations does not prove the falsity of any metaphysical proposition for the reason that, as we have seen, the evidence for metaphysics is not that of generalizations. The latter are only instrumental to, not constitutive of, metaphysics. On the other hand, neither does the assertion of a metaphysical proposition prove that a generalization is false, for here only historical propositions are relevant as evidence. The actual truth of some generalizations cannot be deduced from a metaphysical proposition, only the impossibility of their being true. However, the regulative character of a metaphysical proposition is independent of whether it is true or false. Of course, *if* m_1 is true, then the truth of g_{15} is impossible. But the question is whether m_1 *is* true.

The conflict can never be settled by the experimental scientist and the metaphysician each thinking that his own "truth" disproves that of the other. However, there can be no compromise. Someone must ultimately give up his position. If over a period of time the evidence for a generalization is great, then it can be taken as a *sign* that the metaphysical proposition which would not allow its possible truth is false. But the metaphysical proposition is not false *because* a generalization is asserted as true. *If* the generalization is true and the metaphysical proposition is false, then on further examination it will be found that the latter is false *on metaphysical grounds*. The conflict between the metaphysician and the experimental scientist is solved, then, by each re-examining his own evidence, knowing that one or the other is wrong, and each being ready in humility to accept the verdict, whatever it may be. And if each knows something about the other's kind of knowledge, then each may be able to help the other in discovering who is wrong.

Pragmatism as a species of "scientism" reverses this procedure, confusing "sign" and "cause." A metaphysical proposition is not false because it does not "work out" well as a regulative presupposition in experimental science. It does not work out well because it is false, but its practical failure is a sign.

A naturalistic or materialistic metaphysics and theology. Let us consider the relation of a naturalistic or materialistic metaphysics to theology. We have here a case of intrinsic incompatibility. Naturalism does not allow the possibility of the truth of *any* strictly theological proposition. This is because it does not allow the possibility of any kind of evidence which would be relevant to a theological proposition in contradistinction to a metaphysical proposition. In this kind of incompatibility we face a sharp "either-or" in a double sense, one that is different from the type encountered in the case of the historical and theological propositions. For from the standpoint of the order of knowledge alone there can be no answer as to priority.

In the case of incompatibility of some one historical proposition and some one theological proposition there is a constitutive relation. From the standpoint of the order of knowledge, not of being, priority goes to the historical proposition. For example there must first be evidence for the historical Jesus in order that the Trinitarian doctrine can be asserted. Both the theologian and the secular historian can agree upon this, that the historical takes priority. But in the case of incompatibility between the metaphysics of naturalism or materialism and theology, which has priority? Neither. The conflict is absolute, and from the standpoint of the order of knowledge alone cannot be resolved. A good example of this would be the dialectical materialism of orthodox Marxism versus Christian theology. The impossibility of transcending the conflict lies in the fact that there can be no agreement as to which has priority even on a hypothetical basis. This may be understood by considering the answers the theologian and the materialist must give to each other.

The theologian will say that the materialist holds to his position either "in ignorance" or "by reason of ignorance." The latter means that the materialist's position has been arrived at by some kind of intellectual error. Since the materialist has good will, and the difficulty is merely intellectual, the solution is to correct his errors on metaphysical grounds. Here the locus of the incompatibility is essentially within metaphysics, and only derivatively between metaphysics and theology. On the other hand, if a materialist is "in ignorance," then the difficulty is primarily that of bad will. He is ignorant, not because of intellectual difficulties primarily, but because his lack of good will does not allow him to "see" certain metaphysical truths. While it may be difficult to classify any given person, nevertheless in a pure case of this kind, since reason is inefficacious, the theologian's answer is that nothing can be done by humans except through prayer that the grace of God may touch the materialist's soul.

This is precisely the kind of answer which must be given because the incompatibility is absolute from the standpoint of the order of knowledge. It is also exactly the kind of answer that is meaningless from the standpoint of the materialist. Hence, the double incompatibility of which we have spoken, the increased sharpening of the absolute "either-or." The materialist sees in such an "argument" only a begging of the question. And quite correctly. For the theologian's answer appeals to what it is impossible for the materialist to admit.

Now, what must be the materialist's positive argument? The materialist cannot admit that he holds his position "in ignorance," but he might be willing to consider the question of "by reason of ignorance"; that is, he may be overlooking some evidence. And so he listens to the theologian—but only if the theologian turns philosopher and is willing to consider the truth or falsity of materialism on metaphysical grounds. However, the reconciliation here is only on agreement as to the locus of the incompatibility for the purpose of discussion, the locus which has now shifted. It is no longer between metaphysics and theology as kinds of knowledge, but *within* metaphysics itself. The former incompatibility remains, and will remain as absolute as ever.

Insofar as the theologian and materialist can reason together it must be on the metaphysical level, *and hence the incompatibility between kinds of knowledge remains absolute.* Insofar as reason cannot be appealed to, then the matter is handled outside of any question of the order of knowledge. The materialist liquidates religion by force. The appeal of the theologian *qua* theologian is ultimately to God's power, although he may be forced temporarily to defend himself by using the methods of the enemy.

To the question whether a naturalistic or materialistic metaphysics can be said to be regulative of theology in any sense, the answer must be in the negative. For metaphysics cannot be said to be regulative of any kind of knowledge which it denies. Materialism eliminates rather than regulates theology and hence is a classic form of "reductionism." It is this reductive tendency of materialism, which constitutes its essence, that is responsible for the incompatibility between it and theology.

Is a nonreductive metaphysics regulative of, or partially constitutive of, theology? Metaphysics and theology constitute the two domains of the ontological context. Since metaphysics delimits the possible, and since theology may assert something as actual which from the standpoint of a certain metaphysics is impossible, therefore there can be a conflict. As we have seen, this is the case with materialism. But the incompatibility there arose not from metaphysics in a regulative function, but from metaphysics in a reductive function.

The present question is whether a nonreductive metaphysics can be regulative of theological propositions, thus allowing the possibility of incompatibility. If metaphysical propositions (m_1 . . .) can be regulative of theological propositions (t_1 . . .), then we would have the following formulation:

If t_1 . . . t_{10}, then m_1

and

If t_{11} . . . t_{20}, then m_2.

The "some" theological propositions are only those that have metaphysical relevance. Whether or not there are any other kinds is a question that does not have to be answered at present.

Now, t_1 . . . t_{10} and t_{11} . . . t_{20} must be incompatible, each proposition of the one set as correlated with the other; for if they were compatible, then both would also be compatible with either m_1 or m_2, and the regulative relation would be broken down. More exactly, there is no problem of regulation at all. On the other hand, if the two sets of theological propositions are incompatible, then being singular propositions—which by definition theological propositions must be—the incompatibility must be of the nature of contradiction, i.e., not both true and not both false. Also, either m_1 or m_2 are or are not compatible. If compatible, then they must allow both sets of theological propositions, and hence there is no regulative relation. If they are incompatible, then it may seem that a regulative relation is possible; that is, just as metaphysical propositions are regulative of, say, generalizations—

If g_1 . . . g_{10}, then m_1;

If g_{11} . . . g_{20}, then m_2—

so are metaphysical propositions regulative of theological propositions. However, with respect to metaphysical propositions and generalizations m_1 and m_2 can both be false, and hence g_1 . . . g_{20} be false. In this case, we may then have: If g_{21} . . . g_{30}, then m_3.

The matter is somewhat different with respect to the relation of metaphysical to theological propositions, for m_1 and m_2 cannot both be false. If they were, then none of the theological propositions could be true. The reason for this is that, unlike generalizations which can be contraries, theological propositions must, as we have already seen, be contradictories. Hence if both m_1 and m_2 are false, the alternative would not be m_3 as regulative, but as reductive. The conclusion thus far is that if there is to be a regulative function, then there must not only be an incompatibility between $t_1 \ldots t_{10}$ and $t_{11} \ldots t_{20}$, and also between m_1 and m_2, the incompatibility being the strong contradiction relation, but also there can be an incompatibility between metaphysics and theology

And there the matter would stand if it were not for another factor, one that is unique to theology and which prevents its relation to metaphysics being based on the analogy of generalizations to metaphysics. Since $t_1 \ldots t_{10}$ stands in a contradictory relation to $t_{11} \ldots t_{20}$, whereas generalizations can stand in a contrary relation, neither $t_1 \ldots t_{10}$ nor $t_{11} \ldots t_{20}$ can be interpreted as an indifferent "some," an interpretation which is necessary for there to be a regulative function. Therefore, it is not the case that we have "If t_1 or (indifferently) t_2, then m_1." Rather it is the case that "If t_1 then m_1; and if t_2, then m_1." Also, "If t_{11}, then m_2; and if t_{12}, then m_2." But this is the constitutive, not the regulative, relation.

The conclusion, then, is this, that in the attempt to show how the nonreductive metaphysical proposition may be regulative of theological propositions we find that there can be no regulative relation at all. Rather, the relation is a much stronger one, the constitutive relation. Metaphysics is regulative only of the positive sciences—formal logic (intentional context), mathematics (formal context), and history and experimental science (two domains of the phenomenological context). As one domain of the ontological context it is partially constitutive of the other domain, theology. This is the same relation as generalizations have to historical propositions in the phenomenological context.

Before continuing, a word about the "regulative" relation. When it is said that a kind of knowledge, *A*, does not regulate another kind of knowledge, *B*, it may still be the case that *A* constitutes *B*. Since "constitutes" is a stronger relation than "regulates" it may seem that if *A* constitutes *B* it would also have to be regulative of *B*. But this would require a different meaning for "regulation." According to the definition, *A* may regulate *B* only if it cannot be constitutive of it. As we shall see, metaphysics is partly constitutive of theology. If so, then in partly determining what can be actually true theologically, metaphysics also delimits what is possibly true. But it does so by virtue of its constitutive, not its regulative, function.

The possibility of incompatibility between metaphysics and theology does not occur in the regulative relation simply because there is no such relation, but the possibility remains because of the constitutive relation. Metaphysics is necessary although not sufficient for theology, but because it is at least necessary there is always the possibility of conflict. The question now arises as to which has priority. In the case of a reductive type of metaphysics such as materialism we have seen that the conflict is absolute. From the standpoint of the disputants, if they are consistent, there is no answer as to priority. Or, equivalently, each must insist on his own standpoint as having priority. But the present issue is that of a possible conflict between theology and a nonreductive metaphysics. The answer here may seem to be that, just as in the phenomenological context, singularity has priority over universality. This is not the case, however. Although generalizations are partially constitutive of historical propositions, the latter are wholly constitutive of generalizations. Hence, the priority of historical propositions. But although metaphysical propositions are partially constitutive of theological propositions, the latter are not wholly constitutive of metaphysical propositions—in fact they are not even partially constitutive.

Therefore, on merely a propositional level the incompatibility is just what it is, and there is no question of priority. The problem of priority arises only when one considers what can be done about the conflict, and this has to do with a relation between disputants. We have the formulation "If t_1, then m_1," which is that metaphysics is partly constitutive of theology. The incompatibility may exist within the mind of a person who has the faith or in the mind of one who does not have it. In the former case the person accepts t_1, recognizes the implication, but can only accept m_1 as false. Although on a propositional level the incompatibility remains, for all practical purposes the person must act *as if* t_1 had priority. He must be agnostic about m_1. He must say to himself: "Since the faith requires the acceptance of m_1, and, so far as I can see, metaphysical evidence seems to show that m_1 is false, until the incompatibility is resolved I must keep the faith (t_1) and assume that I am mistaken about m_1 being false, even though I do not now understand how it can be true on metaphysical grounds alone." We say that he must say this to himself, for otherwise he would not be one who had the faith.

In the second case one consistently must take his stand with "reason," metaphysics. But, whereas the materialist must say that it is impossible for t_1 to be true, this person can only say that, so far as he can see, there is no evidence that t_1 is actually true.

Although from the standpoint of the order of being there cannot be any incompatibility between metaphysical and theological propositions, in the order of knowledge there can be an incompatibility between the truth-claims of each. Since reason and faith can be correlated with metaphysics and theology, we see that there is always the possibility of tension between the claims of reason and faith. Historically this has been the case, and since the problem has always been one of the order of knowledge we can see why it must be so—because reason (metaphysics) is necessary but not sufficient for faith (theology). The denial of this has produced the following three errors which also have their historical exemplifications.

(1) Reason is not necessary for theological truth, but is sufficient to show its impossibility. This is naturalism or materialism, and we have spoken of their absolute incompatibility with theology. But it would also be correct to say that there is no incompatibility at all; for if a materialistic metaphysics does not allow even the possibility of true theological propositions, then there can be no *actual* truth-claims to produce a conflict.

(2) Reason is neither necessary nor sufficient for faith. Here there is no relation at all between metaphysical and theological

propositions, which is the same as to say that the relation is one of indifference. If so, then of course there can be no incompatibility. This "solution" has always been a tempting one, at one time leading to the doctrine of "two-fold knowledge." Historically this position of indifference has been closely associated with certain forms of nominalism and anti-intellectual trends. An example of the latest trend would be the theology of K. Barth and certain other forms of the neo-orthodox movement within Protestantism. This is, of course, to be understood as a reaction against the rationalism of modernism in religion. The impoverishment of the latter is corrected by such religious existentialist movements, but at the cost of falling into an anti-intellectualism, which, unfortunately, is sometimes welcomed by those of a practical bent who care neither for reason nor faith.

(3) Reason is both necessary and sufficient for faith. This alternative eliminates faith and theology quite as effectively as materialism. Since metaphysics is based upon abstraction from sense experience, and theology by definition is based upon revelation, to make reason absolute is in effect to deny theology. However, the method is elliptical, not direct as with materialism. If the latter is an *a priori* reductionism, the reduction of theology to metaphysics by "reason" may be called, for the want of a better term, an *a posteriori* reduction. An example would be a rationalism such as Hegelianism. Instead of denying theology directly, theology is admitted, only later to be reduced by the "demands of reason." Instead of theology we have a "religious metaphysics." Christianity becomes "eminently reasonable," no longer the foolishness of which Paul spoke. Existence is reduced to essence, and the nonrational becomes the irrational. Faith is impossible, for there is no transrational object; faith is unnecessary, for rational demonstration is sufficient. Theological faith is reduced to faith in reason, a highly sophisticated form of idolatry.

On this alternative there is no incompatibility between metaphysics and theology, no tension between reason and faith. From the standpoint of theology it is that special form of the sin of pride called "intellectualism." From the standpoint of rationalism the humility of faith is seen as intellectual servility.

If our analysis is correct these three alternatives are errors which come from denying, each in its own way, the principle which seems to be demanded by the order of knowledge, namely, that metaphysics is necessary to, but not sufficient for, theology. Only here do we find the incompatibility, not intrinsic or insuperable, but of such nature as to produce that tension between reason and faith such that reason, in checking theological pretensions, aids and does not destroy the faith which one seeks to understand.

Theological Propositions and Theology

Theology and positive science. A theological proposition can neither be constitutive of, nor regulative of, any propositions of the positive sciences. In other words, the evidence that is constitutive of a theological proposition *qua* theological cannot determine either the actual or possible truth of a proposition in any positive science. In practice this means that a person can pursue his research into history, formal logic, mathematics, or experimental science, all autonomous and positive, without having to worry whether a theological truth might modify or change in some manner the conclusions obtained in those sciences. Nor is theology even instrumental. It is not the case that in order to know some specific propositions of the positive sciences to be true, some (indifferently) theological propositions must be known.

Again, a reminder is necessary that this conclusion is from the standpoint of the order of knowledge, and not of being. The term "true" is used in the analysis of this order as well as that of the order of being. From the standpoint of the latter a quite different conclusion would follow.

The complete absence of any relation of theology to any positive science has often been subject to misinterpretation. The fact is a pleasant one to positivists—those who admit only positive science as knowledge. But this can only be because of a mistaken belief that such a fact is in some way evidence for positivism. On the other hand, the fact has been an unpleasant one for some theologians who have mistakenly interpreted such a fact to mean something derogatory about theology. What has actually happened historically is that the one error tends to strengthen the other. When the theologian "interferes" with positive science the workers in those fields rightly protest. But when they have supposed that therefore positivism follows, with its negation of theology, some theologians unfortunately have reacted with additional interference. The consequence has been a vicious circle of error.

However there are theologians who may not yet be satisfied. The problem now is to understand more clearly why they believe otherwise. The reasons are several.

(1) It may be said that the idea that theology is irrelevant to positive sciences is a conclusion one might expect to get from a nontheological viewpoint. But either there is a theological knowledge or there is not. If there is not, then the conclusion we have come to is simply that of the metaphysics of positivism. If there is, then from a theological standpoint a different answer from ours is possible. The answer to this argument is that there is a confusion with regard to the kind of problem we are dealing with. The place of theology within an order of knowledge is not itself a theological problem. There is no such thing as a "theological answer" to the problem of the order of knowledge. If there is theological knowledge, undoubtedly it is the most important kind. But from its importance one cannot deduce the kind of knowledge it is. Rather, one must know the kind of knowledge it is in order to understand its importance.

(2) But, again, it may be objected that either there is theological knowledge or there is not. If there is, then it necessarily follows that truth can be obtained in the positive sciences only because God created the world. Unless some theological propositions were true a world would not exist in which even some propositions of the positive sciences were true.

This argument may be correct, but it is not one concerned with the order of knowledge. Rather it is a theological explanation of knowledge from the standpoint of the order of being. However, for theology to be instrumental means that if some specific proposition in the positive sciences is true, then some theological propositions must be true. To deny that this is so in the order of being would require a metaphysical thesis asserting some form of naturalism. But to assert that it is so from the standpoint of the order of knowledge implies that a worker in the positive sciences must *use* some theological propositions in order to arrive at the truth of a specific proposition in the positive sciences. But is there any evidence for this?

From the standpoint of the order of being, i.e., in this case from the standpoint of theology itself, the theologian may argue that there would be no natural world at all without the Trinitarian, and not just the metaphysical, God; that whether he is aware of it or not, without the grace of God the worker in the positive sciences could not know anything at all; and so on. On the other hand, from the standpoint of the order of knowledge the worker in a positive science can insist that no knowledge of theology is necessary in order to arrive at the truth of a specific proposition in his science. There is no incompatibility between the two orders; in fact, each demands the other.

The confusion of the two orders is especially serious when considering the proper curriculum of liberal education. The matter is further complicated by the fact that there is also an "order of learning," the "psychological." The three orders, the ontological, logical, and psychological, are all determining in such curriculum instruction. It is part of the problem of the philosophy of education to discover the proper relations among these orders, *their proper functions such that no one of the three is destroyed.*

Theology and metaphysics. Since the evidence from revelation is not necessary in any sense for the truth of metaphysical propositions, the theological is neither instrumental to, regulative of, nor constitutive of, metaphysics. The first two relations would require an indifferent "some" for both theological and metaphysical propositions. But, for reasons already mentioned, such "indifference" is relevant only to propositions of the positive sciences, not to propositions of either ontological domain.

That theology is not partly constitutive of metaphysics may be seen by considering the consequences of the formulation: "If m_1, then t_1," m_1 and t_1 being any specific ontological propositions. In this case the truth of t_1 would be necessary for the truth of m_1. But we already know that the evidence from revelation is not necessary for metaphysical truth, only for theological truth. Furthermore, the truth of m_1 would be sufficient for the truth of t_1, and this is impossible by the very nature of theology.

The formulation for theology as wholly constituting metaphysics would be: If m_1, then t_1; and if t_1, then m_1; the only evidence being for t_1 and there being no independent evidence for m_1. That this is impossible follows *a fortiori* from the impossibility of the relation of "partly constitutive." However, what the order of knowledge does not allow can usually be found historically. Examples would be: (*a*) the interpretation of experimental science only in terms of the theological domain without the mediation of metaphysics; (*b*) a type of ethical absolutism based upon theology in which there is no room for "natural law." This formulation defines what might be called "theologism," a sort of "theological positivism."

This principle of the order of knowledge, that theology is not constitutive of metaphysics, although the converse is true, can be useful in clarifying many difficulties which have plagued the history of the relationship between theology and philosophy. One example may illustrate.

A critic may object that both theoretically and historically it would seem that the very possibility of theology rests upon the principle that theology can be constitutive of metaphysics. In order to strengthen his position he may consider a case involving both Christian doctrine and realism. According to reason alone every accident must inhere in a substance, for if accidents do not so inhere they would become substances. Now, this metaphysical proposition is incompatible with a certain theological doctrine of the Holy Eucharist, for the latter requires that the accidents of shape, color, and extension be deprived of the natural support of the bread-substance and wine-substance after consecration, they being preserved by divine power outside any substance. Since, if the theology is true, there is a demand for the metaphysically impossible, then it is necessary to change the metaphysics obtained by reason in order that it may conform to the theological. So, the metaphysical principle is laid down that the essence of an accident *qua* accident is that it have the *aptitude* to inhere in a substance. It is not necessary that it *actually* inhere. Is this not a perfect example of theology constituting metaphysics, of changing metaphysical propositions so that they conform to theological demands? It would seem, then, that if theology is possible, it must be constitutive of metaphysics.

In answer we may point out that the critic is quite correctly aware of a theoretical and historical difficulty, one that reflects the possibility of incompatibility between metaphysics and theology. This has already been explained. However, the conclusion of the critic does not follow because he has mistaken the locus of the difficulty. In the first place, it may be questioned whether reason demands "actual inherence" rather than "aptitudinal inherence." The issue here is strictly metaphysical. A person of a nominalistic bent may assert the former, although consistently it would seem that one would also have to say, for example, that man cannot be defined as a rational animal unless he is always rational—thus blurring over the distinction between potentiality and actuality.

What is most important, however, is that the critic is actually assuming a principle of the order of knowledge, at the same time wrongly drawing a conclusion incompatible with it. The argument is: If the doctrine of transubstantiation, then aptitudinal inherence of accidents. Then the critic points out that metaphysical evidence requires the denial of the consequent. But the theologians will not allow this. Rather, they assert the antecedent and hence insist on the truth of the consequent even against metaphysical evidence. In short, they deduce metaphysical truth from theology, and this presupposes that theology can be constitutive of metaphysics—a principle which, from the standpoint of the order of knowledge, is impossible.

That the contrary is the case may be seen by analysis. The formulation of the argument is: If t_1, then m_1. *But this is the formulation for metaphysics as constituting theology, not the converse.* As we have seen, t_1 is sufficient but not necessary for m_1, and m_1 is necessary but not sufficient for t_1. Of course, if the theologian asserts t_1 and the metaphysician asserts m_2, which is the denial of m_1, then there is a conflict. But it is a kind that comes because metaphysics is partly constitutive of theology. Furthermore, that t_1 implies m_1 does not mean that the truth of m_1 is deducible from t_1 in any sense which would eliminate the necessity for independent evidence for m_1. In short, by the very formulation of the argument used by the critic the theologians are not saying: "Although there is no evidence for m_1, nevertheless we assert it as true because it has theological usefulness." The argument "If transubstantiation, then aptitudinal inherence" means that the doctrine of transubstantiation presupposes that the nature of an accident requires that it has an aptitude for inherence, that it does inhere in a substance if the omnipotence of God does not decree otherwise; and if otherwise, the essence of an accident is not destroyed by becoming a substance. But this kind of presupposition, of "t_1 presupposing m_1," is exactly the meaning of "m_1 constituting t_1."

That the argument of the critic demonstrates just the contrary to what he thinks may be shown by stating the formulation of theology as constituting metaphysics—which is the critic's conclusion—and by analyzing the consequences. The formulation would be: If m_1, then t_1. But this would mean that the theologian would have to argue that "if aptitudinal inherence, then the doctrine of transubstantiation is true." If the theologian so argued, then it would be a case of theology constituting metaphysics. Now, not only in fact is the argument to the converse, as we have seen, but for one reason at least it must be so. "If m_1, then t_1" means that m_1 is sufficient as evidence for t_1. Not only would this substitute metaphysical evidence for revelation, but it would also imply a reduction of theology to metaphysics.

There is a paradox here. As we know, in the attempt to uphold one error we actually only succeed sometimes in arriving at an opposite error. By a kind of dialectic of error, two errors become really one. (1) Since theology is neither partly nor wholly constitutive of metaphysics, the denial of this leads to the reduction of theology to metaphysics. (2) Since metaphysics is partly constitutive of theology, the attempt to make it wholly constitutive is in effect equivalent to the reduction of theology to metaphysics. The same conclusion or error is arrived at in two ways.

The paradox may be understood if we recall that in reduction of type *A* knowledge to type *B* knowledge, *the latter is destroyed also*. In (1), which is "theolog*ism*," theology as theology is destroyed in the very act of becoming a substitute for metaphysics. But as destroyed it becomes something else, namely, a metaphysics of a peculiar version called "postulational." In (2), the reduction is direct rather than indirect, and we arrive at what has been called "postulational metaphysics," the kind incompatible with the possibility of theology. In both cases metaphysics as autonomous is eliminated. But also, in both cases metaphysics as postulational is implied. In (1) it is generated from theology; in (2) it is generated from experimental science. In both, metaphysics is merely *reflexive* of each and this constitutes not the healthy and fruitful tension between metaphysics and theology which the order of knowledge defines, but rather a war situation between two kinds of "isms," theologism and positivism. Both are kinds of "metaphysics." However, as we will recall, the term now has a different meaning and becomes equivalent to "ideology." Theologism and positivism become two warring ideologies. Reason vanishes from the world. And having vanished the warring parties now co-operate. And so the contemporary world is witness to the end of an era, for now we have not only the "metaphysics of positivism" but also a trend which may accurately be described as the "theology of positivism."

Formal Logic

Logic is the "philosophy of cognitive forms," just as the philosophy of mathematics is the "philosophy of quantitative forms." Historically, a name of a kind of knowledge has been associated now with its positive structure and then with its nature as synthetic. We must make out the best we can with such confusing terminology, and so we have used "logic" to refer to the synthetic science and "formal logic" to refer to the positive science. On the other hand, by the term "mathematics," without an adjective, we refer to the positive science; the synthetic science is called the "philosophy of mathematics." In this respect we have followed customary usage.

As has been shown, there is a ground for such custom. Not all positive sciences are equally so. Mathematics is the most fruitful without metaphysics; formal logic is the least fruitful. It is for this reason that in an antimetaphysical age it seems to some that the barrenness of logic as positive can only be overcome by interpreting it "mathematically," for mathematics as positive is fruitful. Of course, this kind of abstraction can be made. But when it is done, and formal logic becomes the whole of logic, then the science loses its instrumental function in cognition. By this is meant that it ceases to be a science of second intentions and becomes merely another science of first intentions, although it is not at all clear what its "object" is.

Experimental science is an abstraction from natural science, the latter being a synthetic science constituted by metaphysics and experimental science. One can look at positive science from two standpoints. One can begin with experimental science and construct natural science by means of metaphysics. Or one can begin with natural science and break down its components, one of which will be experimental science. In both cases we distinguish "objects" which are inseparable in nature. Now, when this is forgotten, and experimental science ceases to be a component, then it also ceases to be a means of knowing nature and becomes instead a means of manipulating and controlling nature for human purposes. The "science" now becomes an "art." And so with formal logic. It preserves its character as a science only in relation to metaphysics. In complete abstraction from metaphysics it becomes formal in a nonintentional sense. Alternative "logics" are generated. The principle of contradiction is no longer a principle either of thought or of the real. As a positive principle it may be found as a theorem just as easily as an axiom, e.g., as in the first part of Whitehead and Russell's *Principia Mathematica.* Without metaphysics there is nothing left over and above the formal except human "use." And so, if the principle always seems to pop up in formal logical systems, it is because it is very convenient, useful!

As positive, formal logic cannot be either constitutive of, or regulative of, any other kind of knowledge. That is, a specific proposition of a formal logical system is not necessary either for some propositions, as opposed to others, of any kind of knowledge, or for any specific proposition in any kind of knowledge. Or, again, a proposition of formal logic cannot enter constitutively as evidence into any other kind of proposition. It may seem as if formal logic might be regulative of other kinds of knowledge. However, what is regulative is really logic as synthetic. But even this is not quite exact. Whenever a synthetic science is regulative it is really the metaphysical component which is responsible. In this case metaphysics is regulative through, or by means of, logic as synthetic.

It is possible for formal logic to be instrumental in any kind of knowledge, including the ontological. If any specific proposition of any kind of knowledge is true, then some propositions of some formal logical system will be presupposed. This simply means that some formal logic must be used in acquiring any kind of knowledge.

There can be, then, no incompatibility between any proposition of formal logic and any proposition of any other kind of knowledge.

Mathematical Propositions and Mathematics

The term "mathematics," in distinction from the "philosophy of mathematics" refers to the positive science. Since, with but one exception, the same analysis made for formal logic will hold for mathematics, the conclusion can be stated that mathematical propositions cannot be incompatible with the propositions of any other kind of knowledge.

The exception mentioned is this, that while formal logic is instrumental to any kind of knowledge, mathematics is instrumental to the theological only by means of a doctrine of analogy. For example, the number "three" will be applied to the members of the Trinity. However, since the numbers do not have the potency of matter, do not have quantitative being, the number cannot be applied univocally. It is for this reason that a theologian does not have to be first a mathematician, but a physicist does.

Generalizations and Experimental Science

Experimental science as a kind of knowledge is that which seeks generalizations. The relation of generalizations to propositions of other kinds of knowledge has been dealt with sufficiently, so that the relation of incompatibility can be summarized.

Generalizations are instrumental to the other autonomous kinds of knowledge, with the exception of historical propositions. In relation to historical propositions generalizations are partly constitutive. Hence, there can be an incompatibility. In this case, historical propositions take priority because they, in turn, wholly constitute generalizations.

Generalizations have a general instrumental relation to some theological propositions. For example, it can be argued that if Christ was born of a Virgin, then some biological generalizations must be true. The point here is that a miraculous birth could only be understood in terms of the nonmiraculous, the natural laws of nature. But all that is required is "any," indifferently. The "some" is, then, equivalent to "any," and does not mean some group of propositions in contrast to some other group.

Concluding Remarks on the Relations Among the Autonomous Sciences

(1) The instrumental relation is that which predominates in the relations among kinds of autonomous knowledge.

(2) Only the phenomenological and the ontological context have two domains. The constitutive relation is found between the domains in the two contexts; mutual in the phenomenological context, nonmutual in the ontological (i.e., metaphysics is constitutive of some theological propositions, but not conversely).

(3) Only metaphysics is a regulative kind of knowledge.

(4) Theology has no one of the three relations to any other

autonomous kind of knowledge. This explains why workers in the positive sciences can be so successful in their endeavors, at the same time neglecting theological matters. This is the truth that the positivist recognizes, but one does not have to be a positivist to admit it.

The Synthetic Sciences

The philosophy of history, logic, the philosophy of mathematics, and the philosophy of nature are synthetic sciences concerned with kinds of being. Logic as synthetic is the name for the "philosophy of logical forms." Each synthetic science is the result of the integration of the positive science and the ontological (metaphysics and/or theology). The terms referring to the positive sciences are to be taken in "first intention." That is, the philosophy of nature is literally about nature, not about "science." The "philosophy of science," a worthy study in itself, but one which unfortunately is often a substitute for the philosophy of nature, is actually a part of logic. It is concerned with "second intentions," the "philosophy of our knowledge about nature."

Neither theoretically nor historically is it the case that man begins with positive science. One begins and ends with synthetic science, theoretical and practical. This is simply to say that one begins and ends with *being*. On the principle of "divide and conquer" the modes are distinguished, and a division of labor occurs. In integration one attempts to reconstruct in clarity the whole seen confusedly in the beginning. The oscillation between abstraction and synthesis also occurs within each general science. For example, in physics heat and electricity are separated and then united (in attempt, at least) in some over-all "field" theory. In passing it is to be observed that integration within experimental science is a problem of experimental science, not natural science. The latter is the integration of metaphysics (cosmology) and experimental science. In absence of an order of knowledge these two kinds of integration are confused. A physical "field theory" *is not* metaphysics. To obtain a science of *nature* it must be integrated with, and by means of, the ontological. The "ontological" is not the "phenomenological" merely generalized!

The practical sciences are not practical in the sense of being nontheoretical. The term "theoretical" sometimes refers to the principles of the autonomous disciplines, sometimes to those disciplines concerned with *being* rather than *doing* or *making*. Such equivocal use of the term may be regrettable, but it is historical, and we have continued to so use it. Its unequivocal meaning must be grasped in context. The second meaning is relevant in what follows. The practical sciences, such as the social sciences, arts, technology, are practical in the sense that, instead of knowing about *being*, they are concerned with knowing about *doing* and *making*. They are synthetic in that their component parts are the positive sciences and ontology. The metaphysically relevant elements, however, are the transcendental categories, one, good, and beautiful. It is these that are the foundation for the value predicates of the practical sciences. The question arises as to whether logic, concerned as it is with formal and material truth, is a theoretical or practical synthetic science. As dealing with intentional being, it is theoretical; as an instrument in knowing it is "practical." This double nature seems to exist because the objects of logic *as known* are taken in first intention; yet they are second intentions and instrumental with reference to *what* is known *by means of* them. However, being instrumental to knowing is quite different from being instrumental to doing and making. Hence it would be a serious error to conceive of logic as a practical instead of a theoretical science. Knowing about knowing is knowing about a kind of being, intentional being.

A question may be raised about the principle that the practical sciences are the result of integration of positive science and metaphysics or theology. In any moral science is not the factor other than the metaphysical that of the philosophy of nature or the philosophy of human nature rather than that of experimental science or specifically experimental psychology? For example, in personal morality it is the "whole man" to whom metaphysical norms are applied, not the "abstract man" of experimental psychology, which is positive science. This is, of course, correct, but it does not change the principle. Rather, it points to the complexity of moral science as knowledge. Let us say that moral and social science is an integration of ontology and the philosophy of nature (i.e., natural science, including the philosophy of human nature). Now, the philosophy of nature is itself an integration of the ontological and experimental science. Therefore, moral science is constituted ultimately by experimental science (historical propositions and generalizations) and ontology.

The complexity lies in this, that both ontology and positive science are doubly constitutive in moral science. Ontology enters constitutively into the knowledge of the nature of man, and also into the value judgments made about his acts. Experimental science enters constitutively into the knowledge of man (the philosophy of human nature) and also into the value judgments. For example, experimental science may not only give us a true factual aspect of the human situation which is to be evaluated, but may also provide in part the knowledge in terms of which means are constructed in order to eliminate the evil and attain the good.

With this complexity in mind we may still speak of practical science as an integration of ontology and experimental science, the two component parts which, so far as evidence is concerned, are totally constitutive.

Incompatibility and the synthetic sciences. Since a proposition "s" of a practical science must be constituted, so far as evidence is concerned, by a metaphysical and/or theological proposition ("o" for ontological) and also by a historical proposition and/or a generalization ("p" for phenomenological), the formulation may be written as follows, "If s_1, then both o_1 and p_1; and conversely; and there is no independent evidence for s_1"; that is, o_1 and p_1 are both necessary and sufficient for s_1.

A practical science is wholly and completely nonautonomous. Therefore, if there is an incompatibility within a practical science, i.e., between s_1 and s_2, then its locus must be discovered to be between o_1 and o_2 or p_1 and p_2. In other words, all disagreements in the practical sciences are on the level of positive science or are ontological. To give an example, this means that if, say, two psychologists or psychiatrists differ in their value judgments with respect to a patient, their disagreement is either on the level of experimental science or is philosophical. There is no such thing as "psychiatric evidence" in addition to these two kinds of evidence. Therefore, there can be no real conflict between psychiatry and metaphysics or theology. Such a conflict is really on a philosophical level, and should be settled on that level. Again, to use another example, sociology is a moral (practical) science and completely nonautonomous. There is no such thing as "sociological evidence" over and above that of experimental science and the ontological. When there is a conflict between a philosopher and a sociologist, assuming they have the facts straight, it is wholly philosophical—between the philosophy of the philosopher and the philosophical assumptions of the sociologist.

The idea that sociology or psychiatry proves anything philosophical is nonsense of a most dangerous kind, but a kind that is widely distributed throughout our education systems. If a psychiatrist or sociologist thinks otherwise, he is only to be reminded that when he so "thinks" he is not dealing with his own subject matter, but with a problem of the order of knowledge, a problem concerned with the nature of his knowledge-speciality *qua* knowledge.

This analysis of synthetic, practical science holds also for synthetic, theoretical science when the positive factor in integration includes also formal logic and mathematics.

What is the locus of conflict between synthetic sciences? Since they are nonautonomous, any incompatibility is reducible to that which exists between the constituent factors which are autonomous.

NOTES

Chapter 1

[1] Cf. Aristotle, *Metaphysics,* 1069b; Physics, 189b–191a.

[2] Bk. VIII: ch. 1, 1042a, 27–28. Unless stated otherwise quotations from Aristotle are taken from: Richard McKeon, *The Basic Works of Aristotle* (New York: Random House, 1941).

[3] *Metaphysics,* Bk. VIII: ch. 1, 1042b 10.

[4] *Metaphysics,* Bk. VIII: ch. 3, 1029a 19–22.

[5] Sum. Th., I, q. 7, a. 2. Unless otherwise stated quotations from St. Thomas are taken from Anton C. Pegis, *The Basic Writings of Saint Thomas Aquinas* (New York: Random House, 1945).

[6] Cf. E. I. Watkin, *A Philosophy of Form* (New York: Sheed and Ward, 1935), p. 11. Also, John Wild, *Introduction to Realistic Philosophy* (New York, Harper and Brothers, 1948), Part II.

[7] *Metaphysics,* Bk. VII: ch. 8, 1033b 17–19.

[8] Sum. Th., I, q. 110, a. 2.

[9] B. Gerrity, *The Theory of Matter and Form and the Theory of Knowledge in the Philosophy of St. Thomas Aquinas* (Washington, D.C.: Catholic Univ. Amer., 1936), p. 37.

[10] Sum. Th. I, q. 14, a. 1.

[11] Cf. John Wild and J. L. Cobitz "On the Distinction Between the Analytic and the Synthetic," *Philosophy and Phenomenological Research,* VIII, No. 4 (1948): 651ff. For an excellent analysis of the "concept," and the confusion of first and second intentions in recent logic, see Henry Veatch, *Intentional Logic,* Chs. I–IV.

Chapter 2

[1] W. Wallace, *The Logic of Hegel* (Oxford: Clarendon Press, 1892), p. 50.

[2] Henry Veatch, *Intentional Logic* (New Haven: Yale Univ. Press, 1952).

[3] For a logical explanation of these matters one should turn to Henry Veatch's *Intentional Logic.*

[4] There are those mathematical logicians who apparently cannot be classified as nominalists, e.g., A. Church. And there are those who are "Platonists." Admittedly, this raises a problem and perhaps makes our account an oversimplification. But in no fatal respect, for we should uphold the thesis that historically the development of mathematical logic cannot be understood except in terms of the development of nominalism.

[5] Cf. author's chapter, "An Examination of Contemporary Naturalism and Materialism," *The Return to Reason,* John Wild, Ed. (Chicago: Henry Regnery Co., 1953). If this seems to be an exaggerated statement, then I would call the doubter's attention to the statements of naturalists themselves. In commenting on contemporary naturalism Mr. Costello, himself a naturalist, confirms what we have said. The following quotation is from the author's chapter in the volume mentioned, pp. 75–76:

"After pointing out that philosophy must be reductionist and that the new naturalism has at least one liquidationist thesis, namely, that there is no supernatural and that God and immortality are myths, he says: 'So the naturalist now looks up to the great white throne, where once sat great Jove himself, and exclaims, "Thank God, that illusion is gone." But great illusions are not so easy to banish. We must take care lest our suppressed illusions come back to plague us in altered guise, like grinning fiends from out of the Freudian deep.' And then Mr. Costello adds: 'I do not find any great unity, otherwise, among these new naturalists.' "

Chapter 3

[1] The quotation is taken from the book *The Builders of the Bridge,* by V. B. Steinman, and is found in a review of the book in *Saturday Review of Literature,* May 12, 1945.

[2] Cf. Sum. Th., I, q. 5, a. 4; the quotation is from Curt J. Ducasse's, "The Philosophy of Art," as found in E. Vivas and M. Krieger, Eds., *The Problems of Aesthetics* (New York: Rinehart, 1953), p. 368.

[3] Cf. John Von Neumann and Oskar Morgenstern, *Theory of Games and Economic Behavior* (Princeton: Princeton Univ. Press, 1944). The aim of the authors is to describe the endeavor of the entrepreneur to obtain "a maximum of profit" (p. 1). And we are told that the theory of games "is a proper instrument with which to develop a theory of economic behavior" (pp. 1–2). This volume is a good example of the contemporary tendency to substitute mathematics for ethics in economic theory.

[4] In a book review of *Ethics and Language,* by Charles L. Stevenson, *Saturday Review of Literature,* June 9, 1945.

Chapter 4

[1] Maritain has been concerned with the same problem. He says:

". . . the proper matter of the philosophy of nature may have two sources, both of which must be philosophically interpreted: (1) human, primordial, prescientific experience or (2) science, the immense domain of scientific observations and facts by means of which philosophical truths as yet unknown may be discovered or previously established philosophical facts may be confirmed (e.g., the fact that nature gives us examples of substantial changes is confirmed by the analysis of truths established by chemistry and physical chemistry, by the physics of radio-activity, experimental biology, etc., provided that the scientific facts in question be philosophically judged and interpreted). In a word, philosophy may convert into its own substance matter that is foreign to it." J. Maritain, *Philosophy of Nature* (New York: Philosophical Library, 1951), p. 147.

In putting the matter this way Maritain would have to admit, then, that it is possible for chemistry to disconfirm substantial change. Yet the idea that chemistry can prove or disprove something cosmological (metaphysical) is incompatible with realism. Instead of "confirm" we would suggest the term "illustrate." In chemistry we find an *illustration* of that (namely, substantial change) which can be known metaphysically. If one kind of knowledge is instrumental to another the former cannot confirm, but only illustrate, the latter.

[2] C. N. Bittle, *Reality and the Mind* (Milwaukee: Bruce, 1936), p. 169.

[3] *Op. cit.,* p. 170.

[4] *The Logic of the Sciences and the Humanities* (New York: Macmillan, 1947), p. 81.

[5] This analysis, I believe, agrees essentially with Maritain's statement of the relation of the philosophy of nature to "scientific facts"—for example, a statement such as this: ". . . the philosopher uses scientific facts only on the condition that he *treat* them philosophically, deliver them of the philosophical values with which they are pregnant, draw from them facts that have philosophical value." Cf. *op. cit.,* pp. 146–47. However, as we shall see later, we call "cosmology" what Maritain often speaks of as "the philosophy of nature."

[6] *Space, Time, and Deity* (London: Macmillan, 1927), 2 vols.

Chapter 5

[1] J. Maritain, *Preface to Metaphysics* (New York: Sheed and Ward, 1948), p. 44.

[2] Taken from R. E. Brennan, *Thomistic Psychology* (New York: Macmillan, 1941), p. 207.

[3] Cf. C. S. Peirce, *Collected Papers* (Cambridge, Mass.: Harvard Univ., 1932), 2: par. 2.276 and 2.277.

[4] Cf. A. C. Benjamin, *An Introduction to the Philosophy of Science* (New York: Macmillan, 1937), p. 72.

[5] William Wallace (trans.), *The Logic of Hegel* (Oxford: Clarendon Press, 1892), p. 161.

[6] *Ibid.*

[7] *Ibid.*, p. 163.

[8] *Ibid.*, p. 167.

[9] *Ibid.*, pp. 21–22.

[10] *Ibid.*, p. 20; also, p. 16.

[11] *Ibid.*, p. 155.

[12] It is this error that I believe Mr. Northrop makes; cf. *op. cit.*, pp. 80, 113, 123–24.

[13] *Science and the Meanings of Truth* (London: Faber and Faber, 1946), p. 122.

[14] E. L. Mascall, "The Doctrine of Analogy," *Cross Currents*, Summer, 1951, p. 42. We have found this exposition of analogy to be most helpful.

[15] This point is brought out by Mascall, *op. cit.*, p. 44.

[16] Anton C. Pegis, *Basic Writings of St. Thomas Aquinas* (New York: Random House, 1945), 1: 29.

[17] The Scotus view of analogy would be somewhat different. But even for him being is not a genus, although he does hold that the concept, but not the reality, of being is univocal. Cf. C. L. Shircel, *The Univocity of the Concept of Being in the Philosophy of John Duns Scotus* (Washington, D.C.: Catholic Univ. Amer., 1942).

[18] Dorothy Emmet, *The Nature of Metaphysical Thinking* (London: Macmillan, 1949), p. 180.

[19] *Ibid.*, p. 195.

[20] *Ibid.*, p. 194.

[21] *Ibid.*, pp. 197–98.

[22] C. D. Broad, *Scientific Thought* (New York: Harcourt, Brace, 1923), p. 20.

[23] *Ibid.*, p. 22.

Chapter 6

[1] These definitions are taken from L. O. Kattsoff, *A Philosophy of Mathematics* (Ames, Ia.: Iowa State Coll. Press, 1948), Ch. 2.

[2] *Science and Hypothesis* (New York: Dover Publications, 1952), p. 33.

[3] *Review of Metaphysics*, December, 1948, p. 58.

[4] L. L. Whyte, *Critique of Physics* (New York: W. W. Norton, 1931), p. 47.

[5] C. I. Lewis, *A Survey of Symbolic Logic* (Berkeley: Univ. California Press, 1918), p. 360.

[6] *Ibid.*, p. 372.

[7] Paul C. Rosenbloom, *The Elements of Mathematical Logic* (New York: Dover Publications, 1950), p. 96.

[8] Martin Johnson, *Science and the Meanings of Truth* (London: Faber and Faber, 1946), p. 65.

[9] L. L. Whyte, *op. cit.*, p. 160.

[10] *Op. cit.*, p. 22.

[11] *Ibid.*, p. 22.

[12] V. E. Smith, *Philosophical Physics* (New York: Harper, 1950), p. 358.

Chapter 7

[1] F. S. C. Northrop, *The Logic of the Sciences and the Humanities* (New York: Macmillan, 1947), p. 84.

[2] This fact is mentioned by Kattsoff, *op. cit.*, p. 91.

[3] *Op. cit.*, p. 175.

[4] *Op. cit.*, p. 253.

[5] *Op. cit.*, pp. 194–95.

[6] *Op. cit.*, p. 252.

[7] *Op. cit.*, p. 5.

[8] John Myhill, "Philosophical Implications of Mathematical Logic," *Review of Metaphysics,* December, 1952.

[9] *Ibid.*, pp. 185–87.

[10] *Ibid.*, p. 189.

[11] *Ibid.*, p. 192.

[12] For an analysis of the logic involved here, cf. Veatch, *Intentional Logic,* pp. 339 ff.

[13] *Op. cit.*, p. 174.

[14] Bertrand Russell, *Introduction to Mathematical Philosophy* (New York: Macmillan, 1920), pp. v–vi.

[15] *Ibid.*, p. 2.

[16] *Ibid.*, p. 147.

[17] *Ibid.*, p. 154.

[18] *Ibid.*, p. 105.

Chapter 8

[1] Alburey Castell, *A College Logic* (New York: Macmillan, 1937), p. 176.

[2] Norman Campbell, *What Is Science?* (New York: Dover Publications, 1952), p. 63.

[3] A. D'Abro, *The Evolution of Scientific Thought* (New York: Dover Publications, 1950), p. 406.

[4] Henri Poincaré, *Science and Hypothesis* (New York: Dover Publications, 1952), p. 141.

[5] Cf. Martin Johnson, *op. cit.*, p. 66.

[6] Bertrand Russell, *Introduction to Mathematical Philosophy* (London: Macmillan, 1930), p. 204.

[7] C. N. Bittle, *Reality and the Mind* (Milwaukee: Bruce, 1936), pp. 303, 304.

[8] *Op. cit.,* p. 156.

Chapter 9

[1] Moritz Schlick, *Philosophy of Nature* (New York: Philosophical Library, 1949), p. 3.

[2] *Ibid.,* p. x.

[3] Cf. Charles Hartshorn, *Man's Vision of God* (Chicago: Willet, Clark and Company, 1941), pp. 132, 221. In the absence of a doctrine of analogy Mr. Hartshorn advocates the "maximal flexibility of concepts." The problem he faces is that of giving an answer as to how to resolve disagreements when different people "stretch" categories in different ways.

[4] Norman Campbell, *What Is Science?* (New York: Dover Publications, 1952).

[5] *Ibid.,* p. 81.

[6] *Ibid.,* p. 82.

[7] *Ibid.,* p. 85.

[8] *Ibid.*

[9] William Wallace, *The Logic of Hegel* (Oxford: Clarendon Press, 1892), p. 326.

[10] *Ibid.,* p. 394.

[11] *Ibid.,* p. 50.

[12] *Ibid.,* p. 51.

[13] John Wild, "Tendency, The Ontological Ground of Ethics," *Journal of Philosophy,* XLIX (July 3, 1952): 468 [italics his]. This important article shows how certain ethical difficulties derive from metaphysical ones.

[14] Edited by R. W. Sellars, V. J. McGill, and M. Farber, *Philosophy for the Future* (New York: Macmillan, 1949), p. 546 [italics his].

[15] For a volume illustrating this confusion of evidence, cf. Y. H. Krikorian, Ed., *Naturalism and the Human Spirit* (New York: Columbia Univ. Press, 1944). For a critique, cf. the chapter by the author in *The Return to Reason,* John Wild, Ed. (Chicago: Henry Regnery Company, 1953).

[16] E. A. Burtt, *The Metaphysical Foundations of Modern Physical Science* (New York: Harcourt, Brace, 1927), p. 48.

[17] J. Maritain, *Philosophy of Nature* (New York: Philosophical Library, 1951), p. 150.

[18] *Ibid.,* p. 123.

[19] *Ibid.,* pp. 150, 151.

[20] *Ibid.,* p. 151.

[21] George P. Klubertanz, *The Philosophy of Human Nature* (New York: Appleton-Century-Crofts, 1953). Part of this analysis of Klubertanz is taken from the author's article "The Philosophy of Human Nature," *Review of Metaphysics,* VII, No. 3 (March, 1954).

[22] *Ibid.*, p. 4.
[23] *Ibid.*
[24] *Ibid.*, p. 5.
[25] *Ibid.*
[26] *Ibid.*
[27] *Ibid.*
[28] *Ibid.*, p. 4.
[29] *Ibid.*, p. 396.
[30] *Ibid.*, p. 394.
[31] *Ibid.*
[32] *Ibid.*
[33] *Ibid.*, pp. 5, 395.
[34] *Ibid.*, p. 395.
[35] *Ibid.*, p. 396.
[36] *Ibid.*
[37] R. E. Brennan, *Thomistic Psychology* (New York: Macmillan, 1941), p. 51.
[38] *Ibid.*, p. 51.
[39] *Op. cit.*, p. 6.
[40] *Ibid.*, p. 4.
[41] *Ibid.*, p. 5.
[42] *Ibid.*, p. 395.
[43] *Ibid.*, p. 394.
[44] *Ibid.*, p. 394.
[45] *Ibid.*, pp. 388–89.
[46] *Ibid.*, pp. 6, 398.
[47] *Ibid.*, p. 9.
[48] *Ibid.*, p. 8.
[49] *Ibid.*, p. 4.
[50] *Ibid.*, pp. 18–21.
[51] *Ibid.*, p. 397.
[52] *Ibid.*, p. 7.
[53] *Ibid.*, p. 399.
[54] *Ibid.*, pp. 400–401.
[55] *Ibid.*, p. 256.
[56] *Ibid.*, p. 225.
[57] *Ibid.*, p. 320.
[58] *Ibid.*
[59] *Ibid.*, pp. 296–97.
[60] *Ibid.*, p. 420.
[61] *Ibid.*, p. 423.
[62] *Ibid.*, p. 410.